THE ROUTE FROM CULTUS LAKE

A WOMAN'S PATH TO A SOLO CAMPING LIFESTYLE

A. Lynn Ash

THE ROUTE FROM CULTUS LAKE
A WOMAN'S PATH TO A SOLO CAMPING LIfESTYLE

Copyright © 2013 by A. Lynn Ash
All rights reserved.

ILLUSTRATIONS AND COVER DESIGN BY
Barbara Gleason/BGleason Design

MAP/ILLUSTRATION BY
Dave Imus

EDITING BY
Carol Brownson

Library of Congress Cataloging-in-Publication Data
Ash, A. Lynn (1943 –   )
The Route From Cultus Lake: A Woman's Path to a Solo Camping Lifestyle
by A. Lynn Ash —First edition.

1. Camping 2. Travel 3. Birding 4. Feminism

PUBLISHED BY CRANEDANCE PUBLICATIONS
PO Box 50535, Eugene OR 97405
(541) 345-3974 • www.cranedance.com

PRINTING HISTORY
First edition: August 2013

Printed in the United States of America

For Susan

Women have always yearned for faraway places.
It was no accident that a woman financed the first
package tour of the New World, and you can bet
Isabella would have taken the trip herself, only
Ferdinand wouldn't let her go.

—Roslyn Friedman

"What place would you advise me to visit now?"
he asked. "The planet Earth," replied the geographer.
"It has a good reputation."

—Antoine de Saint Exupery

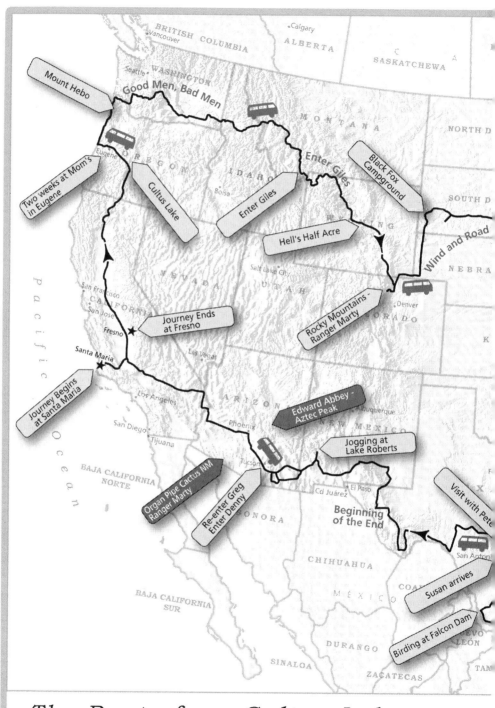

The Route from Cultus Lake

Mount Hebo

Good Men, Bad Men

Two weeks at Mom's in Eugene

Cultus Lake

Enter Giles

Enter Giles

Black Fox Campground

Hell's Half Acre

Wind and Road

Journey Ends at Fresno

Rocky Mountains - Ranger Marty

Journey Begins at Santa Maria

Edward Abbey - Aztec Peak

Jogging at Lake Roberts

Visit with Pete

Organ Pipe Cactus NM Ranger Marty

Re-enter Greg Enter Denny

Beginning of the End

Susan arrives

Birding at Falcon Dam

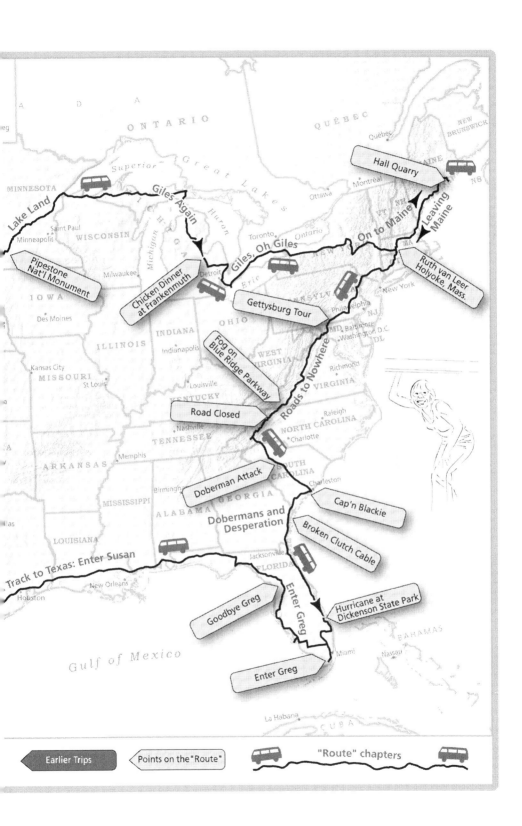

Hall Quarry

Lake Land

Giles Again

On to Maine

Leaving Maine

Pipestone Nat'l Monument

Chicken Dinner at Frankenmuth

Giles, Oh Giles

Ruth van Leer Holyoke, Mass.

Gettysburg Tour

Fog on Blue Ridge Parkway

Roads to Nowhere

Road Closed

Doberman Attack

Dobermans and Desperation

Cap'n Blackie

Broken Clutch Cable

Track to Texas: Enter Susan

Goodbye Greg

Enter Greg

Hurricane at Dickenson State Park

Enter Greg

Earlier Trips   Points on the "Route"   "Route" chapters

x

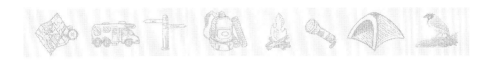

TABLE OF CONTENTS

Foreword

"I'm a local geographer, and I'm not having any luck finding a decent local map. Have you made one?" Those were Lynn Ash's first words to me, via email. When we met at a Eugene, Oregon coffee hangout, Lynn revealed that she was writing her memoirs of solo camping around the United States and Canada.

I learned Lynn's travels had started with a spur-of-the moment trip to an Arizona fire lookout tower to meet her idol, writer Edward Abbey. As two geographers who include Abbey among our favorite writers, Lynn and I inevitably became friends.

Since my geographic specialty is cartography, I suggested to Lynn that her book would benefit from a map showing her route, and that I would be happy to make it. She gladly accepted my offer and traced the path of her trip on a copy of my map, The Essential Geography of the United States of America, and using Post-It, stick-on arrows, she identified the most important locations along her route. Lynn's arrows gave the map a human touch, which I liked and used for the map's design.

The trip Lynn describes in The Route from Cultus Lake: A Woman's Path to a Solo Camping Lifestyle, marks the beginning of what became her way of life for the next thirty years, traveling and camping, mostly alone, searching out the wonders of America.

Always deeply personal, in "Route," Lynn recounts her year-long odyssey through loneliness, isolation, and adventure while never failing to marvel at the beauty she finds tracking down America the USA in a her green VW bus.

—David Imus, cartographer
The Essential Geography of the United States of America

PREFACE

One night in 2008, my sister Susan sat across from me at the dinner table. It was her yearly visit from Arizona, and we were two thirds through a bottle of cabernet. "Lynnie, honey," she crooned, "Do you remember where we were camped when I walked down to a lake shore and picked up some duck feathers?"

"No," I said, and thought a moment. "But I can find out." I jumped up from the table and retreated to my study where I pulled out a farrago of notebooks, diaries, tablets and loosely stapled sheaves of paper from my bookcase—a thirty-year collection of journals I had kept of my solo camping adventures from 1977 to 2007—and hauled them back to the dining room. Thumbing through these, I found the episode she was referring to, and, tentatively, read the entry to her.

Tentatively, because I had kept these journals private for thirty years. Fearful of raised eyebrows or outright ridicule, I had not wanted to share my most heartfelt, authentic thoughts with others, particularly not my sisters. We were not a family with a history of loving supportiveness. But when I finished reading and looked shyly up at Susan, her eyes were shining. "Read more," she ordered. So I found a couple more selections I thought might interest her and read them. This time her eyes were shining *and* moist. "Lynnie, I didn't know you had these journals. These are stories! These are all little stories!" She was excited and a little breathless. "You have to write a book."

I had thought of it before, but until now hadn't mustered the confidence or will to tackle such a project. My sister's unalloyed admiration was the impetus I needed. If she thought the journals had merit, then I would do it.

This is the book, the account of how I became an inveterate solo camper. But lest the reader assumes the author to be some extraordinary, intrepid adventuress, allow me to dispel that notion at the outset.

I am not a brave woman. No, definitely not. I am not one of those women who fly off to foreign countries by myself. I don't celebrate birthdays by bungee jumping from 300-foot high bridges. I won't be jumping from an airplane when I turn seventy; I don't even want to be in an airplane. Nor am I enthralled by the lure of extreme kayaking down perilous gorges. I can get my oohs and aahs studying the drop-to-distance ratio of any gorge from the safety of Google Earth.

I was the family chicken-child, worry wart, and scaredy cat, the prematurely neurotic, hang-back kid always checking out the action from the safety of the sidelines. I didn't walk until I was seventeen months old, and then shrieked when my mother tried to put me down barefoot on the nasty, cold, wet grass. I was the last to learn to skate, to ride a bike, and I was two years behind my friends getting my driver's license for fear of freeway driving. And, terrified of deep water, I could not, and still can't, swim.

However, in spite of these deficits of courage, by the early 1970s inchoate stirrings within me coalesced into a clear and intensely strong desire to get out of town, get into the country, get into the wilderness. Thus began a thirty-year chapter of camping adventures, some of them mere "campfire and s'mores" week-end getaways, but others lasting for a few weeks, some for a month or more, and one lasting from June 1981 to June 1982, an entire year on the road.

I went camping at every possible chance. Fortunately, my career as an elementary school teacher enabled me to travel during spring break and Christmas vacation as well as in the summer. When my school opted to go on a year-round program, every teacher had a three-months-on, one-month-off schedule, which meant I could travel during non-traditional school months: the desert in March or April, the mountains in August and September, the coast at any time of the year. I had the luxury of matching places to seasons.

I traveled alone with only a few exceptions: my sister Susan joined me for a month on my year-long trek and also on other shorter trips. On several occasions my friend Carol joined me at Cabin Lake, our favorite central Oregon haunt, but usually these meetings occurred at some point along the way of one of my longer, solo rambles.

"That sounds like a brave woman to me," you might argue. Not so. My fears and shortcomings were front-seat passengers every mile of the way. You see it wasn't just the lure of wilderness that rallied me to rise above my fears and venture out onto the road alone. It was something else, too, something subliminal, deeply hidden, but powerful: the elemental human craving for recognition, admiration, and stature. I was striving to make myself noteworthy.

This book recounts my early adventures. Part Two tells of my whirlwind trip to visit writer Edward Abbey in 1977, and my first truly solo camping trip to Organ Pipe Cactus National Monument in 1980. Parts Three and Four recount my year-long trip around the United States and Canada in 1981-82. Part Two was written from my recollections. Parts Three and Four, written in journal format, are based on journals I kept as I traveled around the country. They form the backbone of my narrative and will confirm my identity as an ordinary woman: nervous, faint-hearted, timorous, prone to panic, and foolish. But they reveal, too, my passionate nature, a soul overwhelmed by yearning so strong that time after time the impelling force of dream pursuit overruled the sovereignty of fear, banishing doubts to the deep interior of the rear cargo space, below the camp stove, the sleeping bag, the kitchen gear and the water jugs as, once again, I hoisted myself into the driver's seat for another adventure.

PART I:

Introduction

INTRODUCTION

The Kid At Cultus Lake

*A*ll my life I have harbored a longing and a love for wilderness places. Well, if not bona fide wilderness, at least that part of the physical world less inhabited by people: a secret, primitive campsite among junipers and pinyon pines in central Nevada, the rushing upper reaches of Oregon's McKenzie River, or maybe autumn at the summit of a mountain, ablaze with staghorn sumac in Acadia National Park.

Granted, this longing for wild places lay dormant for most of my childhood and teen years. But pulses of that future passion did surface from time to time. When I was seven or eight I would sit on the rickety back steps of our house on fresh summer mornings tossing breadcrumbs to house sparrows and savoring the low-angle sunshine prickling through my body like a warm syrup infusion. I could see the dark green, misty outlines of the Cascade Mountains off to the east. I had not yet been to the mountains, but I wanted to go. They called to me because they were far-off, wild, and beautiful.

We lived in Eugene, Oregon, in drafty and perpetually unfinished upstairs apartments behind the grocery store owned by my father and grandfather. When I was thirteen, we moved into a *real* house. It was out River Road, within a quarter mile of the Willamette River. Remnants of an old filbert orchard stood at the back of our place, and it wasn't long before my sisters and I discovered that we could sneak through the orchard then bushwhack through the tangled riparian growth down to the banks of the river. Many times I went there alone, pushing through the brambles, inhaling the vanilla scent wafting from mystery grasses. At the bank I would lie flat while the river burbled and sighed onward toward its confluence with the Columbia. Above me the blue sky carried rafts of friendly, white cumulus clouds, while green bushy fringes filled my peripheral vision. With no buildings in sight, and no noise but the distant hum of traffic along the north shore, I imagined that I was floating on the river, bobbing along with the mallards and the grebes, hearing only the gurgling of the water, swinging lazily around the broad meanders, and hauling out occasionally to sun myself on an island or sandbar.

I cherished these secret moments of sublimity in my early years, but, being a child, did not recognize them as formative. There was nothing special about a child loving the distant view of the mountains, the timidity of waterfowl, or the flow of a river. My parents would not have taken note. I did not know then that these impulses were clues to who I would become. Only as an adult did I begin to understand that these were defining traits of my emerging character, and that to recognize this was not conceit, as my parents might have viewed it, but validation.

My longing to head for outdoor places had its roots, no doubt, in the same wanderlust that brought my father and his father on a journey westward from Colorado in the mid-thirties. Nosing around, camping, hiking, fishing, looking for prospects, they found Oregon to their liking with plenty of mountains to climb, and clear, rushing streams alive with rainbow trout for the taking. They settled in Eugene and opened a grocery store in the heart of town at the corner of 8th and Monroe–*Ash and Son, Your Friendly Grocer.* They worked six days a week from 8:00 a.m. till 7:00 p.m., taking only one week of vacation a year. Our week came in mid-to late summer, prime time for a camping trip to the mountains.

"Girls, we're going to Cultus Lake," Mom would announce, and we would jump and clap and scurry to our closets to search for suitable campwear. Mom would take us downtown and buy us each new tennis shoes, about $1.98 a pair. At home, we would lace them up and parade along the sidewalk, heads cocked forward to admire the gleaming white rubber against jet black canvas.

Mom would dig out the air mattresses from a dark corner of the laundry room. We unrolled them on the living room floor, releasing the musty scent of last year's camping trip, and checked for leaks. Then came the blankets, which we spread and stacked into bedrolls fastened at the bottom with faded, pink diaper pins, our makeshift sleeping bags.

Early the morning of departure, Dad would hitch the rowboat to our Willys jeep and load it with our gear. The family would pile in the jeep, and Dad would slowly pull away from the curb, testing the load, while we girls whooped and bounced in the back seat like palm-warmed jumping beans.

Out of La Pine, east of the Cascades, we left the paved highway and turned west, driving the last twenty miles over dusty, bumpy, car-rattling road to the east end of Cultus Lake with its lodge and rustic cabins. No crowded resort for us, though. The west end was our destination, our "secret" private campsite, accessible only by boat.

The memory of crossing Cultus Lake still causes me to shudder. Dad would unload our rubber raft, attach it to the rowboat with a rope, and pile it with our supplies. When all was secured, the family would scramble into the rowboat, outfitted with a dicey, three horsepower Johnson outboard motor, for the two-mile trip across the lake. We wore no life jackets, and neither my mother nor I knew how to swim. The trip seemed endless and I was terrified that we would capsize.

We putt-putted ever so slowly across the lake, the water nearly up to the gunwales, and Dad yelling at us to sit still. Submerged trees looming eerily upward toward the glasslike surface only intensified my dread. I was mesmerized by the frightful depth and expanse of the lake, an early impression that nature held spectacles of much greater portent than pretty garden flowers and twittering songbirds.

At last, we could make out the dark strip of shore on the far side, then farther along, the bright curve of "our" little sandy beach, and finally, the opening in the forest that contained our campsite.

What immense relief I felt when at last our boat gently nudged onto the beach, the little wavelets lapping a welcome against the prow as we jumped out and dashed, shouting, arms flung wide, up the sand to embrace our summer Eden.

There was the log that jutted into the lake where we watched crawdads scurrying in the shallow water. There was the rustic table we had built years before. We reclaimed it all joyfully, inhaling deeply the scent of pine as we unloaded the rubber raft and began setting up camp.

On one night my sisters and I lugged our bedrolls down to the beach to sleep at the lake's edge. In the morning, just at dawn, I awoke and peeked out over the edge of my bedroll. A layer of pink fog had crept in and hovered over the lake. To my child's eye it seemed like fairyland had materialized silently, like Brigadoon, unseen, while we slept. I felt as though I was witnessing something I was not intended to see. I watched until it slowly faded into the blue of morn. No one else saw it; this pink-misted fantasy was mine alone.

I remember a time Dad joined me on the beach in the late afternoon to watch the shadows slowly climb the flanks of Cultus Mountain rising from the south shore of the lake. We would take bets on the exact time the shadow would reach the top. His guess was always closer, but I, too, was a winner, having been afforded this brief, and rare, "quality time" with my father.

It was a week of grand sensory input—the bubbling spring of pure, ice-cold water, the scent of breadsticks toasting (or burning) over the campfire, the stinkiness of the latrine, the aroma of trout frying on the grill, the squish of warm sand through my toes—a cache of memories for later days. This was my introduction to camping and the mountain world so beloved by my father.

As I approached adolescence, dreams of wild, outdoor places went underground and would not surface again until my senior year at the University of Oregon. My energies, like those of many teenage girls, were expended in the pursuit of boyfriends and popularity.

In the spring of 1971, a decade after first entering college, I was at last closing in on a B.S. in psychology, finishing up with a seminar in human existential psychology. The seminar met in an antiquated, all-wood classroom on the main level of Condon Hall, a venerable, old brick relic whose dark halls and heavy wooden doors invited exploration. During much-needed breaks from my seminar, I wandered these old hallways and discovered, entombed in the basement, the Department of Geography. An amazing array of maps covered the narrow corridor walls: aerial photos, physiographic maps, land use maps, geologic maps, and topographic maps.

One map in particular, a huge physical map of Oregon, seemed to pull me in. It must have been five feet square, large enough to provide a sweeping overview of the topography of the entire state: the elongated green trough of the Willamette Valley, the hachured cones of the Cascade Mountains lined up north to south, the Columbia River gorge extending to the Wallowa Mountains in the far east, and the Ochoco Mountains, previously unknown to me, perched in the center of the state.

In a glance, my spatial concept of Oregon was overturned. I saw that the Willamette Valley, my beloved and familiar homeland, did not comprise the bulk of the state, as I had imagined. Instead it was a mere thin strip of land in the west, compared to the vastness of mountains and high desert stretching enticingly off to the east. I ran my finger eagerly across the map searching for places familiar to me from childhood, tracing their routes from Eugene, gauging distances and relative locations: Cultus Lake, the Willamette Pass, the McKenzie Pass.

I hunted for a place called Fall Creek where sometimes on an evening after work Dad would take the family on a picnic to get in some fishing during the long daylight hours of Oregon summers. I knew it was somewhere close to Springfield. Scanning all the drainages near Springfield, I found it, a tributary joining the Willamette River south of Springfield. Oh, how that thin blue line on the map brought back vivid memories of little girls scampering over rocks, inhaling the river scent while the sun slowly lowered over Eugene.

I traced our route to the Coast on the mysteriously named Route F, with scary curves so tight I cowered in the back seat of the car with my eyes closed. Now I understood. Route F followed the Siuslaw River, twisting and snaking through the Coast Ranges before straightening out onto the estuary near Mapleton.

Each familiar spot beckoned to me, and all the unfamiliar spots, too. My finger flew across the map, touching down on one symbol after another, tiny green triangles for campgrounds, hundreds of them; miniature fir trees for state parks; small green squares signifying beaches, viewpoints, and recreation areas; hundreds of rivers, lakes, forests and wildernesses, all calling to me, urging me to come.

Why hadn't I been out there exploring these places old and new?

What had happened to me over the last decade? In and out of college, two failed marriages–wasted years it now seemed to me. I had forgotten what was truly important to me–the love of nature instilled in me years ago in the Cascade Mountains. Standing before that map, a flood of sensations came back to me. I could smell the pines, hear the trickle of water over river stones, and the swish of treetops bent to the wind. Suddenly I knew, I *felt*, as tangibly as a beam of sunshine on my face, that out there in the mountains, by a river, a lake, or at the beach, I would find my heart's desire. What I didn't know then, as I do now, was that at that moment, my life quietly, but with certainty, took a turn. I was about to make a choice that would lead me back to Mother Earth.

In the meantime, the university wanted nine more units of course work from me before conferring a bachelor's degree. I had been searching the catalog for the easy ones, but now I knew what to take, geography, of course, the study of Earth. I went directly to the Geography Department and enrolled in Geography of Oregon and Geography of North America, summer term, 1971.

I went on to earn a Master's in geography at California State University. In graduate school I went out into the field with my fellow geography buddies, hiking and camping, poking around northern California, interpreting the physical processes that shape the land, all the time beguiled by the prospect of so much yet to discover.

After completing my Masters, and a fruitless search for a full-time college teaching position, I reluctantly took a job as a city planner. However, four years of writing General Plans and pressing flesh with land developers was counter to all I believed in. Truly, I did not want to develop cities; I wanted to tear them down. I could not countenance a lifetime career as a city planner, stuck in a job I detested, so I took stock of my situation and, guided by my childhood camping memories and love of the land, quit my job and steered a course for the world of sea and sand, cactus, arroyo, mesa, juniper and pinyon pine, prairie, meadow, mountain, valley, glacier, canyon, cliff, space and air.

That is how I began my camping life.

PART II:

Abbey to ORPI

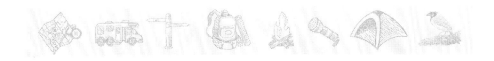

CHAPTER 1

In Search of Edward Abbey

August 15, 1977

Dear Lynn :

Thank you for the very nice letter.
Yes, I'm accessible; are you? I'm working
as a fire lookout on Aztec Peak, Tonto N.F.,
about 40 miles N of Globe, Arizona. Will
be here till October, probly. Yrs,
Ed Abbey
Globe
Arizona

8-15-77

"Soooo, going to spend a romantic night up in a fire lookout with your hero, eh?" My boss Ron wasn't going to pass up a chance for a good time at my expense. He was no environmentalist, and he was fond of razzing me about my "green" leanings and my adoration of Edward Abbey.

"That's not why I'm going, Ron. I admire his work," I said, perturbed. But the more I denied Ron's insinuation, the more he poured it on.

"He's probably tall, handsome, just a touch of gray at the temples, eh? Don't you think?" Ron's face took on a reddish leer. By break time, the senior planner, the clerk, the Director of Public Works and the entire Parks Department knew I was going to go meet Edward Abbey.

I had first read Abbey's *Desert Solitaire* in graduate school, admiring both his writing and his iconoclastic environmental views. He made a desert rat out of me, an Oregon girl raised in the drenching rains of a marine west coast climate in Eugene, a city buried to its rooftops in forests of fir and pine, blackberry tangles and rhododendrons.

I had seen the desert only once before in 1968, cruising down Highway 95 in Nevada toward Las Vegas. The ochre mountains of the Basin and Range appeared denuded, thirsty, unhealthy. I had felt exposed and vulnerable gaping at their sharp outlines. What's wrong with these mountains, I wondered? Where are the trees?

Now a convert, I devoured each of Abbey's books as soon as they hit the market. Abbey voiced so exquisitely my own views, he became an obsession with me. Starry-eyed and full of fantasies, I sent him a fan letter asking if he was accessible, and even though I strongly denied to my friends, and to myself, any sexual motivation–the man was known to be "accommodating," especially to younger women–I knew full well the overtones lurking in the word "accessible."

I pictured us at the base of a fire lookout, sitting on sandstone slabs surrounded by cactus and sagebrush, and gazing out at a vista of distant mesas. He would be wearing a dusty cowboy hat, a red bandana tied around his neck. I would be listening enrapt to his stories of box canyons, quicksand-mired cows, and moon-eyed horses.

I did not know where or how to reach him, but I knew he had worked at Arches National Park near Moab, Utah, so I simply mailed my letter to Edward Abbey, Moab, Utah. That, I thought, would be the end of it. Two weeks later, to my astonishment, a postcard arrived with a note that could only be construed as an invitation. I knew at once that I would go, so I hastily made plans and dashed off a postcard.

Dear Ed Abbey,
Thanks so much for your card. I will fly to Phoenix early September 9, rent a car, and arrive probably in mid-afternoon. Is the road to the lookout passable; do I need a 4-wheel drive vehicle?
Sincerely, Lynn S.

Then a week later:

Friday, September 9, 1977

It was still dark when I left for the Sacramento Airport this morning to catch an early flight to Phoenix. I had my sleeping bag and Thermarest air pad stashed in an old army "pimple pack" borrowed from Hal, the crusty public works chief. My plan was to bed down for the night at the base of the fire lookout on Aztec Peak, like a supplicant to my idol in the tower.

At Sky Harbor Airport I hurried to the rental car area. A small car could handle the road, Abbey had said, so I chose a Ford Pinto, a bit low-slung for the job it seemed, but the best the dealer had to offer. I navigated through Phoenix to Highway 60 and headed east through miles of stop lights and strip malls toward Apache Junction, passing the jumbled, cactus-strewn Goldfield Mountains where finally the city began to fall behind. From

Apache Junction to Globe, the desert materialized before me exactly as I had imagined: green sage and cactus punctuating the topaz cliffs beneath an intensely blue sky. I drove along gawking at the unexpected beauty of the desert. At Globe I turned northwest and, after a few miles, found Route 288 heading north across the Salt River and up onto the sandstone and quartzite cliffs of the Ancha Range.

The narrow, red dirt road up Aztec Peak began smoothly enough, but soon steepened and became more rock than dirt. With a death grip on the steering wheel, I drove slowly, maneuvering the Pinto over rocky slabs and hoping the rough part would be short. Instead, the road worsened, becoming narrower, rockier, and deeply rutted. I pulled over and got out to scout the road ahead, wondering if I should stop and walk the rest of the way, not knowing how far it was. It was then I heard the unmistakable burr of a Volkswagen engine below me. Looking back down the road, I saw a VW van steadily rattling up around the curves. The driver slowed as he approached, and asked me if I needed help. He was young and alone, and I resented him immediately, knowing he would get to Abbey before me. I didn't have it in mind to share my hero. Even though I was doubtful that I could actually go much further, I thanked him and waved him on.

Back in the Pinto, hunched over the steering wheel, I held my breath and pushed up over ever larger rocks.

"The last three miles are rocky," Abbey's warning came back to me.

You'd better stop, Lynn, the smart voice inside me was saying, but I didn't. In the next moment, with a loud, ringing *clang!* the Pinto struck rock, hard, and came to a stop. A jolt of red-hot alarm seared in my chest. An ominous hot smell rose from under the Pinto's hood. I jabbed at the key in the ignition, turned off the engine, and sat, half-stunned, trying to think.

Oh God, I hope I haven't ruptured the oil pan, I thought, even though I wasn't sure what or where the oil pan was. I forced myself to get out, to look at the greenish black puddle I knew was spreading out below the undercarriage. To my enormous relief the road under the car was dry, but what other damage had I done? Mangled an axle, ripped off the tailpipe? Whatever had happened under there, I was too chicken to bend down and look.

I did a three-hundred-sixty degree scan of my surroundings, desperately seeking some solution to my predicament, as if help would come marching out of the pines or clamber up over the edge of the cliff. I looked up the road to assess the distance to the top, and there at the bend in the next switchback was the VW. The young driver had stopped, gotten out, and was gazing at the view. He looked pretty useful to me now. I hollered, but he didn't hear. I hollered again, waving my arms wildly. Suddenly, panicked at thought of being stranded, I grabbed my backpack from the car, slung it over my right shoulder and began running, flailing my arms and yelling, lurching up the road, as if in a nightmare, trying to reach him before he drove away. He was just getting back in his van when, at last, he heard me yelling.

I must have looked like Quasimoto, the pack hunched and thumping against my shoulder as I staggered as fast as I could up the road to my rescuer. His name was Dave, and he was happy to give me a lift the rest of the way up the mountain. I threw my pack in the back and climbed into the passenger seat, enormously relieved and grateful.

"You going up to the lookout?" Dave didn't seem to know about the famous person up there.

"I'm going up to visit Ed Abbey," I informed him. Dave offered no comment, no flash of recognition. "You know who Ed Abbey is?" I queried. He didn't, and I didn't bother to enlighten him.

Queasiness festered in my gut as we rounded the summit. I was about to meet Edward Abbey, my idol, and I was in a stammering fear, rehearsing what to say, how to act. And I was anxious about Dave. How could I discourage him from hanging around? I definitely didn't want to appear as though I had arrived with a boyfriend. When we pulled up at the base of the lookout, I blurted anything I could think of. "Thanks a lot for the lift, Dave. Wow, look at those clouds closing in! Looks like we're in for some heavy rain. This road's going to turn to mud!" I yanked my pack from the van and turned away, thinking go away Dave, scram.

From the sign at the bottom of the lookout I gazed up four switchback flights of stairs to the square box sitting atop the tower. A catwalk ran the perimeter. A man in a long jacket and a western hat stood silhouetted at the rail looking down.

> Tonto National Forest
> Aztec Peak
> Elevation 7964 FT.

I called up, "Are you Ed Abbey?"

"That's what they call me."

"Well, I'm Lynn S., and I've come from California to visit you."

"Bring your friend and come on up."

"Oh, um, I don't know him. He just gave me a ride up the mountain." It was a lousy thing to do, but I was beyond redemption. I struggled to hoist the bulky pack to my shoulders.

"Just leave the pack down there. Unless you're planning to stay the night," he called.

Oops, I thought, but at forty-one feet above the ground I was fairly certain Abbey couldn't see the sudden reddening of my face.

"Oh, um, sure," I stammered, and headed for the stairs.

I was half way up the first flight when I turned to look for Dave. He was gone. All I saw was the tail end of the VW and the red on-and-off flicker of brake lights as the van disappeared through the trees back down the mountain.

"I have a bottle of red wine if you'd like some," Abbey offered after greeting me with a warm handshake. I just shook Edward Abbey's hand, I was thinking, standing next to him, tongue-tied and stupid with fear. I had decided to try and impress him by quoting from *Desert Solitaire*—a disparaging remark he had made about tourists who expect the comforts of home while visiting wild places.

"Where's the Coke machine around here?" I gave him a knowing grin, but Abbey didn't seem to know what I was talking about, and I lost substantial "cool" points by having to explain myself. Nevertheless, he poured two plastic cups of wine and we stood at the railing, looking out over the forest and mountains beyond. "I'll take you for a walk and show you around and then you'll be my guest for dinner. I was planning on that. I'm pretty good at potatoes and green chili."

We walked out over the rocky platform of the summit, Abbey pointing out and naming distant peaks, mesas and buttes. To the east and south, looming thunderheads darkened and drifted ominously nearer, slashes of lightning ripping through them. Presently Abbey said, "We'd better head back to the tower unless you're good at dodging lightning." Back at the base of the tower I surreptitiously sized up my sleeping situation. There was no sheltered spot for me to throw down my sleeping bag. I had no tent, no car. Just as I was resigning myself to a long trek back to the stranded Pinto, Abbey said, "You'd better sleep up in the tower tonight." More embarrassment and angst, where exactly do I sleep? But Abbey was ahead of me. "There are two twin beds in the tower."

Back in the lookout, Abbey began slicing potatoes while I sat stupidly on one of the beds trying to think of intelligent things to say. We drank red wine and chatted, but every word out of my mouth—far too many, I was sure—had the taint of inanity. I had imagined us engaged in conversation about environmental issues, but the persona he projected foremost was that of a writer. He had a vintage typewriter, and reference books and sheaves of paper were scattered around. It surprised me that I hadn't thought of him this way but, of course, he must spend a lot of time writing, as prolific as he was. So the conversation turned that way, and I relished this new image of him.

After dinner, Ed lit candles and tuned his short-wave radio to a classical music station. A faint edge of sunset lingered on the western horizon, thinly visible through the gathering darkness of night and storm. He apologized for not being a better host, and asked if I wanted to play a game of scrabble. I assured him he was an excellent host and I was very happy just to sit in the darkness listening to the music and watching the electric show with him. He said he preferred that, too.

Just then, a blinding streak of lightning blazed across the catwalk outside the window, inches from us, followed instantly by a deafening crack of thunder that shook the tower and jettisoned my drumming heart to my throat. Sinister green-black thunderheads hovered over the catwalks hurtling their worst, bombarding us with billions of volts of electricity, and nothing to do about it but sit and be battered. Low, growling, drum rolls of thunder crescendoed into ear-splitting, angry explosions. With each percussive report the tower shuddered, rattling and straining against the hissing wind.

"Do you think we'll be struck?" I asked Ed.

"Probably already have been," he answered. "Several times."

I thought of the four spindly steel legs holding up the tower, and pictured them buckling like toy beams in a child's erector set, the flights of stairs pancaking as the tower collapsed. In the dark, I tried to read Ed's face for signs of fear, but he seemed to be completely unruffled.

I slunk into my sleeping bag, but there was no sleep for me as I strained to detect any lessening of the assault. Throughout the night the storm raged, a malevolent beast intent on annihilating us. I tried to take heart from Ed's apparent lack of alarm, reminding myself that summer thunderstorms are routine in the mountains, and fire lookouts are no strangers to them.

By morning the storm was gone; the skies cool and clear. Birds were singing; rain droplets clinging to leaves sparkled in the sunlight, then gently plopped onto the soft earth. Serenity had returned to the tower. If Ed hadn't slept, I couldn't tell. If he was ill at ease and anxious to be rid of me, I couldn't tell. But I did have the good sense not to overstay my welcome, if I hadn't already–my mother had always stressed the importance of not being a nuisance. So I planned to leave right after breakfast. Instead, Ed suggested a hike to an abandoned apple orchard below the tower. His work schedule didn't allow him to go with me, but he said by following the trail a way, then bushwhacking downhill, I couldn't miss it. In company with Ed's black lab, Ellie, I set out to find it. It felt good to be out of the tower, free from the pressure of presenting my best side to my idol, yet still within his territory. The air was fresh and trembling as I headed down the trail. Just out of sight of the tower, I stopped. Soft, sweet notes as delicate as mist came floating down from some mysterious height among the trees. Transported, I listened to the hidden musician, a water nymph perhaps. I peered into the woods around me, but could not find the sprite. I tried to recall if there were any dwellings around where songsters might reside, but there were none.

I found the orchard, but did not linger. A restlessness and unease troubled me. I had planned to spend the second night at nearby Roosevelt Lake, sleeping in the back of the Pinto, but now that prospect held an element of dread as I pictured myself alone in the dark in an unfamiliar wilderness.

Soon after reaching the orchard I called to Ellie and turned back up the mountain. At the last turn of the trail I looked up to the tower. Ed stood at the rail, a flute at his mouth, and again the soft stream of notes floating down. When I reached the platform he asked if I had heard him playing. "Yes," I said, "so you were the phantom musician."

As I began to pack, Ed asked if there was anything of his I would like as a souvenir. I had noticed his cap with the words "Hayduke Lives" hanging on a nail. That's what I wanted, but I couldn't ask; it seemed too much. So, instead, I asked if I could take his photo.

"Don't you know that you rob a part of a person's soul when you take his photo?" Abbey chided. Chastened, I hurried to finish packing. Abbey walked downstairs with me. I thanked him, shouldered my pack, and began to walk away. "Lynn," he called. "Don't you want to take my picture?"

"I thought it would it would rob you of your soul," I said.

"Well, I was really only just kidding you." But it was too late. I was embarrassed and didn't want to leave him with the impression that I was a shallow, camera-toting, snap-and-run tourist. So, I demurred. Abbey smiled. He came to me and kissed me quickly on the mouth. "Goodbye, Lynn S.," he said.

"Goodbye Ed Abbey."

I set off the way I had just come and found the orchard again. But after that I wasn't sure which way to go. Ed had said I would intercept the road by heading straight downhill from the orchard. But, which way downhill? I didn't know and again I felt the acid pang of fear as I stood looking around me, trying to determine what to do.

"Straight downhill, Lynn," Ed had said.

Straight means straight, not right or left, I told myself and continued in my original direction hoping I wasn't walking in circles like half-crazed, half-starved, lost people do. I pushed on and soon enough it did appear. But then I didn't know if I had come out above or below the car. I opted for above, and began walking downhill. About the time I thought I had misjudged, I saw the abandoned Pinto glinting in the distance. A quick inspection showed everything to be intact, and when I turned the ignition key the engine purred to life with no complaints.

A rush of relief poured through me on the way back down the mountain. It was easy going now and I made good time heading back to Globe. By the time I pulled into a gas station I had already decided to try and catch a flight back to Sacramento that afternoon. From a pay phone I called the airline. They had a flight leaving in two hours. It was eighty-five miles back to Phoenix, but I thought I could make it. I booked the flight and hung up. The gas station attendant had been listening. "Can I make it back to Sky Harbor in two hours?" I asked.

"Do you know how to drive mountain roads?"

"Uh, yeah, I do. Sort of." Seemed like I remembered something about accelerating in the curves and using compression to brake. Whatever, I would have to push it. I made it back to Phoenix in an hour and forty minutes. Twenty minutes before departure I pulled into the rental car area. I urged the check-in clerk to make haste, grabbed my rental receipts, and dashed for the gate, arriving just as my flight was boarding. I found my seat and plopped down.

It was all such a rush, such a perfect, exhilarating finish to this extraordinary weekend. Once we were at altitude, I ordered a scotch and mellowed into a glowing recapitulation. I did it! By damn, I actually did it. I had whipped up a first class dream and transformed it into a first-rate adventure, shunting aside fear, and racing off to meet my idol. I began to scribble some notes on a cocktail napkin, but my head and heart were too full for one napkin, too full for one cocktail. I wrote feverishly until my tray was covered with moist, sticky cocktail napkins. Then I rested my head against the seat back and gazed into the space of the cabin. I envisioned a long stretch of road reaching away from me, but instead of narrowing to a distant focal point, it widened into the distance, beckoning me to come, come.

CHAPTER 2

Organ Pipe Cactus National Monument

April 5 – 11, 1980

Left Santa Maria early this morning on my first, truly solo camping trip. Can't count my trip to Arizona in 1977 to meet Ed Abbey. No campout on that trip since I spent the night in the lookout tower with him, ditched my plan to camp the second night at Roosevelt Lake, and lit out for home instead.

It is because of Abbey that I have chosen Organ Pipe Cactus National Monument as my first solo camping destination. He worked there in 1968 as a ranger. Thanks to Abbey, I loved "ORPI" before I had ever been there. At home with his book propped on my knees, I envisioned the thorny palo verde, the ocotillo, the spiny cactus, the shimmering baked rock, and the enormous spaces in between he so hauntingly evoked.

I wanted to cover the ground that Abbey had walked, see the landscape he described. I wanted to hike the Bull Pasture Trail, intrigued with his tale of the mysterious disappearance of one Carol Turner who, in February of 1971, went hiking alone up there and never came back. No one learned what happened to her, no body was ever found.

I had read everything I could find about ORPI, but ultimately armchair traveling became more angst than enjoyment, and I resolved to go.

First thing needed was a tent. I didn't own one, so I rented a flimsy pup tent from a local sporting goods store. Next came provisions. It didn't occur to me to plan meals, and I had no idea how much food I would need for a five-day camping trip, so I packed three cardboard boxes with canned goods. I stuffed my ice chest with bacon, eggs, hotdogs, beer, sodas, and, for good health, some green stuff.

I stashed boots, hats, binoculars, birdbooks, water jugs, air mattress, sleeping bag, and every other conceivably useful camping item I could think of in the crannies of the back seat and trunk of my trusty canary-yellow Dodge Colt. The night before I left, I restudied my maps, memorizing my route, then went to bed, a knot of apprehension centered in my stomach.

The morning dawned sweet with early spring sunshine. I was on the road by 8:00 a.m., driving through the Los Padres National Forest, keeping a sharp eye out for California Condors, to no avail. I swung south around the Carrizo Plain, across the San Andreas Fault, and connected with Interstate 5 south of Bakersfield.

There wasn't much traffic as I exited east onto State Highway 14. The off-ramp swept down onto the highway in a broad curve, and I was accelerating smoothly into it when suddenly the hood on my car sprang free of its latch and banged upright in front of my windshield. I slammed on my brakes, but without forward vision there was little more I could do. Luckily, I was in the right-hand lane and could see a broad gravelly shoulder out the passenger window. I pulled over, braking hard, and holding my breath that I would not run out of shoulder and before I came to a stop. Thank my lucky stars, neither happened and I stopped safely. I got out and slammed the hood down, then tested it a few times by pulling up hard on the front. Satisfied, I pulled out slowly, keeping a lookout for places to pull over in case the hood sprang again. After a few miles I felt fairly sure it was down for good, and I relaxed into the drive.

It was a lovely, sunny spring day and now dense patches of golden poppies began to appear along the roadside and far across the fields in vast, plush carpets of golden orange. I drove on through the towns of Littlerock and Pearblossom–such lovely names–and into the empty desert world I had imagined. East of Pearblossom, I squeezed up between the San Gabriel and San Bernardino Mountains at Cajon Pass, then plunged down into the miasma of the east Los Angeles basin and on to Interstate 10, the Los Angeles to Palm Springs "Smogway," a one hundred mile corridor of gray-brown gunk.

Driving this smudgy freeway, I found myself–as often happens when I am driving solo–reciting an abridged geography lecture on temperature inversions to an imaginary class of intensely interested tourists.

Beautifully situated on a curve of Pacific shore, Los Angeles is, nevertheless, pestered by sneaky rollers of cool, marine air which slip in beneath warmer air aloft, flipping the normal arrangement of air temperature, and trapping air pollutants in the cooler layer close to the ground. This creates smog, which can't escape vertically because cold air doesn't rise, and it can't get out sideways because the surrounding mountains block it. So, it is channeled eastward, all the way to Palm Springs and beyond. Unless winds and storms can upset this layer cake, folks in the Los Angeles Basin are forced to breathe some of the world's dirtiest air.

Class dismissed.

I kept peering intently through my windshield looking for encouraging hints of blue sky, trying to outrun the grime. By the time I reached Highway 62 north of Palm Springs, the sky was blessedly clearer. Here I turned north for a side trip to Joshua Tree National Monument. Weary from driving through smog and heavy traffic, I found a cheap motel on a hill overlooking the town of Joshua Tree.

When the sky turned dark I grabbed a beer and pulled a chair outside my motel room to watch things. Never before had I seen a skyscape of such chilling clarity, an empire of black velvet, vast and deep beyond comprehension, spangled with billions of stars glittering like chipped ice. It seemed as though all the heat output of the hottest desert day would be nothing but a flint spark in that icy realm.

In the morning I continued on through the town of Twentynine Palms. At its eastern edge I turned south toward Joshua Tree National Monument. It was a perfect desert day, blue and bright, verging on hot, but not scorching. At the visitor center I picked up an armload of brochures and a few books, then wandered along the "Oasis of Mara Interpretive Trail" behind the visitor center to familiarize myself with the plants and animals of the desert. Later, sitting on a bench reading my brochures, a roadrunner appeared at the edge of the pavement just a few feet from me. I saw what a beautiful little guy he really is, with patches of blue and red behind his eye. I made chucking noises at him and invited him over. He looked at me, thought it over maybe, but did not accept.

Continuing south through the monument, I stopped at the cholla cactus garden, in the transition zone between the Mojave and Colorado Deserts, so said the brochure. Chollas are squat, multi-armed cacti with fine, soft-looking bristles which diffuse sunlight and give them a glowing effect. Walking through this shimmering array in the early morning, I couldn't keep from smiling at these friendly, gnome-like plants, so fuzzy-looking, so huggable. No wonder they are commonly called teddy bear cholla. Darn cute, but beware. Each bristle is sharply barbed, and the merest light brush with this teddy bear will find you with a needle piercing your skin. I discovered this for myself when I accidentally touched one with my left hand, then reflexively grabbed with my right, only to transfer the painful barb to my grasping hand. Without pliers or heavy gloves, there's no way to win with a teddy bear.

Finally, I passed the Cottonwood Visitor Center at the southern end of the park and reconnected with Interstate 10. I pressed on to the east, my destination for tonight, Blythe, California, situated on the Colorado River at the border with Arizona. After one hundred miles of dun-colored desert, I was unprepared for the verdure of Blythe. From five miles out, I looked down on well-watered green fields of alfalfa and cotton. Amazing the transformation a river can bring to an arid place, but how strange, how tenuous that slash of green agriculture in the desert. Blythe, to me, sits inharmoniously on the land, dependent as it is on the overused, overmanaged Colorado. Life as a Blythean would be unpalatable to me. I would feel too much the usurper living in such a place.

I started early the next morning, driving over the Colorado River and into Arizona. I wanted to finish most of my day's drive before the Sonoran desert heat made my un-air-conditioned Colt intolerable. One hundred monotonous miles later, I finally reached Highway 85 and turned south off the interstate. But with the temperature already in the 90s, and another 100 miles to Organ Pipe, I opted to stop in Gila Bend for the night and finish the drive in the freshness of morning.

I left early and continued south on Highway 85 passing between the Sauceda and Crater Mountains, a couple of the more than two hundred small mountain ranges in the Basin and Range province of the western United States.

All was cactus, plain and mountain, devoid of human habitation. And not just because of heat and aridity, but also because the first thirty-five miles traversed the Luke Bombing and Gunnery Range, training ground for aerial gunnery, rocketry and other military maneuvers. A small road sign cautioned, *low-flying aircraft*.

I wasn't giving much thought to aircraft, though, until, in the middle of a reverie about the stark beauty surrounding me, a sudden screaming roar directly over my head nearly jellied my innards. From out of the serene desert morning, a fighter jet had streaked low over the hood of my car, ripping the sky apart, and was now disappearing down the road ahead of me, leaving me shaking at the wheel, my heart pounding in outraged beats. When the thumping quieted and I could think, I smelled a rat. Betcha anything this wasn't a coincidental flyover, but an invitation for a little target practice on the part of some ace pilot who spotted the bright canary color of my little Dodge Colt as it moved down the arrow-straight highway. I drove the remaining miles into Organ Pipe hunched over the steering wheel, scanning the sky in cringing preparedness for another surprise attack.

But it didn't come and soon I was out of the bombing range approaching the copper mining town of Ajo. From several miles out, great ridges of ash-colored tailings marked the town like map pins, and I anticipated a charmless, gray little place subdued by the gritty dominance of the Phelps Dodge Corporation.

Once in town, I pulled off onto a side street to study my map and take a look around. It was a gray little town, a curious little town. I locked my car and set out on a walking tour. Ajo's residential area consisted of several blocks of small, stucco bungalows with lawns of gravel within chain link fences. Strangely, though, the place was not charmless. Instead, it had a peculiar allure. The streets seemed to doze dreamily under the mid-morning sun. There was a hint of ease in the dusty light, a kind of settled, hometown feel. I walked on toward the center of town, attracted by an incongruous splash of bright green. It was Ajo's historic central plaza, an oasis of green grass ringed by tall palms and bordered on the backside by a U-shaped row of commercial buildings. A beautiful arched wall framed a continuous walkway in front of the markets and the railroad station. I strolled around the plaza, peeking through windows and savoring the feel of old Mexico.

After leaving Ajo, I passed through the quirky town of Why and soon arrived at the Organ Pipe visitor center. I stopped to snag as many books and brochures as I could afford, and choose a campsite from the map of the pear-shaped campground, which consisted of 208 sites in closely packed parallel rows. I expected the campsites would be nothing more than exposed, concrete slabs, more like a parking lot for RVs, but I was prepared to accept that.

From the visitor center it was another couple of miles to the campground. I pulled back onto the road and almost immediately noticed a change in the plant life. The saguaros and organ pipe cacti were suddenly and astonishingly much larger than those I had seen coming into the monument. They towered, green and lush, above the road like lords of the desert. How could this be, I wondered? These fellows are way too enormous and green for the scantiness of rainfall here. What could account for this, and why this sudden appearance at the national monument boundary? I pondered this for a while. Then a little ray of light managed to break through the fog of my brain. "Oh, heh, heh, I get it," said the dullard to herself. The saguaros and organ pipes don't just *happen* to be larger here in the national monument, it's a national monument *because* they are larger here. That still didn't answer my question, though, about why they were so big, but I guessed I would find out soon enough.

I was in for a surprise when I arrived at the campground. Yes, the sites were close together, but each was screened from the others by combinations of stout saguaro cactus, organ pipe cactus, lime-green paloverdes, creosote, and brittlebush, offering much more privacy than I had expected. I pulled in to my designated spot, hauled out my tent and prepared to pitch it, acutely conscious of my greenhorn status.

Appearances were everything, assuming as I did, that all other campers were observing me and knew telepathically that this was my first attempt at pitching a tent. I placed a peg in a grommet, and with my mallet drove solidly, competently, through the center of the peg head, expecting to feel the soft parting of soil as the peg penetrated. Instead, the thin surface soil shattered like brittle piecrust as the mallet ricocheted back at me with a metallic *boing*. I tried again, and again, each time moving the peg slightly to find softer ground, but to no avail. Then I remembered from graduate school my professor's lecture on desert environments. I was trying to pound through *caliche*, a rock-like, hardpan layer that develops just below the surface in deserts. Most of the other campers were in RVs and couldn't care less about caliche, but if I wanted any privacy, I had to erect this pup tent, and I had to show anyone watching that I knew how to do it. So, devil take caliche, the tent must go up. I pounded so hard the pegs bent, but eventually I managed to secure a couple of guy lines firmly enough to raise each end of the tent about three feet. The roof sagged like a saddle, allowing just enough room to push my sleeping bag inside. Once the tent was, er…pitched, I stood back, hands on hips, examining my expert job, hoping to convey the impression that this was what I had intended to do and that, obviously, I possessed some esoteric rationale for leaving a twelve-inch dip in the roof of a tent pitched in the desert.

Once camp was established, I took my first walk around the campground perimeter. The park rangers' trailers were near the entrance to the campground and as I passed by them a young ranger helloed and stopped for a brief welcome-to-ORPI chat. I asked him several questions about the park and he was happy to enlighten me. He was dark and slim, but not particularly good-looking. He seemed a bit goofy to me, a kind of backwater yokel, still, in spite of myself, I felt some feminine skills coming into play. It would be pleasant to have some personal attention from a park ranger. He introduced himself as Marty.

The next day I walked the 1.3-mile Palo Verde Trail to the visitor center. On the way back as I was passing by the ranger trailers, I saw Marty. I was hoping to run into him again, and I'm pretty sure he was planning on running into me the way he was hanging around his trailer not doing much. He came up and asked how things were going. I told him I had just finished a 2.6-mile hike and was feeling pretty hot and sweaty. "Hey," he said, "you're welcome to come up and take a shower in my trailer." I'll just bet I am, I thought. I didn't think rangers should be inviting park visitors into their residences, and I didn't think his supervisor would much like it either, if he knew. "Tell you what," he went on. "If you want to take a shower later, I don't mind. Then if you like, we can drive down into Mexico for dinner. I know a good little place." That scared me a bit. Marty, a stranger; Mexico, a foreign country. I had heard stories about gringo mishaps south of the border. Still, I figured Marty, having worked here for a while, probably knew what he was doing, so I agreed.

Toward dusk, I grabbed some toiletries and a towel and headed up to Marty's trailer. As I walked from the campground up the path, I felt as though every eye inside every R.V. was watching, and every tongue was tsk tsking at this obvious and blatant indiscretion. Inside Marty's tiny trailer, the shower wasn't *exactly* in a bathroom. Instead it was more of an *area* in the rear, but Marty assured me he would keep his eyes averted. By this time I had pretty much pegged Marty as too nerdy to be dangerous, just a bit socially off kilter, not exactly what most women would call a cool guy. I arranged curtains and doors to maximize privacy and took my shower. Marty was true to his word. I sensed that he wouldn't have known what to do even if he had been carnally motivated.

By the time we were ready to go, it was dark. Marty said before dinner he wanted to take a quick ride out to an overlook to scan for illegal aliens coming across the border from Mexico, a hazardous-sounding proposition to me, and a rather strange prelude to a date. But, again, I figured this was part of his job and he knew what he was doing.

Marty's favorite illegal alien lookout was along the twenty-one mile, one-way, graded dirt, Ajo Mountain Drive. At a rocky outcrop he stopped his pickup, got out his binoculars, and started scanning the southern terrain for distant flashlight beams. I wasn't sure if this was part of his job description, but he seemed to be getting a big kick out of it, because he continued to scan for half an hour while I sat in the cab of his truck drumming my fingers on the dashboard. By the time he was ready to push on, I gently suggested that maybe it was a little late to drive down into Mexico for dinner, and that I had plenty of canned goods that we could make a fine meal out of. He agreed.

Back in his trailer over a dinner of eggs and Vienna sausage, Marty told me his last name was Garcia-Gunther, hyphenated. He said his mother was Garcia and his dad Gunther, and that he used his mom's surname because he believed the "Garcia" would enhance his job opportunities, affirmative action-wise. Dream on, I thought, but kept it to myself.

I told Marty about Ed Abbey and about Carol Turner on the Bull Pasture Trail, and that I planned to hike the trail tomorrow. He offered to go along and take his pickup, which sounded all right to me. It wouldn't hurt to have ranger Marty along just in case Carol Turner's Fates were still haunting the trail.

The Fates, if there were any, seemed to ignore me, but they tempted Marty a couple of times. As we were walking to the Bull Pasture Trailhead, I spotted something orange and black moving slowly across the road. "Marty, look! A gila monster!" Nocturnal and rarely seen, this rare and beautiful reptile is the only poisonous lizard in the United States. I was ecstatic at my good fortune. The gila monster was making its way to the shade as quickly as possible after its night of hunting. I knew prolonged exposure to direct sun would cause it to overheat and perish. These creatures move slowly, but I knew that when riled they can react quickly, biting down hard, and relentlessly grinding venom into its molester.

I knew to keep a respectable distance. Not Marty, though, who should have known better. He grabbed it behind its neck, and picked it up. "Marty, put it down! Put it down!" I cried. He hung on to it, grinning like a fool, while I stared in disbelief at the thrashing animal. Finally Marty put the creature down and it crept off to find shelter. I confronted him. "What the hell are you doing?" I sputtered. "Gila monsters are endangered. It's illegal to molest them. You should know that, Marty. You're a ranger. You caused that animal a lot of stress, and you could have been bitten."

"I just wanted to get a better look," Marty pouted, looking sheepish.

"You should know better, Marty. That's what stupid tourists would do. You're supposed to be protecting these animals."

Marty was proving my suspicions that he was lacking in good judgment and maturity. He wasn't really a malicious guy, just thoughtless. We continued on to the trail. Marty hiked fast and soon left me behind, saying he would wait for me up at Bull Pasture. That was fine with me. I didn't want to hurry through that amazing surround of rock and sage. Ahead of me I saw movement in the shadow of a ledge in the trail. I stopped as a snake slithered out and rested momentarily on the slab taking in a little morning sunlight. A sidewinder, maybe. I watched it awhile, glad that Marty wasn't there to provide me with a closer look, then continued on up the trail.

At last I stepped out at the top of the trail into the Bull Pasture, a broad basin in the top of the mountains, once actually used as a cow pasture by early cowboys. Marty was waiting, as promised. We sat for a while drinking in the silence, gazing out over the sagebrush and eating our lunch. I assumed we would hike back down the trail then, but Marty had other plans.

"I'm going to hike across to the other side and climb the ridge," he announced. "If you don't want to come with me you can stay here or wait for me back in the truck. I won't be gone long." I suspected Marty's idea of not long would be meaningless once he started out. And I also sensed that it would never occur to him to consider my feelings about his plan. I didn't want to go scrambling up the opposite cliff with Marty's backside disappearing over boulders a quarter mile ahead of me, and I didn't want to sit around up there twiddling my thumbs waiting. Nor did I want to hike back down and wait in his truck, either. I at least wanted to keep track of him through my binoculars. Clearly, all of the options meant I was in for a worry, and there was nothing I could do about it. I opted to wait at Bull Pasture while Marty went off to play mountaineer. Maybe, just maybe, he really did mean to come back soon.

I watched Marty walk across the basin and start up the other side. Then I followed him with my binoculars until finally he vanished among the rocks. To pass time, I wandered off on little mini-hikes, not straying far from the trailhead. I studied plants and rock formations. I waited. It was past mid-afternoon and I was sure Marty would be heading back by then. I scanned with my binoculars, but couldn't find him. I strained to glimpse his white T-shirt, but saw only buff-colored rock. I waited some more, becoming increasingly anxious and angry. As deep afternoon turned to dusk, I became really worried, and tried to think of the best plan of action. Should I walk back down the trail and go for help? I had the keys to Marty's truck. But, if he came down when I was gone, he would be stranded. What if I stayed and he was hurt or in trouble and couldn't move? We'd both be up here all night with no protection. I strained my ears to listen for a distress call, but received only silence. Stars were beginning to appear, but no sign of Marty. I couldn't stand the tension any longer. I grabbed my daypack, scrambled to my feet and turned toward the trailhead. Just then I heard a clattering of rock in the basin below me. I peered down into the shadows and there at last I saw Marty's dark head bobbing up the slope.

Neither my anger, nor my repeated explanations about the stress and concern he had caused me, had any impact on him. What was the big deal, he asked. He merely misjudged how long it would take him to cross the basin, climb the ridge, and get back. We hiked back down the trail by flashlight. I fumed silently all the way back to camp, icily refused his invitation for dinner, and hurried back to the comfort of my own little camp chair, a tuna sandwich, and a cold beer from my cooler.

I avoided Marty on the last days of my vacation. I drove the Puerto Blanco Drive, a fifty-three mile, one-way loop circling the colorful Puerto Blanco Mountains. At the southwestern corner of the loop along the Mexican border, I found Quitobaquito, a one-acre, natural pond surrounded by cottonwoods, bulrushes and mesquite–a haven for birds and therefore birdwatchers like me. I stopped to bird for a long time, picking up several new bird species for my list of birds seen, my "life list."

Early the next morning I took one last walk from the campground to the visitor center and back. I sauntered along identifying the plants: there's a brittlebush, there's bursage, that's Engelmann prickly pear…The desert had gotten under my skin. I loved the lacy, lime green branches of the palo verde, and the gray-brown smudge of the smoke tree. I loved the soaring dominance of the saguaros and the organ pipe cacti. This is a place I must return to, I thought, and the sooner the better.

Back in camp as I was folding the tent and packing up two and a half boxes of canned food, I saw Marty slowly circle the campground twice in his government pickup. On the third loop he pulled up to my site.

"Getting ready to leave?"

"Yep. Time to go." I didn't really want to encourage conversation, but when I looked into Marty's goofy brown eyes my heart softened. Marty meant well; he didn't have a mean bone in his body. He was just a bit obtuse. So, I thanked him for showing me around. We each tore off little pieces of note paper and wrote our names and address on them and said we ought to keep in touch. Marty said he wanted to leave ORPI soon and find a job with the Park Service in some other beautiful place. I never expected to see him again, but as I drove away from the campground, little did I suspect that my farewell to him would not be the last. All thoughts of Marty Garcia-Gunther quickly faded as I turned the canary Colt north and retraced my route on Highway 85, back past the forbidding Cabeza Prieta Wildlife Refuge, through the gunnery range, and on into the stark, indifferent radiance of the open desert.

PART III:

The Big Trip: California to Maine

June 22 – October 2, 1981

CHAPTER 3

Feasibility Studies

July 9, 1981
Ready, Set, Go

Sitting at mom's sewing machine sewing a yellow and white striped awning for my Volkswagen Westfalia. Arrived a week ago after ten days on the road, stopping to visit friends between Santa Maria, California and Eugene, Oregon where my mother lives. I'm here to spend time with my mother before leaving on my journey. And also to gear up, anticipating all my needs for a year on the road living in my little pea green VW, the Greenhouse.

I have busted out, broken loose from the oppression of my job as a drudge in the Advance Planning Division, City of Santa Maria, California. After struggling with the pros and cons of quitting my job at the brink of middle age, the ayes and nays finally settled into place heavily on the side of the ayes, and it was clear that spending the rest of my working life as a city planner would be a sellout. Even though I was in my late thirties, even though my inbred sense of responsibility argued for bucking up and settling down, I could not endure that fate. The wisdom of too many philosophers, dreamers, and social advisors resounded in my head: follow your dreams, live life to the fullest, march to the beat of your own drummer, etc.

In Santa Maria every morning was the same. I would arrive at work early before the others, pour a cup of coffee and sit down at my desk, staring at the pages of rough draft and outlines in front of me. I was responsible for writing two elements of the General Plan, which I did with my best technical writing skills, although little did it matter as these documents were given only the minimally prescribed attention before being rubber stamped by the City Council and shelved in the city's archives along with all the other yellowing general plan documents.

Alone in the silent office, I began my customary pre-work daydream with a question: What would I rather be doing right now instead of sitting at this cold desk in this dank, windowless office? I would close my eyes and look inward as though lying on an analyst's couch, trying to visualize myself in my idyllic spot. The materializing image was a solitary campsite along a murmuring stream. It is morning and I am sitting in my camp chair on a little sandy bar, coffee cup in my hand, gazing at the sparkling waters, sunlight warming my skin. I hear the morning titter of songbirds. A forest of fir and pine forms a backdrop.

I performed this exercise daily, closing my eyes and concentrating. Each time, images flashed through my mind, like pages in a cartoon flip book, and each time the flickering images settled back onto the streamside camp. No doubt about it, I would rather be camping at this very moment.

Camping, however, is not a viable lifelong pursuit. It can last a week or two, maybe, depending on weather, bugs, boredom, and things like that. Still, what if I could just take off and go wherever I wanted, for as long as I wanted? Traveling around visiting national parks, cruising back roads, exploring campgrounds, and stopping for the night wherever I pleased? Imagine doing that for, say, a year.

Sometimes an idea delivers a lightning bolt punch. This one did–a sudden blitz of an idea. Why not, just for the sheer amusement factor of it, try to figure out what it would cost to finance a year-long camping trip. Just for the hell of it.

I grabbed a pencil and a blank sheet of paper and began scribbling:

Year-Long Camping Trip Feasibility Study

	Est. Expense
Vehicle: Used camper, VW pop-top	$2500 – $3500
Per Month: gas, food campgrounds eat out, laundry, stamps, postcards, wood, etc. $400 × 12, rounded up	$5000
Equipment / Gear	$500
Post-Trip Reserve	$3000
Total	$11,000 – $12,000

As I added the last digit, I gaped in disbelief at the bottom line. Surely it must be wrong. I had expected some exorbitant, unattainable figure, like thirty, forty thousand dollars, which, for me, might as well have been a million. But eleven or twelve thousand dollars was not so much. A person could raise that amount of money. But, how quickly, I wondered. Could I raise that amount in, say, a year? I grabbed more paper and started figuring again:

Year-Long Camping Trip Feasibility Study

Estimated Savings for One Year	
Half city planning paycheck $525 × 12	$6300
Part-time college teaching, two semesters	3500
Sell Dodge Colt	1200
Total	$11,000

My mouth dropped open when I saw the bottom line, so eerily matching my estimated expenses, as though fudged by an obliging fairy god-accountant.

These morning scribblings had been strictly for amusement; they weren't supposed to line up like this. But there it was, the budget, staring at me from yellow-lined paper, shouting, feasible! feasible!

I should have been exhilarated, but instead I was struck with a profound fear. I couldn't just quit my job and drive away. At my age it would be grossly irresponsible, too wild, too reckless. Wouldn't it? I grasped desperately for the "cons" against such a crazy idea. Surely there must be some blaring reason why it wasn't possible. But there wasn't. There was nothing to prevent me from going but the heart-palpitating fear of it.

Like a sudden shake into awakening, the debate ended. My heart thumped loudly in my throat; my breathing came shallow and perforated, like strained wind. I looked up from my desk at the bare, brown wall in front of me. The words seemed to come of their own accord from some submerged font of confidence in me.

"I am going to do it."

CHAPTER 4

Prepare for Departure: Home Sweet Greenhouse

I couldn't wait to tell Callie and Jill, my office mates, that I was going camping for a year. The next morning I arrived early at the office and waited for them to come. "Hurry up. Hurry up," I chanted, pacing the floor and anticipating their faces when I popped the news. I planned a sort of casual, off-handed glide into my announcement when they arrived. Just a small item slipped into our usual pre-work, first-cup-of-coffee confab. But I knew I wouldn't be able to contain myself very long. When it comes to sensational news, I am a spillway.

Callie and Jill sat very still in their chairs, wide-eyed, polite smiles affixed to their faces. I could sense them trying not to cast skeptical glances at each other. It was plain they were torn between incredulity and the courtesy of sharing my excitement. That was all right. I didn't blame them for their doubts. Time would be my champion.

I put my plan into action immediately, stopping all extraneous spending and stashing $525 a month into a savings account. I taught nights and Saturdays at the local college, and fattened the fund with that income. Daily, I scanned the classified ads in the *Los Angeles Times* for campers. I began a list of all that I would need for a year's journey, everything from tools to toenail clippers.

In the evenings I settled on the sofa with a National Geographic coffee table book, *America's Wonderlands*, marking X's next to the photos of places I wanted to visit, so many I wondered if a year would be enough time. I considered several routes, drawing colored lines all over the map. I contemplated different ratios of driving-to-camping days: drive one day, camp three; drive to a national park, stay a week, drive to another national park, and so on. When my obsessive planning began to feel like a full nelson around my neck, I finally threw my pencil down and gave myself a talking to. Enough. Go where you want to go, when you feel the hell like it. I loosened the stranglehold a little and chucked all travel scenarios except the general route I would take, a northerly, clockwise circuit around the country.

One day in late winter, scanning the *Los Angeles Times* classifieds, I found an ad: *1978 Volkswagen pop-top Westfalia. 20,000 miles. $2200.* I called the party and made arrangements with a friend to drive me to L.A. the following weekend. The pea green camper was in nearly perfect condition with low mileage. The interior was paneled with a brown, faux wood veneer, and the seats sported green and yellow plaid burlap upholstery to match the pea green paint. Green burlap curtains covered the windows. I snagged it for $2200 and drove it back to Santa Maria. I couldn't wait to explore the nooks and crannies of the interior and push the pop-top up for the first time.

When I arrived home, my neighbor Bill came out to see my new rig. He poked around the interior and sat dutifully watching as I prepared to raise the pop-top. It was not as easy as I had thought. It required pushing hard on a horizontal metal brace to force it up and lock it in place. I gave it a heave, got it half way up, and ran out of steam. I didn't have the arm strength to snap it into the upright position, and besides, I was too damn short.

"Try again," Bill urged. I pushed as hard as I could, but clearly I wasn't strong enough or tall enough to do the job. I tried stepping on the back bench seat, but that put me too far away from the bar.

"Shit! I can't do it!" I collapsed onto the seat, tears springing to my eyes. I saw my dream vanish before I had even gotten started. "I should have known something would go wrong."

Poor Bill, I vented all my anger and humiliation on him, as if it was his fault. Bill knew me pretty well, though, and wasn't about to brook any "poor-me-I'm-just-a-helpless-female" whining. He shrugged and walked back to his apartment.

Sulking, I sat alone in my camper pitying myself. Eventually I calmed down and started thinking rationally. There had to be a solution. There were tools after all, levers, pulleys–that sort of thing. There must be lots of ways to solve this problem. I went into my apartment and fetched the footstool I used to reach anything above six feet high, and placed it on the floor of the camper. Looking around to make sure no one was watching, I stepped up on it and grabbed the metal bar. Reminding myself to lift with my legs, not with my back, and bending my knees to get maximum thrust, I heaved forward with a Herculean effort, and whap! the thing snapped firmly into place. Sunlight filtering through the canvas released the same smell as the old tent Dad used to pitch at Cultus Lake, and of the moldy laundry room where it was stashed fifty-one weeks of the year.

"Yes!" I yelled, which brought Bill back out of his apartment. He found me sitting on the bench seat, beaming. I pulled the top back down and pushed it up again, for practice, and to demonstrate for Bill.

On Monday morning I drove my camper, newly dubbed "The Greenhouse," to work. At lunchtime my co-workers gathered around as I slid back the side door and gave them a tour, popping the top to reveal the upper bed and unfolding the bench seat into the lower bed. They exchanged dubious glances at each other, no doubt wondering if I would be foolhardy enough to actually undertake such a preposterous journey. But then Callie, who had been sitting on the bench seat spoke softly. "You're really going to do this, aren't you, Lynn?"

"Yes," I said, "I am." I had never known such excitement before. This was far beyond the scope of anything I had ever imagined I would do. But it was too grand a dream to be ignored. From that moment on there was never any wavering, never a doubt, never a backward glance.

For the rest of the year I adhered to the budget I had set for myself, and put all other funds into savings. I added items to my camping list and outfitted my camper with a propane cook stove and a five-gallon propane tank. The tin icebox set into the top of the galley counter had no drain, so I elected to use it solely for storage and keep my perishable food in a portable ice chest. To add comfort to the hard mattress of the bench seat I bought a thick foam pad to use under my sleeping bag.

I packed cookware, clothing, maps, tools, first aid kit, solar shower, toiletries and everything else I needed into the closet and cupboards and under the bench seat.

Every night in bed before drifting off to sleep I pretended to be in the greenhouse, comparing the dimensions of my bedroom to the dimensions of my camper, trying to envision my head and feet in proximity to the front and rear windshields, assessing the "coziness" factor.

The days passed quickly. At last my departure date arrived, June 22, 1981. I drove the outfitted camper to the office one last time to say goodbye. My friends gathered around my "rig." I snapped a group photo, gave warm hugs all around, and drove away.

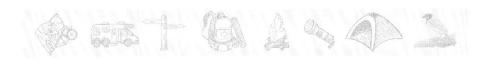

CHAPTER 5

Pacific Northwest: Good Men, Bad Men

Thursday, July 16, 1981
Eugene, Oregon

*W*oke up this morning feeling anxious. Today I begin my journey. Spent the morning packing, stuffing clothes into the camper closets, cramming the cupboards with food. As soon as I go for a run I'll be ready to go.

At 2:00 this afternoon I said farewell to my worried-looking mother and sister, and drove through west Eugene toward the coast, anxious about finding a good place to camp. Following directions in my campground guide I found North Fork Siuslaw campground 13½ miles northeast of Florence. But it was occupied by a seedy-looking group of youths playing loud music on their car radio. It was only 4:00 in the afternoon, and I didn't think I would enjoy spending the rest of the day worrying about hooligans, so I left and continued on to Highway 101, not knowing where I would rest.

At Florence I turned north and stopped at the first campground I came to, Sutton Creek Campground. As soon as I settled into a good site, I went for a short walk along a nature trail and met a friendly young couple from Seattle, Dean and Suzette. We talked for quite a while; Suzette was distressed by the number of rude people she had encountered on their trip, "freaks and weirdos," she called them. I sympathized with her and figured I would meet a few of them myself over the coming year.

Each campsite at Sutton Creek was thickly enclosed by darlingtonia, thimbleberry, ferns, wildflowers, fir and pine trees, affording complete privacy. As I sat in my camp chair, chickadees and swallows darted about in search of supper. A small, wren-looking bird–a wrentit maybe–picked through the bushes, but I couldn't tell for sure. I sat drinking in the sounds of birds and the resin scent of pine trees until dusk overtook me and I stepped into the camper for my first overnight on the road.

I'm in the greenhouse now. It's as cozy a cabin as I could ever want, like the cabin of a tiny boat. The light is paling and it will be dark soon. The breeze is blowing a chill through the air, and a fog hangs to the east. But I am snug in my cot, curled up on the bench seat looking around my miniature apartment glowing with candlelight. It's just right. I feel safe and warm here.

Expenses:	$10.80	gas
	5.00	phone calls
	4.00	campground

Friday, July 17, 1981

It took me an hour to get things set up for breakfast, eat, and clean up. In my apartment kitchen at home I knew where everything was. I knew which way to turn to reach a spatula and where to set the hot frying pan. Now, instead of having ten feet of counter space, I had thirty-six inches and a very tiny table for workspace. It was disheartening at first, dimming the likelihood of early morning quick starts. But then, I was never an early morning, quick-start kind of person anyway, and besides, the routine would become familiar soon enough.

Outside my camper the day offered fog and drizzle, standard fare for the Oregon coast. A shaded trail led from the campground through the forest to the beach. I walked into the green gloom listening to the muted birdsongs. I heard the "*Madge, Madge, pleeease put on the kettle,*" of the song sparrow, and the high, lisping whispers of cedar waxwings. From deep in the bushes came the ping pong ball song of the wrentit, "*pit...pit....pit...pitpitpit*" accelerating into a trill at the end, and I stood patiently, the way we crazy birdwatchers do, until the elusive, yellow-eyed bird briefly popped into the open to show me his long, upwardly cocked tail.

I emerged from the woods into an expanse of small lagoons, which I had to cross to reach the shore. All was enshrouded in a bright fog melding sand, sea and sky in monochromatic unity. Shapes normally identifiable as trees or rocks now were blurred into hazy dark smudges. Sand hummocks fringed with grass separated the lagoons from the ocean. I crossed the lagoons on driftwood logs and brushed through the hummocks onto the broad beach. Far out, the frothy line of low tide glittered milk-white on the lip of the ocean. I stood a long while, until my own edges blurred and blended into the silence and the fog. Then, invisible, I turned and walked back to camp.

In the evening I built a campfire and cooked a meal girl scout-style. I wrapped hamburger, carrots and onions in aluminum foil and waited for the fire to recline into coals. Then I buried the packet in the glowing embers and baked it for half an hour. My supper was perfectly cooked, succulent and tasty. Contented, I sat close to the waning warmth of the fire and listened to a hermit thrush's plaintive, flute-like calls coming from deep within the forest.

Saturday, July 18, 1981

I left Sutton Creek early this morning and continued north. The sun was shining, the sky blue, the sand bright. Every wayside, beach, park, and picnic table beckoned to me. There were so many. I stopped at Devil's Churn where the surf behaves like a powerful geyser when it is squeezed into a narrow slot in the rocks and explodes upward with a tremendous boom. I drove the steep road up to Cape Perpetua, 800 feet above the ocean, for a dramatic view of the coast stretching away to the north and south.

In the small town of Yachats I stopped to buy groceries and mail a letter. The town hadn't changed much since my last visit years ago, a few more restaurants, but still tiny and charming. I was surprised at how little traffic there was along Hwy. 101, especially for a Saturday in the middle of summer. It heartened me. The Oregon coast still looked wild and unspoiled.

I pulled in at the first campground north of Yachats, Tillicum Beach, and soon met the campground host, Jack Gannon, a very friendly, obliging man who directed me to a campsite. As I set up camp, my neighbors struck up a conversation, elderly folks who seemed to perceive me as needing advise and succor, as though it wasn't my fault or my choice that I was alone on the road . . . adrift, helpless, and forlorn.

Later, I strolled down to the beach. The sun was shining through a light mist floating in from the sea. I stayed there a long time, spellbound by the warmth of the sand and the brilliance of the surf and air.

Back in camp, I cooked a pot of beans in my pressure cooker. This time, kitchen operations were much easier and faster. I was getting the hang of it and gaining confidence. I discovered a way to hang my solar shower above my tiny sink to wash dishes or my hair with relative ease. Everything was working out fine. I love my little greenhouse.

Sunday, July 19, 1981

Arose late this morning. Made pancakes with peanut butter and syrup for breakfast, my favorite. Sticks with you all morning. Went looking for a vacant, oceanside campsite, and got lucky.

Jack Gannon, the campground host, is getting real friendly. In fact, he let me know very plainly that he would like to fool around. I let him know very plainly that I would not. He said okay, and didn't seem too upset. He invited me to go crabbing the next day at Waldport with his eleven year-old son, Brandon.

Monday, July 20, 1981

Jack, Brandon and I left about 11:00 a.m. to go crabbing at the bay in Waldport, something I would never have done on my own. I enjoyed the crabbing, but not Jack's company. Out of Brandon's earshot, he leaned toward me and said, "These crab legs are good-looking, and so are yours." He kept up the scurrilous comments and threw in a few dirty jokes for extra effect, forcing me into a lot of verbal sidestepping.

Later, while sitting in my camper writing in my journal, I looked up to see Jack approaching. At my open door he presented me with fresh, cooked crab he had caught that morning. He made no move to leave, so I invited him to sit in the front passenger seat, which was rotated to face the interior. I sat on the opposite bench seat which I had hastily strewn with blankets, books, and clothes to preclude his sitting beside me. It didn't take him long to get to the point I already knew was coming. He spoke in a low, self-conscious voice, as one does when he is about to reveal an intimate desire.

"I would like to kiss you," he murmured. Only it came out "kith," as though he were too embarrassed to pronounce the s's.

"I'm sorry, Jack, that's not going to happen. I don't feel that way about you." I tried to keep a pleasant smile on my face.

His proposal rebuffed, Jack backed off, but, nevertheless, invited me up to his trailer for a drink that evening. Knowing that his son would be there, I didn't think any harm would come of it, so I accepted. It turned out to be a lively evening. Jack toned down the suggestive comments and the three of us talked and told jokes until 10:45 when, in a mellow mood, Jack and Brandon walked me back to my camper.

Tuesday, July 21, 1981

The Specter at Hebo Lake

This morning I packed up my camper and said goodbye to Jack. Drove the few miles into Waldport and had breakfast at the Drift In Café. I'm heading for Hebo Lake today, six miles north of Pacific City. Hope the campground isn't full.

It's a long, steep, twisting road up here to tiny Hebo Lake. The campground is moist and heavily wooded with fir, spruce, and red alder, and quite isolated and primitive compared to Tillicum Beach.

It is dark here in the woods, with ominous gray mists from off the ocean sneaking through the trees like malicious, snooping neighbors. And silent, except for the intermittent soft tap of swollen water droplets falling leaf to leaf, leaf to ground.

I felt uneasy as I began setting up camp, as though someone in the screening gloom was watching me. I finished arranging gear on the picnic table, turned to step into my camper, then stopped. A few yards upslope, as silent and motionless as the firs around him, a man stood staring intently at me. He was ancient and gaunt with eyes like dark, hollow pits. Startled,

I called out a cheery hello, attempting to mask my alarm with a forced air of insouciance. He did not speak, but lurched toward me, jerking his arm upward, and emitting a short, guttural cry, like a paralyzed man trying to shout. Then he was silent and still again, but continued staring with those ghastly, cadaverous eyes.

A horrible vision of a crazed old man crashing down slope toward my camper in the dark of night, a long, sharp knife in his upraised hand, spurred me to action. As quickly as I could I reloaded my gear back into my camper and drove to the opposite side of the lake, nearer to the only other, and more normal-looking, campers in the place.

I desperately needed a crackling campfire to comfort me and banish the image of the man in the trees. But I could find no dry firewood and did not know the tricks to starting a campfire in wet woods. Finally, after multiple attempts and prodigious squirts of starter fluid, the fire was blazing. I cooked chicken, carrots, onions in foil, and sat by the fire peering into the shadows, alert for unwanted visitors, until weariness won out and I retired to the greenhouse.

Wednesday, July 22, 1981

After breakfast I prepared for a hike up the flank of Mt. Hebo. I layered on sweaters and shirts and topped them with my waterproof Gore-tex raincoat, grabbed my binoculars and bird book and headed up the trail through a mossy, green wonderland. Birds were everywhere. I spotted a western flycatcher first. Then several gray jays, (aka "camp robbers"), came gliding in close to inspect me. One landed on the limb just over my head and peered down at me for a long time, cocking his head back and forth in that bold, curious way of gray jays.

I saw a varied thrush, hairy woodpecker, Wilson's warbler, juncos, many chickadees, and, best of all, a winter wren—I knew it by its short, stubby tail, hopping and bobbing through the undergrowth, loudly scolding and chattering.

I returned to camp around 1:00 p.m. and ate lunch. Nothing else to do on such a gray, cold, and drizzly day but study field guides and write in my journal. If only it was sunny, I could heat water in my solar shower and bathe. I felt so dirty.

I never did see the old man again. Likely, he was just a lonely, slightly off-kilter old fellow, harmless, and perhaps disabled. And perhaps it would have grieved him if he knew the fright he had given me. But I will never know.

Thursday, July 23, 1981

"Spectacular!"

The process of setting up and breaking camp is becoming tiresome. The mere matter of feeding myself requires planning and far more work than it would in a fully equipped kitchen. And there are a lot of niggling little chores, too: buy gas, buy groceries, check oil, wash windshield, start fire, wash dishes, write letters, write journals and keep records. I am feeling hungry and out of sorts.

I drove down from Lake Hebo this morning and pulled into Nehalem State Park, north of Tillamook, a state-of-the-art campground with paved roads, paved campsites, showers and electrical hook-ups. I feel much better, which is strange, because I haven't used either showers or electricity yet. Although the sky is overcast, the gray layer is a blanket holding warm air close to Earth. Compared to Hebo Lake, this feels like a steamy sauna.

I'm sitting in my camper relaxing with a beer, enjoying the hazy warmth, my curtains partially drawn for privacy. I am listening to the muted sounds around me—bits of conversation from folks strolling by, waves washing up the beach, birds twittering in the bushes outside—when the chirpy voices of two little British boys playing nearby ring out above the ambient sounds. I lean forward a little and spy on them.

They are pretend golfers, about seven or eight years old, exchanging chatter about the magnificent imaginary shots they are making. They have real golf balls but sticks for clubs. I hear the "thock" of the golf ball they are putting around the pavement. Then I hear "thunk" as a misputted ball rolls up against the front wheel of my van, and the sound of hurried footsteps as one little boy runs over to retrieve it. I can hear him panting just outside my thin camper wall as he fumbles to extract it from behind the wheel. I hear his soft grunt as, unaware of my presence, he takes a mighty swing with his stick club, launches the golf ball all the way down the pretend fairway, to the imaginary green, and…it's a hole in one!

"Spectacular!" he exclaims as he charges away to rejoin his friend.

Friday, July 24, 1981

Astoria, Oregon

Astoria is visually and historically fascinating, being the oldest city in Oregon, and near the terminus of the Lewis and Clark Trail. The city is dominated by the famous Astoria Bridge. The sight of it alone, soaring across the mouth of the Columbia River, dizzies like a ride on a roller coaster.

In spite of these highlights, my experience here has left me downhearted. The arterials are clogged with traffic and it's difficult to find a quiet, safe, and, since the town is hilly and the streets steep, *level*, place to park for the night. As a money saving measure, I had planned to overnight once or twice a week on quiet, residential city streets, but here in Astoria I encountered an unexpected street sign that would require some future adjustments to my plans:

NO OVERNIGHT PARKING
City of Astoria
Code Section 5.900

So much for the street-parking idea. I would have to look for other overnight arrangements. I had been told by other RVers that mall and church parking lots were good places to spend the night because they are well lit and usually patrolled.

I began cruising the main street of Astoria hunting down a suitable spot. I found it at the local hospital. I made a circuit of the parking lot and found what I thought was an inconspicuous corner spot under a tree. It seemed my best bet. Glad to have my bed place staked, I went off to find some means of amusing myself until dark, which comes late at this time of year and this far north.

The lot was lit like a tennis court when I returned, and patrolled, too, all night long, as I discovered. After I pulled in to my corner spot, I waited until well after dark before slipping into my sleeping bag, but I was reluctant to give in to sleep, fearful of just about everything. At regular intervals, I peeked out my window only to observe a patrol car slowly circling the lot. I lay tense and sleepless, expecting to be routed at any time by a banging on my window or the rude sweep of a flashlight beam into my tiny home. But neither happened. The guard must have seen me—it was impossible not to—but he must have figured a pea green pop-top VW meant a weary, anxious traveler, and had chosen to leave me alone.

At last the sky lightened, and I hauled out of my sleeping bag a tired, but savvier camper.

Saturday, July 25, 1981

I left Astoria in early afternoon, the weather sunny and beautiful. I planned to drive inland from the mouth of the Columbia River today looking for a good place to stay tonight before going across the river into Washington. Choosing the town of Clatskanie for tonight's camp, I thought it wise to check with the local constabulary regarding camping on city streets. A very nice police office directed me to a regional park where I could set up for the night. He told me it would be safe and that he himself would be patrolling it. His reassurance, and the beer now in my hand, helped to restore my mood.

Sunday, July 26, 1981

Randy

Today I arrived at Lewis and Clark State Park, off Interstate 5 in Washington. It's a pleasing, well-tended place and there's a Mt. St. Helen's Visitor Center here featuring exhibits, information, and an excellent film about the eruption of the mountain last year.

I must admit that loneliness is starting to affect me. I notice single male campers; I spy on them secretly, and wonder where they have come from and where they are going. I wonder if they notice me. One such camper arrived on a motorcycle and chose a campsite between me and the restroom, which made it necessary for me to pass by him regularly, stealing sideways glances. On one of the passes, we exchanged hellos, and soon he was seated across from me at my campfire. His name was Randy, from Texas, a big, shaggy, gentle guy, much younger than me, and he was doing what I was doing, just rambling around. We talked amicably for a long time and agreed to go hiking together the next day.

Monday, July 27, 1981

Today Randy and I hiked the "Trail of the Deer." He was easy-going and comfortable to be with. Along the way we decided we would share a campsite for the remainder of our stay—it would save money. We hung out together for the rest of the day and became intimate by evening. It was wonderful to have a lover again.

Tuesday, July 28, 1981

I rolled over in my sleeping bag this morning to see Randy, a stranger, asleep beside me. A moment of sickening remorse gripped me. What had I done? I felt a sudden panic of entrapment, of my freedom being stripped away, and also, of shame. Randy stirred and turned toward me, releasing the scent of body warmth from his sleeping bag. He was all comfort and ease with no hint of expectation in his awakening. He murmured good morning as he lay on his back, yawning, smiling. There was no lasciviousness to Randy; he was guileless and sweet. I slipped in beside him and was drawn firmly into his arms. I inhaled the faintly milky smell of his hair and chest and stretched out along the length of his body, feeling the slight rasp of the hair on his legs as I slid mine along his. Our bodies blended together naturally into unhurried lovemaking as the hours passed unnoticed outside the tin walls of my home.

Wednesday, July 29, 1981

How can it be that in two and a half days I should feel so close to a man, a boy, actually, who is essentially a stranger? Again this morning we nestled together as though we had known each other a long time. But today Randy and I would part—no lingering embraces or false promises. We did not try to make anything more of our affair than what it was, a sweet, brief encounter. The goodbye was quick and we were on our separate ways: Randy rode off to the west, and I headed east.

Monday, August 3, 1981

Just short of 4700 feet, Cayuse Pass on the east flank of Mt. Rainier is high enough to be in the fog. Still, rounding the bends of scenic State Route 410, I catch glimpses of the magnificent, snowy triangle of Rainier's summit piercing through the gray layer into brilliant sunlight. Wildflowers bursting open on the slopes are charged with color, dashes of electric red and blue, vivid pinks, magentas, all intensified by light refracted from the foggy sheen.

Near the summit I stop at a vista point, mostly clouds today. Many folks have stopped here; something besides the mountain has captured their attention. Least chipmunks are standing on their tiny hind legs eating from people's hands. Gray jays and Clark's nutcrackers, tame as house cats, beg for handouts. Although it distresses me to see people feeding wildlife, I confess I am captivated by these antics. I grab my Pentax K1000 camera and enter the scene to take a few snaps. I arrange my assortment of lenses and gadgets in a semi-circle on the ground around me, little servants at the ready waiting for duty. It occurs to me folks might think I am a professional photographer, the way I confidently kneel on one knee, shift my position, turn my camera sideways then lengthwise, focus, expertly change lenses, refocus. I prolong these maneuvers to . . . well, to achieve the most artistically advantageous position, of course, then freeze and raise the viewfinder to my eye. At the precise moment my finger is about to trip the shutter for a prize-winning shot, a cocky gray jay flies down and lands squarely in the middle of my head. A silly bird atop a silly poseur.

It is a 3600 foot descent from Cayuse Pass to Yakima, Washington, with a drop in average annual precipitation from 44 inches at Mt. Rainier National Park to just over 8 inches at Yakima, only 50 crow-flying miles away. This dramatic drop in average annual rainfall is a testament to the effectiveness of the Cascade Mountains in blocking moisture-rich westerly winds from the Pacific. Towering thunderheads rear up on the western Cascade flanks unleashing frequent deluges on the windward slopes. Then, wrung nearly dry, the winds overtop the summit and surge down the leeward side, warming and drying as they descend, creating semi-arid conditions for Yakima. The vegetation responds in kind. Leeward, the dense forests of fir and pine rapidly thin out yielding space and supremacy to the sagebrush and scrub of the semi-arid steppe of eastern Washington, the vast basaltic Columbia Plateau, and the dune-like hills of the Paluse in the southeast.

Following the Naches River down from Rainier, I found Sawmill Flat campground and pulled into a sunny spot near the river. Male and female spotted sandpipers on the rocks, and belted kingfisher perched on overhanging branch. Spent a peaceful night.

My travel days are settling into a routine. Each morning over coffee, I gather my maps, brochures, and campground guide, and contemplate my movements for the day. I unfold the small table in my camper and spread out the map. First, I decide how far I want to travel, what I feel up to. Some days it might be two hundred, two hundred-fifty miles. Other days, one hundred miles would seem like a long haul. I have learned that a drive of over two hundred-fifty miles in my underpowered, unstable VW is a bad plan. Long miles behind the wheel leave me buzzing and disoriented, affecting my ability to cope with exigencies. When this happens I am likely to pull off the road and sit in despair, unable to decide what to do.

I study the terrain, analyzing the topography of various routes. I want to know the elevations of mountain passes, how curvy the roads are, how steep, whether they are gravel or paved. The beginning of each day's journey always holds an element of anxiety, and I find myself planning a route that is least likely to pose difficulties. If the weather looks threatening, I want to avoid high mountain passes where I could get caught in hail or snow. If I am low on gas, I want to avoid long stretches with no services, and I definitely want to avoid large urban areas with heavy traffic. Also, before I leave each morning, I must know where I am going to stay that night. I never leave that up to chance.

Tuesday, August 4, 1981

Bad Day in Yakima

Woke to bright sunny morning. Feeling tranquil. Left camp around 10:30, heading for Yakima Sportsman State Park and looking forward to the security and amenities of a state facility.

There is something unkempt, slightly sleazy about this campground. It should be nicer, being a state park. The campsites are patches of matted brown grass encroaching on each other as if they didn't care. Randomly placed picnic tables slouch on broken legs, fire rings are garbage cans. Dust and disorder overlay the scene with a filtered tinge of perversity. I can't say why exactly; maybe it's negative vibes emanating from the other campers who speak loudly and coarsely, and who do not smile or say hello.

But I doubt the scientific validity of "vibes," so I cast the feeling aside and put out my camp chair, ice chest, and a few other things to mark my place. I filled my solar shower with water and laid it on the ground in a sunny, but hidden, place. Then I headed back into town to do laundry and buy groceries.

When I returned to camp and went to retrieve my solar shower, it was gone. Just disappeared. No one paid any attention as I shot glances around trying to detect a guilty look on someone's face.

My solar shower is indispensible. Basically a large, rectangular, plastic bag, clear on one side and black on the other with a hose and nozzle attached to one end, I fill it with water and place it in the sun. A few hours later, I have three gallons of piping hot water for a shower or shampoo. But now it was gone. Disheartened, and knowing that there was a thief around put me ill at ease, so I popped a beer to lighten up.

Before long a camp employee approached on an electric cart, making his rounds collecting camp fees, I figured. I was hoping sympathy from an amiable, courteous park ranger or camp host would dispel my unease, but the man riding the cart didn't look the part. He was wearing faded jeans and a T-shirt. Young and good-looking with tightly curled blond hair, he greeted me, but he was not smiling. There was a tightness, a hint of brutality about his mouth, as though he didn't give a damn for rules or niceties or whether I paid my campground fees or not.

Tom was his name, and the sight of my open beer seemed to trigger an almost angry reaction. "I could use one of those right now." It was almost a growl, not a remark I would expect from a park employee. "Well, you're welcome to come back after work and have one," I offered. As soon as the words were out of my mouth I regretted the invitation and wished I could retract it.

"I'll be here," he said, and drove off to the next campsite.

I sensed he would be here, and I wasn't comfortable with the prospect. A state park employee drinking with a park visitor would definitely be against the rules it seemed to me, but this guy had no compunctions about it. I chastised myself for not being more circumspect, but it was too late. Oh well, I thought, chances are it would be all right, and anyway, there were lots of people around. I would make sure to keep the camper door open and keep the conversation light.

The rest of the day I lolled around camp, birding, writing in my journal, and keeping a lookout for someone hefting a black plastic solar shower. Shortly after 5 o'clock Tom showed up. He didn't wait to be asked, but stepped into my camper with a firm tread, as though he owned it. He sat on the bench seat opposite me and, without a smile or thanks, grabbed the beer I offered.

"I'm not really supposed to be drinking," he said as he slammed the door closed behind him. The closed door made me jumpy, uncomfortable, but I didn't want to send out any distress signals. It just didn't seem like a good idea.

"Why not? Employee rules?" I asked.

"I'm not an employee. I'm on work furlough from prison."

"*Prison*." The word hit me like a jab to the solar plexus. My instincts had been correct.

"Oh," I said, trying to sound casual as though this bulletin didn't alarm me. "Um, what was the charge?"

"Assault on a cop. I bloodied him up pretty good, too." He bragged.

Christ almighty, Lynn, what the hell have you gotten into? I thought. Sitting across from me was a violent person, a convict who had been denied access to women for who knew how long, and I was shut inside a small camper with him. I needed to get him out of there, but carefully, with finesse.

I sat dumbly nodding my head, saying nothing, trying to think of a plan for extracting myself from my predicament. Tom filled the silence.

"There's a good swimming hole about a mile up the river. Sometimes I ditch work and go there. Nobody's ever there. I'll take you there tomorrow."

I had an image of what could happen to me alone with this man at an isolated swimming hole. "Well, I'm really not a swimmer," I stammered, weakly, but Tom wasn't the least bit discouraged.

"That's all right. You don't have to swim," he said, barely masking his intent and the impatience in his voice.

I should have said no thanks, firmly, but I didn't know how he would react. Clearly he was capable of violence, and I didn't want to rile him; I didn't want him to see how scared I was, and, foolishly, in spite of my fear, I wanted him to think I was cool, worldly. Tom swigged his beer and said nothing for a while, sizing me up with a menacing gaze. Then he shared his thoughts. "I'd like to put my head between your legs right now."

I felt the blood drain from my face and the ice-cold slap of reality: this was dangerous; I was a fool. For a few wavering seconds, I was a child, uncertain what to do, ignore his remark and continue the hip, savvy chick ruse, or destroy my image and boot him out? Fortunately, good judgment won out and I opted to act like a grown-up. I leaned forward toward the door, anticipating an assault, prepared to scream. But Tom didn't move. I heaved the door back. Sunlight flooded the camper like a wash of salvation.

"I want you to go now," I said.

"Why?" he demanded.

"No discussion, please. Just go." I tried to steady my voice, be assertive, but inside I was withering. "If you don't leave, I will," I added. I had no idea where I would get help, but apparently he didn't want to risk dealing with the park authorities or police, because he stomped out of the camper, scowling. The eviction didn't faze him or alter his plans for tomorrow, though.

"I'll be here early tomorrow morning to go swimming," he snarled and walked away before I could object.

I locked all the doors quickly and waited for my heart to stop pounding. I sat warily peeking through the curtains for a long time, afraid to go to sleep and worried about tomorrow. Finally, I set my traveler's alarm for 5:30 a.m. and settled into my sleeping bag. By 8:00 o'clock the next morning I was an hour away from Yakima Sportsman State Park heading east on Hwy. 12 toward Idaho.

Wednesday, August 5, 1981

Driving out into the Palouse, miles and miles of dune-shaped hills constructed long ago from wind-driven, glacially-deposited silt. I drive along Highway 124 across the treeless, wheat-sown land, putting many miles between me and the bad taste of Yakima. I will stop in the town of

Dayton, Washington, and inquire about a safe, and legal, place to camp.
The necessity of approaching strangers for help, and the fear of rejection
or ill treatment always fills me with apprehension. That's how I feel today:
worried, scared, not knowing what's in store.

Dayton has a friendly face. It is small, there's little traffic, and the streets are easy to navigate. I pulled into a gas station and turned off my engine, no other customers around. The station door opened and the attendant, a thirtyish blonde woman in overalls, emerged. She was chunky, freckle-faced and a bit hard-worn looking, but she was smiling broadly. It was easy to begin a conversation with her. She introduced herself as Ellen. I asked if she knew of a campground or safe place I could park for the night. She said I could park in front of her house, and gave me directions. "My son will be there. He's ten. Just tell him mom said you could stay there for tonight. Feel free to go in and use the bathroom if you want."

Ellen was unconditionally trusting of me, as if she saw wings on my back and a halo over my head. Allowing a stranger access to an unchaperoned, ten-year old boy was not a wise parenting move in my book. I was a bit worried about alarming her son, but accepted the offer anyway, knowing Ellen would claim me as her guest in case the local cops came around looking to bust someone for vagrancy.

Accommodations for the night secured, I backtracked five miles to Lewis and Clark Trail State Park to spend the rest of the afternoon birding. I saw my first eastern kingbirds there, new birds for my "life list."

Back in Dayton I found Ellen's house easily enough, a small ramshackle cottage set back from the street and fronted by a large, matted, former lawn. A gravel driveway ran down one side of the house. I shut off the engine and let the quiet surround me. No one was around. It was a lovely day, warm and peaceful. After a while, I relaxed and opened my sliding door to let in some of the loveliness. A small tailless cat sauntered up and sat at my doorstep disinterestedly licking his fur. "Come on in, cat," I ordered. "You know you want to." Cat tossed a languorous sneer at me over his shoulder and went back to licking. At length, his ablutions completed, he casually turned and leapt into my camper. Finished with pretense, my new friend, a born cuddler, was soon purring passionately in my lap, very domestic. Like home.

That's when I saw the little boy slowly walking down the driveway, hands thrust deep into pockets of junior-sized overalls matching his mom's, and glancing up shyly in my direction as he approached.

"Hi," I smiled when he was within earshot. "Are you Ellen's son?" He nodded sweetly, an angelic, tow-headed little hayseed. "What's your name?"

"Ivan." He looked up at me with large, trusting, brown eyes. I wondered if he had ever been warned about talking to strangers. I wanted to invite him to come closer, have a chat, not only to set him at ease, but because I was lonely and wanted the company. I allowed Ivan to take his own time making up to me. It didn't take long, though, and soon he was at my door telling me lots of things.

"Did your mom tell you that I would be coming?" I asked. He nodded yes, and I felt better. "Is your dad home?" He shook his head the other way.

"He doesn't live here," he said.

Oh, divorced, I thought. "Where does he live?"

"He lives in prison."

I flinched at the word *prison*, especially after my encounter with "Yakima Tom" yesterday. "Well, I'm sorry to hear that." I wondered if that was the right thing to say to a ten-year old boy in such a case. I should have left it alone, but my curiosity got the best of me. "What's he in prison for?" I pried.

"Rape and murder," he said flatly. I wondered if those words had any emotional content for him. They did for me. If Ellen's taste in men ran to rapists and murderers, what kind of boyfriends might she have hanging around, and should I maybe just move on down the road?

I soon found out. Late in the afternoon a battered car pulled into the driveway, and a long-haired, scruffy-looking young man dressed in overalls like Ellen's and Ivan's got out. He greeted Ivan by swinging him high off the ground in a grand hug. When he saw me, he grinned and introduced himself, saying no one would bother me there and he would watch out for me. I asked if there was a store close by where I could buy beer. "Don't bother," he said. "I've got lots in the fridge. I'll get you one." He came out and handed me a cold beer, then said, "see ya later," and left me alone. Good for Ellen, I thought. Looks like she made a much better choice this time. Gradually, my safety reasonably assured, I relaxed into a peaceful and quiet afternoon and night.

Thursday, August 6, 1981

Left Dayton about 7:45 after a good night's sleep. It's warm, and today, for a change, I feel good. No anxiety. Entered Idaho at Lewiston and continued east along the Clearwater River. Idaho so beautiful through here. Passed through Orofino, Kooskia and Lowell. After Lowell, I found Glade Creek Campground, only four spaces, no drinking water, but it is so lovely. Glade Creek trickles by my campsite and empties into the nearby Lochsa River, its banks dotted with small, sandy beaches. A little trail follows the creek down to the Lochsa. I follow it and bathe in the cool water.

CHAPTER 6

Montana, Wyoming, Colorado: Enter Giles

Friday, August 7, 1981

I continued up the Lewis and Clark Highway this morning, along the Lochsa, a river of flowing diamonds. Sparks of light glinted from the water, distracting me. I wanted to stop at each splendid little creek spilling into it.

I crossed Lolo Pass on the border between Idaho and Montana, and stopped at the Lolo Pass Visitor Center where I talked to "Smokey" the helpful host there. From there I dropped down into the town of Lolo, Montana along the Bitterroot River. The day is very warm, the sky is blue and oh so big–no wonder it's called "Big Sky."

I'm camped at Flint Creek campground, buzzing and tired after a long day's drive. On my second beer, just surveying the place. Chipmunks are ransacking my camp, cheeky little varmints. Hebgen Lake next, and then Yellowstone. Hoping to hunker down somewhere for a few days.

Expenses:	$8.10	gas
	1.62	breakfast

Saturday, August 8, 1981
Giles and John

BEAR COUNTRY, announced the sign at Beaver Creek Campground. Store food in metal bear boxes, tents not advised, dispose of garbage in bear-proof cans, do not feed bears. The postings were apparently effective because, although virtually in Yellowstone's backyard, the campground was empty, not a single soul around.

"It isn't bears scares 'em away," explained the ranger on his circuit through the campground, "the ladies are afraid of earthquakes." He was referring to the big one, about 7.3 on the Richter scale, which shook southwestern Montana in August of 1959, causing eighty million cubic feet of mountainside to plunge into the Madison River below, damming the river and creating a new lake, "Quake Lake." Downstream, Lake Hebgen still bears scars on its banks from water sloshing back and forth due to the ground's rocking motion during the earthquake. Fault scarps along the trail to Quake Lake look fresh enough to have occurred yesterday rather than twenty-two years ago.

I'm one lady not worried about earthquakes—I'm from California—but bears? Bears concern me. As soon as I shut off my engine I began worrying about whether or not to pop the canvas top of my camper. I envisioned a bear on his hind legs, dancing with my rig, shredding the canvas on my rooftop like wrapping paper off a gift. In fact, from what I had heard about bears, even metal camper sides would be no obstacle for an amply motivated bear.

I sat, rigid, in my closed camper for a long time, keenly aware of my aloneness, and peering through the windows, tense and alert for dark forms emerging from the silent forest surrounding me. Gray stratus clouds press down in sultry gloom.

Just as I began to relax, I heard the unmistakable sound of crunching gravel and the ominous drone of an engine. A car was approaching, and I didn't like the looks of it, a low-riding, gunmetal gray job idling at the entrance to the campground. "Please don't come in, please don't come in," I chanted. It was so like me to assume any newcomer would be bad news. Like an animal sensing my fear, the car advanced through the gate and began slowly circling each loop, sniffing out each site like a near-sighted beast tracking human scent. The car paused three spaces down from mine. "Keep going. Keep going," I breathed, but the car pulled in and stopped.

The doors opened and out stepped two men.

Slouched low in my camper, I propped my binoculars on the dashboard and peered as they began unloading gear. One man was medium build with thinning, brown hair, about in his mid-thirties. The other was dark-haired, slim, about the same age. They were dressed in cargo jackets, chinos, and sporty hats, a good sign. Dangerous men would not be so nattily dressed. Probably.

From the trunk they pulled four long, rifle-shaped canvas bags. Men with rifles, though, that is not a good sign. I had vivid flashbacks to my nightmarish incident with Tom at Yakima State Park. Maybe I should move to another site, or even another campground. Or is this just silly, being so skittish? The men had now emptied the trunk and were unzipping the long canvas cases. I watched intently, but instead of rifles, out came four slender fishing rods! Oh, sweet relief, they were fishermen. Nothing to fear.

They began pitching two small, flimsy-looking dome tents. Tents? In bear country? Could they possibly have missed the warning signs? Maybe I should go warn them. Then again, maybe not.

Before long, the medium-build, balding man came up the road carrying a bucket for water and heading for the nearby water spigot. As he neared, I studied his face. It didn't look like a mean face. This seemed to be a good time to make my inevitable appearance. They would know soon enough I was a woman camping alone. As he returned past my camper, I casually stepped out and began arranging gear on my picnic table. This was the critical moment that would determine my relationship with my new neighbors. I glanced up as he passed.

"Hello," he said, smiling. I returned his smile, signifying consent to engage in conversation. He walked into my campsite, and we began chatting with the usual camper's questions: Where are you from? How long are you staying? What do you do? He had an accent, like American actors in 1940s movies effecting British speech, saying "dahling," instead of darling, drawing out the a's. I couldn't tell if it was real or put on, but either way, I was charmed. He was from Canada, down for fishing with his buddy. The two of them had just finished a fly-fishing course and wanted to test their skills on the Madison River, apparently a good one for that.

"You're camping in tents? Aren't you worried about bears?" I asked.

"I really don't think it will be a problem," he said.

"Well, I guess I won't worry about my canvas pop-top, then," I laughed, "Because bears will go straight for you." He grinned at that, and I saw the two dimples on either side of his mouth.

He introduced himself as Giles, from Toronto, and invited me to his camp to meet his friend John. Both men were professionals; Giles had his own communications company in Hamilton, Ontario, and John was in government service. I liked them enormously, two witty, affable campmates. We chatted away the afternoon, bonding quickly as though we were old buddies. At dusk I retreated to my own camper for supper. Giles had suggested we have a party at my place later. We had tallied up our joint supply of beer and agreed we had the makings of a festive evening. I tidied up my rig, stuffing random clothing and gear into tiny compartments. I lit candles, and rotated the front seats inward to create a "conversation pit."

After supper I waited as the black of night slowly enveloped me. Then two whispering voices behind two thin, probing beams of light approached. Giles and John materialized from the dark with six-packs in hand. They entered my tiny den, and in the glow of candlelight we begin snapping caps off beer bottles. We drank lots of beer and tried to scare each other with bear tales. We drank more beer and took turns telling our life stories, placing our deep secrets into one another's trust, howling at the funny parts, noddingly sympathetic and sappy at the sad parts. We were boon companions, perfectly, cosmically, drunkenly in tune with each other, a cadre of two, "dangerous" fishermen, and a footloose gal camper, sending shouts of merriment outward from a tiny pinpoint of light into the vast Big Sky.

Sunday, August 9, 1981

Giles and John invited me to breakfast this morning. Afterward Giles asked me to go for a walk with him. "Why don't you come with us for the next few days?" he suggested as we walked. "It would be a lot of fun." When I declined, he tried to sway me with blandishments, shooting down all my objections, not the least of which was that he was married. "Please come," he begged. "We can explore Yellowstone. I'll take you to dinner."

"Have you consulted John about this?" I did not think he had.

"It'll be fine with him. Come."

I held firm, but said I would see them again tomorrow before they left. Giles had told me he and John would be moving to another campground a few miles down the highway and closer to the Henrys Fork of the Snake River where they planned to fish. It wasn't far he said, and I could find them there if I changed my mind.

It took a bit of self-wrenching to say goodbye to my Canadian pals. I watched them drive off, and later went into Yellowstone on my own. I stopped to look at Norris Geyser, but didn't have the heart for a full tour. Dark storm clouds threatened thunder and hail. After only one evening and one morning with Giles and John, my veneer of independence was faltering. I missed them, and wanted more of the flattering attention Giles seemed all too willing to bestow. So, I turned back toward Hwy. 20 and drove to the campground where I hoped Giles and John would welcome me.

They were not at the campground when I arrived. Out fishing, no doubt, and who knew how long they would be gone. I waited all afternoon wondering if I was at the wrong campground, or if they had changed their plans. Just before dark, I saw them finally pulling into the campground.

Monday, August 10, 1981

Giles convinced me to stay and go to Yellowstone with him for the day. This was supposed to be a fishing trip with John, and it seemed he was being rather cavalier with his friend's feelings, upsetting the plans so frivolously, but I consented nevertheless.

We left in his car after breakfast and drove to the town of West Yellowstone. From the beginning it was clear Giles wanted to spend money on me. After traveling for two months in austerity mode, I was embarrassed by his show of generosity, but Giles would hear nothing of my feeble complaints.

We browsed in a gift shop where he bought me two books, a dictionary and a novel. We lunched at a coffee shop, then went on into the national park. On our way back to camp that evening, we stopped for a romantic dinner and drinks in West Yellowstone. He kissed me many times and told me he loved me, underscoring this by lightly touching my nose and murmuring, "and that's the truth." I knew it wasn't the truth, but Giles was irresistible, sweet, witty, intelligent. And that damned Canadian, Scottish, whatever-sounding accent, those damned dimples. I was a goner.

Giles asked me to spend the next week with him, just ditch John and go off with him. He asked me to come to Toronto.

No. No. No. The man is married.

Tuesday, August 11, 1981

Reluctantly, I left Giles and John this morning. Giles left a note in my camper, "I love you 'dahling,' remember me."

It was hard to be alone again, especially after Giles's lavish treatment. I drove through Yellowstone, my foul mood heightened by idiotic tourists screeching to a halt in mid-road at the sight of an elk or bear. Even worse, jumping from their car to chase down the poor animal for a Kodak moment, unmindful of the traffic backed up far down the road behind them. I was hoping for a Kodak moment too: an angry black bear hot on the tail of a camera-toting boob beating feet back to his car.

At last, leaving the heaviest traffic behind me I made my way into the beautiful and much less crowded northeastern part of the park. I found a campground near the park entrance and settled in. After supper, sipping wine and missing Giles, I reached for the dictionary he had bought me. It was inscribed:

> *Dahling,*
> *In your hands is your novel. The only*
> *thing left for you to do is....rearrange the*
> *words.*
> > *Love, Giles*
> *P.S. Words can be used more than once.*

Thursday, August 13, 1981

I left Yellowstone in early afternoon and took the Dead Indian Pass cutoff southeast toward Cody, Wyoming. The road was unpaved, rough, and slow-going through the Absaroka Range and over the 8,000-foot pass. But the scenery was spectacular, red and yellow rock sculpted into buttes, ledges, and jagged peaks.

There's a spot on the map under the M in Wyoming called Hell's Half Acre. I will certainly have to stop and see what's hellish about it on my way through the state. Tonight I will hunker down at Buffalo Bill State Park.

Friday, August 14, 1981

Hell's Half Acre, Wyoming

Here I sit at Hell's Half Acre, smack dab in the center of Wyoming far from any sizeable town. I'm alone completely except for a white-tailed rabbit grazing five feet from me. Driving all morning I had hoped to find a picturesque campground, but found only a down-at-the-heels restaurant with a few pathetic campsites fronting what looked to be a barren, desert wasteland beyond. But I had no other camping choices, so I settled in, turned my camp chair away from the restaurant, opened a beer, and began a thorough survey of the place.

I hadn't seen it when I drove in, but now looking out I noticed a sharp, gray line, like an edge–the brink of something–in the distance. Curiosity won the moment, and I got up to investigate. As I approached, a gaping chasm in beige and mauve opened before me, a gash in earth's crust, deep and wide, with crumpled walls and jutting ledges, and naked rock spires thrusting upward from a floor of rocky phantasms sculpted over the eons by water and wind. Here, to be sure, was a first cousin to the Grand Canyon, and I would never have seen it if I hadn't turned my chair away from the road. I stood gazing at the spectacle for a long time before returning to my camper.

Now, from my "front porch" looking out over the chasm, the sun is setting behind a dark, billowing storm cloud. In the distance gray-brown veils of rain dampen other parts of Wyoming. Mountain bluebirds, those lovely high altitude denizens, are everywhere, flitting from fence post to power line, the males brilliant sky blue, the females drab brown with a wash of blue on the tail and back. They hover like flycatchers as they search for insects.

A mule deer has silently emerged from the mangled depth of Hell's Half Acre and has paused on the brink, browsing for a moment, silhouetted against the sky, then, just as silently, slips back down into the pit, to what abode I can scarcely imagine. Now the approaching clouds offer some moisture to my campsite. A light sprinkling. I cover my backpack, table, and chair with my tarp, and step inside the greenhouse. To the east, through the front window, a full, cheddar moon has risen above the horizon.

Saturday, August 15, 1981

I left Hell's Half Acre this morning and drove to the Casper post office where I had arranged to have mail sent general delivery. I was surprised to see a letter from Marty Garcia-Gunther. Since my visit to Organ Pipe Cactus National Monument in 1980 we had exchanged letters. I had told him about my travel plans and said he could write to me care of general delivery at Casper. He said he was now working as a ranger at Rocky Mountain National Park in Colorado, and would love to have me stop to visit him. He had a cabin there and I was welcome to stay as long as I wanted.

I pushed on south to Laramie where I opted to rent a motel, the first of my trip, for the night. By the time I arrived, I had decided to accept Marty's invitation; it would be nice to perch in one place for a while and do some hiking and birding. I called him from the motel and told him I would arrive in Estes Park tomorrow.

I started out for a run around the university, but soon felt very weak and breathless. When my legs became rubbery and my heart beat accelerated I began to worry that something was wrong. Then I remembered, Casper's elevation is over 5000 feet. I had a right to feel awful. I walked back to my motel and flopped on the bed, excusing myself from exercise today.

I miss Giles.

Sunday, August 16, 1981
Rocky Mountain National Park

I pulled into Estes Park just as the sky broke loose in a fearsome storm with rain so heavy I couldn't see through the windshield. I took refuge in the parking lot of a convenience store and hunkered low in my seat beneath the hammering from the lightning and thunder directly above me. Staring through the windshield, I had the sensation that I was higher than the rest of Estes Park, as though I stood on the bridge of an ocean liner. All I could see were the battleship gray swells of clouds and flashes of lightning through them.

Finally the storm abated and I saw that I was, indeed, perched at the top of a rounded knoll, the worst place to be in an electrical storm. Most of Estes Park was below me.

I found my way to the park visitor center and asked for Marty. No one seemed to know where he was, but I found him at last in the ranger residential area behind park headquarters. He was living in a log cabin set in a yellow pine forest. It was good to see him again. Good old goofy Marty.

Monday, August 17 - Wednesday, August 19, 1981

My camper is parked outside Marty's cabin, and he says I can stay here as long as I want, no charge. This is the perfect setup, under the trees and stars, but near a toilet and shower. The only drawback is Marty's pesky roommate who, drunk after a night of partying, rapped on my window last night and asked to be admitted. He was persistent and belligerent until I told him to get the hell lost or I would start honking my horn. He never showed up again–something about being stationed in a different part of the park, according to Marty. Fine with me, I was glad to be rid of him.

Marty, and his young ranger friends Carol and Diane and I hiked up Specimen Mountain today, a beautiful hike above timberline and into the alpine tundra. We were rewarded with sightings of four bighorn sheep and two yellow-bellied marmots, in addition to all the juncos and chickadees along the way.

After the climb, my capacity for socializing with twenty-something-year-olds was spent, and I was looking forward to the privacy and comfort of my little greenhouse. But as we climbed into Marty's car, Carol announced, "I need to stop at the drugstore."

"Oh, shit," I muttered under my breath, but managed a dose of big girl patience and smiled wanly.

Pulling away from the drugstore, Diane suddenly remembered, "Oh, I need to get some new boots." Scrunched in the corner of the back seat no one heard my exasperated sigh. I had become a non-entity, captive to the caprices of the young folk. So, for the next half hour I sat, fuming, holding empty shoe boxes in my lap while Diane tried on every pair of size seven, waterproof, Vibram-soled boots in the place. Back in the car again, Carol had a great idea. "Let's go to the bookstore." I wanted to scream, "Hey! What about me?" I didn't though. Instead, feeling like an old fogey, I meekly asked if they would take me back to my camper first.

Oh bliss, Tuesday was all mine. I went out early to have the oil changed in my van. This gave me time to walk, deliciously free of companionship, around Estes Park, so lovely in the early morning. Later, I did laundry, a little shopping, then came back to Marty's cabin and spent the rest of the day and evening there.

Wednesday, a gloriously beautiful morning, I drove to the Wild Basin Ranger Station for a hike to Calypso Cascades and Ouzel Falls. Huge granite boulders and slabs loomed majestically above the trail as I pushed up through the shimmering green of aspen and fern. Everywhere birds enlivened the forest, singing and hovering so alluringly, so cheerfully. Snow White had nothing on me.

I stopped at Calypso Cascades, a series of stony steps over which the waters of St. Vrain Creek tumbled and thrashed into a milky froth. After a few shots with my fully manual, trusty Pentax K1000, I moved on to Ouzel Falls, aptly named for the pudgy little gray-black bird known for scooting through the water just inches below the surface in search of his meals.

Thursday, August 20, 1981

Today it was post office, post cards, coffee mug for Marty, groceries, and back to the cabin. I cooked up a pot of beans for supper. Marty had been good about letting me stay here, even though the national park rules didn't allow it. He wasn't really a cheating kind of guy, just oblivious to certain fine points about ranger conduct.

We had bean burritos for supper, and afterward Marty put on some disco music. "Do you want to dance?" he asked.

"I love to dance," I said, but didn't mention that I only love to dance with good dancers, and that kind is hard to come by. You can tell them the minute they take your hand. They exude *savoire faire*, as they lead you on to the dance floor. Probably that was not Marty. Still, it was worth a try.

"Do you know how to do the Swing, Marty?"

"What's that?"

"It's easy. I'll show you." I stood and walked through the basic steps. "You just count: one . . . two . . . quick-step." Marty got the one, two part, but the double-time, quick-step was too nuanced for him.

Unlike guys who can't dance and say so, Marty was a trouper, chanting, "one, two, quick step," in something like waltz time, but not exactly. He flung me jubilantly out to arm's length, throwing us even further from the beat. I tried to guide him back to two-step by wrangling the lead from him, but he was in dance heaven, grinning, gleaming with sweat, a dark lock hanging limply over his forehead.

The dancing ended late, both of us flushed with the effort of it. I was ready for sleep and made for my camper. As I gathered up my jacket and bag, Marty piped up.

"Why don't you sleep inside tonight? It's warmer in here."

This was odd. Why would Marty suggest I stay inside? "It's not cold out there, Marty. Besides, there's no place for me in here."

"You can sleep in my bed with me. Just sleep. I won't do anything."

Marty's innocent eyes! All I could do was chuckle and shake my head. "Marty, that's ridiculous. Why else would you want me in bed with you?"

"No, really, it would just be nice to have you in bed with me. I promise I won't try anything."

I looked at him in disbelief, still smiling and shaking my head.

"Really, Lynn, I won't bother you." Marty was begging. "Please."

"No, Marty, I'm tired. I want to sleep." Was it possible he really believed he would be content with just my proximity? I asked him that question.

"I promise I won't bother you. I'll leave you alone. It would be nice just to have you there."

Somehow I was won over. Marty was so amazingly guileless, so simple, so clueless.

"All right, Marty. But I am going right to sleep, understand?"

"I understand," he said, nodding.

Dressed in everything but my shoes and jeans, I slipped between the covers, scooting to the far edge of the bed and turning away from him. This is absurd, I thought. I could feel his body heat, sexual tension crackling like static electricity across the sheets. I waited, tense myself, but he did not stir. Several minutes passed. Well, true to his word, I thought, and I began to drift away into sleep. Then.

"Lynn?"

"Whaaat, Marty?" I groaned.

"Would you like me to massage your clitoris?"

I threw back the covers and began groping for my jeans and shoes, shaking my head, sputtering. "I am leaving. Good night." I felt my way to the door and out to the holy solitude of my camper. Oh, Marty, poor, clueless soul.

Friday, August 21, 1981

Drove early this morning to Beaver Meadows, beautiful with its green grass, quaking aspen, and pine, all encircled by the towering peaks of the Rockies. At the picnic area birds were everywhere, too many and too active for me to identify them all, very frustrating. I saw flycatchers, but what kind? Two birds on the fence wire, jay-sized and kingbird-shaped, with long, notched tails, completely stumped me. They turned in unison when the wind blew, then flew off. Saw sparrows I couldn't figure out. Saw pine siskins, mountain bluebirds, and chickadees, but my best find was a pair of female red crossbills poking around in the ashes of the fire grill. Their strange-looking bills look like they have been twisted sideways with pliers. They have to tilt their heads to sip water.

Came back to the cabin early, frustrated by too many "lost" birds. Marty and I are going to dinner, then dancing tonight. He already knows I will be sleeping in my camper.

Saturday, August 22, 1981

Marty and I drove to the Glacier Junction trailhead early this morning for a hike to Sky Pond. From just under 9200 feet, the trail climbs gently to Alberta Falls, then twists up and continues on to The Loch, the first in a series of tarns, small lakes occupying depressions gouged out of the mountainside by glaciers. This sparkling beauty was ours alone today, and we lingered, silent and reverent in the thrall of such ineffable splendor.

A steep climb lay ahead of us to Timberline Falls where we emerged onto the mountain's highest reaches, the alpine tundra. Here storm clouds gather, harsh winds rage, and soil moisture is frozen too long for trees to grow. Lichens and mosses crouch low, clinging to rocks, seeking protection from the gales. The rocks themselves bear scars from the passage of ancient rivers of ice.

Ahead of us the route was evident, but the trail had disappeared. Now it was a scramble, rated strenuous by the park service, over boulders and waterfalls up to Glass Lake and Sky Pond, tarns strung along Icy Brook like beads on a rosary—"paternoster lakes." I struggled upward, picking my way through crevices and over huge rocks, my confidence flagging with each step. This was dangerous territory, way beyond my skill level. Marty was already far ahead, and not likely encumbered by concerns about me.

Finally I reached Glass Lake. I rested and looked up toward Sky Pond, only a quarter of a mile farther, but across another vast jumble of house-sized boulders. It looked to me like a thousand chances to break a leg. Maybe I could make it, but I was too scared. I called up to Marty to tell him I was turning back. He waved and went on toward Sky Pond.

The traverse back through the boulder field to Timberline Falls was easier this time. Having crossed it coming up, I now had "expertise;" I was an accomplished mountaineer, and the boulders almost seemed to draw back to allow my passage.

After resting awhile, I sauntered on down the trail, taking my time, knowing that Marty would take his. Better to prolong the pleasures of the trail than sit in the cab of Marty's pickup waiting. At The Loch I glanced back up toward Sky Pond and was unnerved by the sight of dark thunderheads spreading over the mountaintops. Marty was up there in the high country, exposed, and lightning was starting to flicker through the clouds. I hoped he would have the sense to get down to low ground.

Fat raindrops were starting to splatter on the trail, and I knew I was in for a drenching myself if I didn't hurry. I jogged the three miles back to the trailhead, slowing only at the switchbacks. It was pouring rain and almost dusk when I arrived at Marty's pickup. Luckily, I had persuaded Marty to allow me to carry his keys, so at least I had shelter from the storm.

Darkness fell. I waited, not too concerned at first, but more anxious as time passed. I knew Marty would not be daunted by a mere mountain thunderstorm, but I also knew he was not invincible. There was nothing to do but sit, peering into the darkness toward the trailhead, straining to detect movement. It was almost nine when, at last, I saw the ghostly metallic glint of a silver thermal blanket lurching up through the gloom, sheltering a tired, but unperturbed Marty.

Sunday, August 23, 1981

Started my period. Feeling too lousy to leave today. Decided to stay one more day. Into town for groceries and a phone call to Mom. Sisters Jane and Susan were with her, so talked to them also.

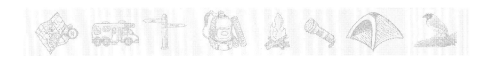

CHAPTER 7

Nebraska, South Dakota: Wind and Road Rage

Monday, August 24, 1981
Scotts Bluff

I left Rocky Mountain National Park today. Humming along Highway 287 heading north toward Cheyenne, I was casting glances casually off to the right, off to the left, surveying the landscape as I usually do. Suddenly I realized I was driving along a clearly delineated boundary between two distinctly different physiographic provinces and the economic bases associated with them.

Geographers understand that boundaries between adjoining regions are usually transitional, and often subjective, but not here. Out my left window, to the west, rose the commanding front range of the Rockies, with Denver as its hub for tourism and commerce, and home to a university. Out the right side window, to the east, the gently rolling high plains, dotted with wide-spread cattle ranches, and sugar beet and grain farms, stretched far away to the horizon. The line between the mountains and the plains was sharp and visible, and I, the exultant geographer, was driving along it.

Entering Nebraska from Cheyenne I am undeniably out of The West, into the Great Plains, far from home, and a bit breathless about it. Nebraska is lovely under a cornflower blue sky. The land is flat to rolling, very pretty, and covered with cheerful sunflowers. Heading north from Kimball toward the town of Scottsbluff and Scotts Bluff National Monument.

From out of this rolling landscape, the bluffs would rise, but although I was constantly scanning the plains, I saw no sign of them, until about twenty miles south of the town of Scottsbluff. Then, gradually, the road's embankments rose into highly eroded, cliff-rimmed bluffs of some kind of fine-grained, light-colored material, sandstone, maybe. The rock looked soft and crumbly, as though a night's worth of vandalism would reduce them to mounds. These were the Wildcat Hills, not Scotts Bluff, but once part of the same rock layer laid down millions of years ago. I will find out for sure tomorrow.

There was camping in the Wildcat Hills, my campground guide said, so I drove up into them. But I discovered that, although intriguing, the place did not look welcoming, and there were no designated campsites. I elected to continue on into the town of Scottsbluff in hopes of finding a place to stay there.

The town of Scottsbluff rests gently on the land, easygoing, unassertive. It greets its visitors with light traffic and easily navigable streets. I found a pleasant municipal campground near downtown, across the North Platte River from the national monument. It was nearly empty, and only $4.50 a night. Once I settled in, Jim, the caretaker, came to greet me. He supplied me with brochures and maps of the town, and asked where I was heading and with whom. He was surprised when I said, just east, just me, and wanted to know all about my journey, and why I was traveling. Admiration glowed in his eyes; I liked that.

I telephoned Giles today. He was so happy to hear from me, and I, too, was gladdened. We planned to meet in Michigan near Port Huron in about three and a half weeks.

Expenses:	$10.04	gas
	0.34	grapefruit
	2.80	beer
	4.50	camp

Tuesday, August 25, 1981

A broad, looping road leads to the base of Scotts Bluff, a huge, buff-colored jib of an eminence. Today I hiked the trail to the top and got a better look at those crumbly rocks. They are, as I suspected, ancient deposits of sand and mud, consolidated over the eons into sandstone and siltstone, and interlaid with volcanic ash. A cap of limestone, more resistant to erosion, tends to keep the bluffs flat-topped.

My path led through weirdly sculpted sandstone structures then veered toward the top. I scanned upward with my binoculars, following the trail as far as I could. Near the top it appeared to stop abruptly at a vertical wall as though sliced through with a cleaver. Drawn by this peculiarity, I continued on. I had to satisfy my curiosity about this disappearing trail. I walked on and on, but even as I neared the "vanishing" point, I still could not see the endpoint of this trail. Was it simply going to disintegrate among the crumbly rocks? There was one more turn in the trail; I rounded it and saw the wall into which the trail butted. Mystery solved. A tunnel had been punched through to the other side, and the trail continued from there. From below, the tunnel had not been visible, only a seemingly impervious rocky rampart.

I stepped through the tunnel and emerged at the summit where a red-tailed hawk and white-throated swifts were soaring overhead. I looked out over the plains, once an unimaginably boundless short grass prairie, now transformed into farms and ranches. Away off to the east unfamiliar lands beckoned to my peripatetic soul.

Wednesday, August 26, 1981

Black Hills

After breakfast, gas fill-up, and grocery shopping, I was on the road by 10:30 a.m. headed for the Black Hills of South Dakota and Wind Cave National Park. I didn't feel as chipper as I did driving into Scottsbluff two days ago. Gauzy gray had replaced the blue in the sky and the drive over the rolling plains was monotonous. Only 160 miles to go, but it felt like a longer haul today. At last at the entrance to Wind Cave National Park, I was greeted by a herd of bison and two pronghorn antelope, exquisite animals.

I am now at Elk Mountain campground waiting for the ranger to come collect camp fees. It's not a great campground, open and windy, but it's better than some, and I am within walking distance of the visitor center.

Thursday, August 27, 1981

Biscuits for breakfast sounded good to me this morning. From the back of a drawer I pulled out my 1950s campfire cookbook, yellowed with age. In it was a recipe for campfire biscuits, which required the construction of a reflector panel. I can do this, I thought. By bending a coat hanger into a rough rectangle and covering it with aluminum foil, I fashioned an oven "wall" that more or less stood upright inside my campfire ring. Next I made biscuit dough and placed the cutouts on a cookie sheet, which was then placed on the fireplace grate in front of the reflector panel.

Simple in concept, but flawed in execution, as I discovered. I sat waiting expectantly for the biscuits to puff and brown. But nothing doing. The pathetic little blobs of dough refused to inflate. Obviously my oven wasn't hot enough. I covered the biscuits with foil and placed the cookie sheet back on the grate. Still nothing. As a last resort, I flipped the cookie sheet over and placed it directly onto the coals. Five minutes later, the result: soggy-centered mounds of dough with burnt outer edges. Damned, though, if I was going to toss the whole mess out. I nibbled the crumbly perimeter of each biscuit down to its pulpy center, then, relegated the remaining goo to the fire.

Later, I wandered down to the visitor center to see about a cave tour. I'm not really keen on caves, being somewhat claustrophobic, but I did take an interest in the guide, one of those few men who share my first name, Lynn. He was articulate, poised, attractive, and a birder. Perhaps I would see him at the amphitheater program tonight, and perhaps I would ask if he would like to go birding with me.

Friday, August 28, 1981

Geography of the Plains

Up there on the ridge behind my camp, the prairie and the forest come together, another boundary between different physiographic provinces, but this one is not abrupt; it is a transition zone.

Out on the prairie, flowers in abundance—salsify, aster, goldenrod, and prickly poppy, intermingle with the grasses—buffalo grass, grama grass, switchgrass, and rye. The pine forest marches down the hills to meet them. At its front margins, a vanguard of smaller pines venture boldly into less hospitable territory. Tender green pine seedlings, no taller than the grasses, and widely scattered, advance bravely in an attempt to overtake the prairie. They would succeed, too, but for aridity and fires, natural and manmade, which favor the grasses.

Another prairie surprise. Cactus. Miniature prickly pear and barrel cactus nestle among the pines and grasses, perfectly at home and comfortable far north of the desert Southwest where we usually expect to find them. In spite of the cold winters, the climate of the central plains is semi-desert, averaging less than sixteen inches of rainfall yearly. South Dakota is a long way from the Pacific Ocean and the westerly winds that suck up its moisture as they cross. Those winds are intercepted first by the Sierra Nevada and Cascades, and the Rockies after that. As a result, the rain is dumped on the mountains' windward flanks, not "mainly in the plain." This "rainshadow effect" allows a hot, dry summer climate to extend as far north as southern Canada. Hence the appearance of cactus on these northern plains.

Ranger Lynn and I went birding. He is a good birder, and with his help I added gray catbird, white-winged junco, black-headed grosbeak, and western wood pewee to my "life list." Back at camp I rested and studied maps. At dusk I walked again up on the ridge behind camp and took some photos. Felt depressed and lonely tonight.

Saturday, August 29, 1981

I'm off to see Mt. Rushmore today. I am skeptical about visiting this national monument, since I prefer my mountains uncarved—by human hands, anyway. But being this close and not stopping would somehow seem like an unmet obligation. So I mingled with the hordes, gawked at the four presidents hacked perversely into the mountainside, took several photos, and scampered away. I continued on through Keystone and Hill City, small tourist towns on opposite sides of Mt. Rushmore.

I settled for the night at Whispering Pines Campground near Silver City, recommended to me by Randy, back at Lewis and Clark State Park in Washington. He was right. It is a comfortable place to rest. In the evening I went to the recreation room to shoot a few games of pool with a fellow there. Won one, lost one, lost one.

Sunday, August 30, 1981

Rochford and Black Fox Campground

The sun was warm this morning. I lingered over a hearty breakfast of juice, ham, French toast, and coffee before leaving at 11:30 for Strawberry Hill Campground farther north along my route. It was listed in my campground guide as having amenities, and it was close to the highway.

When I reached the tiny town of Merritt, I saw a sign with an arrow pointing west: Rochford, 11 miles. Ranger Paul back at Mt. Rushmore had said something to me about Rochford. "It's a neat little village," he had said. A neat little village? Off the beaten path? My taste exactly. I cranked the steering wheel westward, off on a tangent again, and exhilarated by the impetuosity of it.

Paul was right. Rochford *is* a neat little village. Driving down the gravel road, I came upon it almost unexpectedly. No fringe of outlying buildings prepared me for its sudden appearance. An old gold mining town with little more than a general store, saloon and forest service office, it occupied its forest clearing as though it had just been set down there, like a marker on a gameboard. It seemed to have an ephemeral quality, like a fairy tale village that might shimmer into nothingness if I failed to keep an eye on it.

A middle-aged woman emerged from the general store. She had long, wavy gray hair, piercing, blue-gray eyes, and a riveting smile that insisted on conversation. I told her I had taken a sightseeing detour on my way to Strawberry Hill campground. She listened, tilting her head sideways, sizing me up.

While I spoke, she smiled, inwardly, as though she knew something I didn't, but wasn't sure if she wanted to share it with someone who preferred cushy RV campgrounds. Ultimately, however, she must have sensed that a solitary woman traveling and camping far from home would be *something* of an adventuress.

"There's a better campground nearby," she offered somewhat hesitantly. "Black Fox Campground, over where the south and north forks of Rapid Creek join." She pointed her thumb over her shoulder. "It's isolated, not fancy, but a lot prettier than Strawberry Hill. You might like it."

"That sounds wonderful," I said. "How do I get there?"

"Keep on this road a couple more miles," she said. Turn here, turn there, look for the sign.

How could I resist a place with an alluring name like *Black Fox*? I turned my rig where the woman had pointed and bounced on down the road, hoping Black Fox Campground would be a place to linger for a few days.

Like its namesake, Black Fox Campground sat shyly, half-hidden, in the forest. It was small, only a few campsites nestled companionably along Rapid Creek, which lent its tinkling music to the otherwise silent scene. There were only two other people there, a couple in a small camper, so I had my choice of creekside spots. The creek was narrow, but spritely, bounding over rocks, and dappled with sunlight. A vibrant green tangle of low-lying willows and ash trees lined its banks. I chose a site close to the creek and set up camp. For a long time, I sat quietly listening to the creek's voice and the soft rustling of leaves. Now and then the breeze shivered across my arm, feather-like. I sat until I was no longer a stranger.

Late in the afternoon, after a thirty-minute run up the canyon road, my thoughts turned to supper. The mid-day warmth had succumbed to a pre-autumn chill. Rummaging around the campground, I stockpiled twigs and forest duff for a fire, arranged them over wads of newspaper and topped them with larger twigs. They caught the flame of my match hungrily, unwaveringly, as though commanding, "bring on the logs, now!" Soon my fire was gnawing the logs into embers. I placed a can of tamales and foil-wrapped corn in the coals and sat nursing a beer waiting for my meal to cook, and thinking Brava! Lynn, a one-match fire.

The sun had departed from all but the treetops, still glazed by the low-angle rays. Up there, the first leafy reds and golds foretold the on-coming season. I sat gazing hypnotically into the pulsating red-orange coals, listening to the soft crackle of the fire and the occasional sighing of the breeze through the trees.

Then something else caught my attention. Another sound, like the breeze, but stronger, and steady, a distant wail overlaying the soft, low registers of the fire and creek. It seemed to be coming from up-canyon, and strengthening, like a far-off gathering of something. I sat upright and strained to listen. Yes, it was unmistakable, there was a noise, and it was coming closer, moving straight down between the canyon walls. I felt a surge of adrenaline as I rose from my chair to face the unknown. I peered up the road into the dark, but could see nothing. Now the sound was loud, harsh, and scraping, as though the canyon walls, too narrow for the invisible thing, were being scoured as it passed. Something unstoppable was rushing down the canyon, and I was in its path with nowhere to run. I braced for the onslaught of—what?

Then, rushing out of the canyon, a gale force blast of wind ripped through the campground, sending embers and sparks eddying violently up from the fire, rattling the trees, raking down showers of leaves, and hurtling my camping gear into the bushes. Like a single swipe from the arm of an angry giant, the gust swept away every pot, pan and dish on my picnic table. I grabbed for my camp chair and turned my back to the wind, covering my head and eyes from the dust, waiting for the buffeting to end.

One sweeping rush and it was over, like a powerful wave crashing on shore. All was silent again, and calm. I roused myself from shock and gathered up the strewn kitchen. I doused the fire and secured my camp stove and propane tank. Then I went into the greenhouse and sat, alert, for a long time. At last I slipped into bed and lay awake thinking, sorting through all that I knew about canyon topography, air pressure dynamics, local winds, etc., trying to understand what would cause that powerful, one-gust storm. But it eluded me. My geography failed me this time, and there was nothing I could do about it but accept my scientific limitations and go to sleep.

Monday, August 31, 1981
Chipmunks and Kinglets

Last day of August. Awoke cold. Sun shining, but windy and cold. Hands and feet stiff with the chill. Needed my parka. Talked to my neighboring campers, nice folks. We're the only ones here. Fine with me.

Flocks of red crossbills, dozens of them, are gorging themselves on spruce cone seeds. Thought they were pine grosbeaks at first, thought I saw the white wing bars.

I have seen no black foxes yet, but there's plenty of other wildlife: birds, red squirrels, and least chipmunks, especially the one that hopped up on the log beside me this morning while I was drinking my coffee. There he sat, a marvel of quivering life, his ears tiny soft pads, like miniature mistletoe leaves. Fine brown and white lines framed his face; black and white stripes ran the length of his back. Not a single strand of white fur intruded on the black, nor black on the white. How does nature know to do this? How is it possible any creature could be so fine, so delicate, perfect? The morning sunlight shimmered in the chipmunk's fur as he sat on his hind legs with his front paws drawn together under his chin. I could only shake my head. The ungraspable reality of his existence was more wonder and joy than I could contain. Why would anyone need more than this? Why would anyone seek spirits, or sprites, or fairies? How could any spirit or fairy manifested in flesh, be more awesome than this?

By mid afternoon, summery warmth had pushed back the cold. I went for a long hike up the road beyond the campground, thinking, irrationally, maybe I would find Aeolus's mustering ground, an arena bearing scars from last night's windy rampage–broken tree limbs, shredded bushes, disturbed soils. I chuckled at myself for entertaining such fanciful ideas.

As usual, I had my binoculars slung over my shoulder as I walked, swinging them up to my eyes at every bird sighting. Most of the time, I recognized species instantly, but then a trembling in the bushes off to my left caught my eye, the slight fluttering of only three or four leaves. I knew the bird hidden in there was small, and I was determined to see it. I kept my eyes on the spot where the leaves had moved and slowly brought my binoculars–my trusty Pentax 10 x 42s–to my eyes. These binoculars gather a lot of light, so I knew I would be able to see deep into the dark interior of the bush. There it was, the tiny bird. I could see the short, stubby tail and the frequent upward flick of the wings. "Ah, a ruby-crowned kinglet," I breathed. But at that moment the bird darted out of the bushes into the open. I saw a patch of bright red-orange sharply bordered by black on his crown, and on his face a snow-white stripe above his eye. Not a ruby-crowned, it's a *golden*-crowned kinglet! It was the first I had ever seen. A beautiful, three and a half inch jewel flitting among the leaves. Even after the bird disappeared, I stood shaking my head in amazement at the artwork on the creature's head. For the second time today, I wondered why nature, in her evolutionary efficiency, would unfold in the direction of such beauty.

When I returned to my camper, three young men had arrived and were setting up camp. Their behavior was loud, raucous, putting me ill at ease. How dare they inject ominous undertones into an otherwise perfect day?

The evening turned cold. I snuggled into my sleeping bag very early and kept watch on the boys, but they seemed to settle down as the chill deepened, so I ended my vigil and went to sleep.

Tuesday, September 1, 1981

Arose around 7:00 a.m. Very cold this morning. Ice on the windshield, picnic table, and ground. Donned many layers of clothes. Brewed a cup of hot coffee and wrapped my hands around the mug. A patch of sunlight broke through the forest by the creek, and I walked over to it, seeking warmth. The ray of sunlight was bright, but hardly warmer than the shade. A water dipper splashed through the ripples of the creek, so cold. How can he stand it?

Doesn't look like the three fellows are getting ready to leave this morning, but they aren't so loud today, and they really haven't been a problem. Guess I'll go gather firewood.

I tried to run today. I made it about 24 minutes, but the lack of oxygen did me in, and I had a serious attack of intestinal "backtalk" afterward. What I needed was a shower, but how do I take a shower in a campground without that convenience? This is how: I heat water on my stove and fill my solar shower. Then I fasten a grosgrain strap around the handle of the water bag and toss the strap over the crossbar that supports the pop-up. I position the shower over the sink, tighten the strap, and, there it is. Of course there is no tub to stand in, so I place a towel on the floor. Then, by leaning over the tiny sink, I can spray deliciously hot water from the hose over my arms and even my shoulders. By sitting on the counter, I can just squeeze both feet into the sink and wash them. Ah, the skin-tingling luxury of hot water over frozen feet! The rest of the operation is a sponge bath affair sans flowing hot water, but effective nevertheless.

I felt better after my shower. I made guacamole and spent the afternoon snacking and reading. Later, the lady in the next campsite invited me to come have hot dogs with her and her husband tonight. Of course I will. I love these happy encounters with people along the way, this adopted feeling.

Wednesday, September 2, 1981

My friendly neighbors brought me two gift trout this morning, which I fried up for breakfast, a delicious alternative to the usual. After breakfast I broke camp and left around 9:00 thinking, my sojourn here the last three days has proven that the idyll I envisioned so long ago sitting at my desk in Santa Maria, is, indeed, attainable.

I stopped in Rochford on my way out to buy ice and make a phone call to Giles. He had encouraged me to call him any time, and often, and each time I did he had been overjoyed to hear from me, as he was now. In high spirits, I rolled away from Rochford, doing forty along the gravel road out to the paved highway, heading for Rapid City and the Badlands beyond. How fine to know someone is thinking about you, glad to hear from you.

Must be getting close to the main highway, I think. I check my rearview mirror and see a large truck advancing behind me. He must be doing fifty or more. He won't want to stay in my dusty roostertail, but I don't think he'll pass me at that speed on this gravel road. It shouldn't be too much farther to Merritt and the paved highway. The truck in my rearview mirror is now almost on my tail.

What the? . . . He whips out around me and throws a fan of gravel up from his wheels, splattering rocks everywhere. One bullet-like ping and my windshield shatters into bifocals. "You son of a bitch!" I yell at his tailgate. "You couldn't wait till you got to the highway!" Through his dust stream and my broken windshield, I watch him disappear ahead of me. I slow to a crawl, afraid my windshield will give way. After a few more miles I am still cursing him, incensed that he got away never to hear what I have to say to him.

I think I see a building up ahead, yes, the roadside café at Merritt, a place to stop and survey the damage. To my astonishment, the very truck that passed me is parked outside. "Yes!" I shout, feeling vengeful heat rise in my chest. In a fury, I pull in and park boldly within inches of the bastard's rig. Too angry to exercise discretion, I jump down from my van and storm into the café.

"Hey!" I yell. He's sitting on a stool at the counter, about to tackle a hamburger. "Hey! Come see what you did to my windshield!"

He's a big fellow, rough-looking, and it's just dawning on me that restraint would probably be the wiser course with this dude, but it's too late. He turns toward me, but his gaze is unfocused, as though he's following the buzz of an irritating insect around the room.

"You broke my windshield, jerk!" He's focused on me now. "You sprayed my windshield with rocks when you just had to pass me."

If I had any inkling of danger from this man, I needn't have worried. He is utterly dismissive. "Oh, that happens all the time on this road," he says, casually. He turns back to his hamburger and chats breezily with the wide-eyed waiter, leaving me sputtering and impotent in the middle of the room, crumpled, like the greasy, wadded napkin beside his plate.

I march out of the café, still raging. I glare at his truck, wondering what damage I can inflict, but there's nothing a lady my size can do to a semi, especially with its brute of a driver within bone-crushing distance.

In abject humiliation, I climb back into my van. So, there is to be no restitution. Well, the windshield can be replaced, I have insurance, but the scratches on my psyche? I wonder if Allstate's "good hands" will cover that. I pull out and continue on down the gravel road to the highway leading to Rapid City.

By the time I arrived in Rapid City, I had calmed down. On the way into town I spotted an auto glass shop, and, luckily, they had the right windshield for my VW in stock. I made an appointment for tomorrow morning to have the windshield replaced. With that settled, I had the rest of the day for errands and sightseeing. I went to the Chamber of Commerce for a city map, the first thing I do whenever I arrive in a new town. Next, I found the insurance claims office. The claims adjustor took one look at my windshield and filled out the paper work on the spot. So easy, I thought. I hadn't expected a smooth transaction, even though I had no reason to believe otherwise. I had paid my car insurance premiums, on time, for years. But, owing to my general self-view of unworthiness, which I had carted around since my youth, I was sure the agent would find cause to reject my claim. Instead, I left the claims office with my problem resolved and the prospect of a pleasant day ahead. I headed for the Mt. Rushmore Mall.

At the mall I gazed into shop windows at the latest fashions, wistfully comparing them to the *haute couture* stuffed into the crannies of my camper: jeans, sweatshirts, T-shirts. I ate cheese-on-a-stick and slurped an Orange Julius. For a finale, I walked into a beauty salon and was taken in hand by a sweet girl who cut and styled my hair.

In the afternoon I headed back out of town to a pleasant little private campground I had seen as I drove in to town. It was situated near a large pond, the perimeter of which made an ideal running track. After several circuits around the pond, I took a real hot shower and did my laundry.

Thursday, September 3, 1981

Badlands

I dropped my car off at the auto glass shop at 8:00 this morning. As I was starting to leave, a thought occurred to me, and I turned back to the service man. "All my belongings are in my van," I said. "I have no choice but to trust you. I'm at your mercy."

"Don't worry, lady," he replied. "This isn't California." I smiled at this. He must view California as a west coast hotbed of iniquity, a place of twenty-four million cynical and corrupt people, all of them intent on sticking it to each other. I didn't try to disabuse him of the notion; actually I was reassured by his implied integrity. I left and went across the street to breakfast at Sambo's. By the time I finished, my van was ready, the new windshield clean and sparkling. After a stop at Safeway for groceries, I was back on the road again.

I had been seeing signs advertising Wall Drug for the last one hundred miles, but I hadn't intended to stop, knowing it was a tourist trap, and probably a cheesy one at that. But, after all, it *was* a famous place, and the signs announcing "only ex more miles to Wall Drug" were appearing more frequently. I could feel myself caving. What the heck, why not stop and see what it's all about? I'll probably never pass by here again. So, I joined the flow of tourists streaming in to the long, low wooden building. I took a quick tour of the gift shops, gaped at oddities, and ordered a buffalo burger, my first taste of buffalo meat. That was enough of Wall Drug for me; I was eager to move along. Down the road were the Badlands of South Dakota, one of the places I was especially keen to see.

From Wall, South Dakota, State Highway 240 slices south through Buffalo Gap National Grassland, and then into Badlands National Park, where there are two campgrounds, one to the east near the visitor center, and a primitive one to the west, Sage Creek Campground, ten miles down the gravel Sage Creek Rim Road. I chose the primitive one.

There's a good reason why the road is called a "rim" road; it runs along the very cusp of the Badlands and offers panoramic views at Haybutte and Sage Creek Basin Overlooks, where the grandeur and magnitude of the Badlands are revealed. Three hundred eighty-one square miles of ruler-straight sedimentary rock layers have been carved into staircases and ridges. Millions of years of erosion have whittled the ridges into triangular peaks, thin as wafers, with razor-like edges. Bands of pastel tan, peach, cream, and mocha delineate each tier. Why, I wonder, do millions of years of deposition and erosion result in a landform that looks like a chocolate and whipped cream torte?

By contrast, Sage Creek Campground is open prairie surrounded by distant hills. A few picnic tables and garbage cans are scattered throughout the area, but there are no other camper facilities, and no designated camping sites. You park your tent or camper wherever you like.

I chose my spot on the open plain, popped the top of the greenhouse, and set up camp. I liked this arrangement. There were very few people, and I anticipated a peaceful and private camping experience, in spite of the openness of the place. Most people would probably choose the other campground with its water and electrical hookups, I figured.

Out here on the prairie, I was struck by the immensity of two elemental layers: earth and sky. The blue sky, fusing with the green earth below, stretched to the distant horizon, flat and unbroken except for the far line of low hills rising like a blister on the skin of the prairie. Hawks I couldn't identify were wheeling in the blue above. Prairie dogs and bison roamed freely on the earth below.

By dusk many other campers had arrived, and my hope for privacy had died. But there were compensations. The low evening sun had cast a golden blanket over the prairie, burnishing the grasses in reddish light. I sat in my camp chair with a beer, of course, facing the setting sun and gazing at the fire-tinged grasses. As I watched, a round cluster of them seem to be rolling down a narrow dirt path before me. I blinked my eyes and looked again. Yes, there was definitely a ball of grass, and it was moving slowly away from me. This required investigation. I rose and approached cautiously, wide-eyed, wondering, as usual. A porcupine! Of course. His upraised, backlit quills formed a spiky, yellow halo around his darker body as he skulked away from the indignity of my intrusion. This was my "ball of grass." I watched him for a while, delighting in yet another of nature's compositions: animal, color, light, texture. "Is that incredibly beautiful?" I said aloud. "Or is it just me?" I wandered back to my camp chair, continued nursing my beer, and waited to see what program the night sky had in store.

Friday, September 4, 1981

The wind and flies are about to drive me crazy. I've moved to the campground near the Badlands visitor center. Wind howling at gale force with no let-up, a battering ram trying to rip out the canvas sides of the pop-up, the noise nerve-wracking. Don't like this place, in spite of the intriguing surroundings. Ventured out once for a two-mile hike along the Castle Trail.

Saturday, September 5, 1981

I passed the 100th meridian today and crossed the wide Missouri River, historically significant as the route of Lewis and Clark, and the "river of no return" for thousands of westward-bound pioneers in the middle of the nineteenth century. I stopped to take two photos of this impressive river, then moved on toward Mitchell in eastern South Dakota. Tonight I treat myself to a motel room.

CHAPTER 8

Minnesota, Wisconsin: Lake Lands

Sunday, September 6, 1981

I stayed up late last night enjoying the novelty of television in the comfort of my modest motel room. But in spite of sleeping in a real bed, I didn't sleep well. I awoke early and showered, but when lifting my hair dryer to my head, a sudden pain shot through the upper left part of my back around the shoulder blade—a pinched nerve, maybe—severely limiting my range of motion. Each time I tried to take a deep breath, wracking pain prevented it. I was fearful of trying to drive, but I couldn't afford to spend another night in a motel. So, hurting, and tired, too, I pulled myself, wincing, grunting, up into the driver's seat, and anxiously started out.

Gradually, I was able to breathe normally, and the pain in my shoulder blade abated a little. I had entered Sioux Indian country and no doubt about it. It was evident everywhere in the landscape: road signs, place names, parks and monuments. Near the South Dakota-Minnesota border I stopped at an especially modern rest stop and tourist information center, which boasted a concrete, teepee-shaped sculpture as its focal point. Here I gathered a library of brochures and fliers advertising places to see in the region. One of them described a place called Pipestone National Monument not far away in southwestern Minnesota.

I crossed into Minnesota, turned north, and headed there. I was curious about the name "Pipestone." What did it refer to? For some reason I was picturing ruins of old cabins, burned, with charred chimneys poking up from ashes. I had no idea what was there, but I was tremendously interested in finding out.

The monument turned out to be a quarry site for red pipestone, the soft rock used by Indians to carve their prayer pipes. Indians considered the site sacred to this day, and quarrying, with a permit, still continues.

I would have lingered at Pipestone, but I was hungry, tired, and grumpy. And my shoulder still hurt. I was anxious to stop for the day, so I pushed on to Granite Falls to a nearby municipal campground on the Minnesota River. I found the campground in a rural area outside of town along a paved side road with no traffic. The campground was deserted. The campsites, lined up along the sides of the road, looked as though they were closed for the season, a decidedly "out of service" look. In spite of this, they appeared to be well maintained, and each site was equipped with a water spigot and electrical hookups. I pulled into a spot and turned off the engine, sitting for a while, as usual, to get the feel of the place.

I slid back the camper door and stepped out to explore my surroundings. The sky was gray, the air sultry and full of mosquitoes. I wandered around looking for the pay station, but could not find one, not even a sign posting the fees. There was no "No Trespassing" or "Closed" sign, or any other indication that I shouldn't be there, so I returned to my camper, and began setting up camp, quietly, with many furtive glances around the place. I felt exposed, and had the slightly guilty feeling that I was getting away with something. I was afraid someone had seen me, and was on his way right now to evict me.

But all remained quiet, and when it was apparent that I wasn't going to be ousted, I relaxed. Lucky me, free camping. Out of curiosity, I pulled the electrical cord from its compartment and plugged it into the hookup, not expecting any current. But, to my surprise, the juice was flowing. Double lucky me, camping and electricity at no charge. I didn't know why, but I wasn't going to bother worrying about it.

No one ever came to collect fees, and no other campers came, either. I finished off the day with my usual: birding, journal writing, reading, beer, supper, and bed.

Expenses:	$13.00	gas
	13.60	motel
	3.40	breakfast

Monday, September 7, 1981

Labor Day dawned blue and crisp, a true nip of autumn in the air, which I love. Drove from Granite Falls northeast up through Minnesota today. What a beautiful, neat and tidy state. Saw a few of the 10,000 lakes they brag about here, sparkling, pure and green; wanted to stop and stay at every seductive little lakeside resort I passed, but I've been spending a lot of money on gas due to too many consecutive driving days. Have to stick to my budget. I will be glad to stay put somewhere for a while. I really don't like rushing through this country, but I'm eager to get to my rendezvous with Giles.

My pinched nerve is hurting me again, so can't go for a run, although I badly need the exercise. But this campground is beautiful and rich in birds. Campground lady says there are pileated woodpeckers here. Hope I see one.

Tuesday, September 8, 1981

Awoke to a bright, sunny day. Over coffee, I grabbed a scratch pad to do some pencil and paper figuring of expenses. Money was a constant worry to me. I had allowed myself a budget of only $400.00 per month, and staying within that amount was difficult. I reached in the drawer for a pencil, but the leads of the several I had brought were all worn down to the wood, and I couldn't find the small pencil sharpener I had brought along. I would have to find some place with a pencil sharpener along my route today.

After breakfast, I broke camp and continued on toward Duluth, feeling once again the breathlessness of adventuring so far from home, and about to see the Great Lakes, well, one of them, for the first time. Soon after leaving camp, I stopped at a rustic gas station in Rutledge. A craggy-looking old man wearing a woolen hat approached. He wore a deadpan expression as I asked for a fill-up. Without saying a word he filled my gas tank, then appeared at my window.

"Ten dollars," he said, his face a blank, but I thought I detected just a slight twinkle in his eye.

"Would you happen to have a pencil sharpener?" I asked. He gave me a queer look, as though to say, "We only do gas here, lady."

"Yep," was his terse reply. I expected to be pointed into his grimy little office, but instead he barked, "Where's your pencil?" As I handed him my pencil he reached into his pocket, pulled out a pocketknife and flipped it open. Three or four quick swipes of the blade and he had whittled the business end of my pencil into a miniature Matterhorn. I looked at the multi-faceted point and gave him a wan smile. I'm not sure, but I think maybe he had a slightly defiant look on his face, although his eyes were still twinkling.

I drove on through green, green Minnesota. Green grass, quaking aspen, poplar, maple and pine, one of the loveliest drives of my trip so far. At Duluth I pulled into a large visitor information center with huge windows overlooking a spectacle of endless water. From the northwest the St. Louis River spilled into Duluth Harbor, which widened and joined the west end of Lake Superior. As I gazed through the windows, I recalled that as a youngster I had tried to imagine the enormity of the Great Lakes as described by my teachers. Now I could see for myself. Water everywhere I looked. I might as well have been standing on the shore of the Pacific Ocean.

I phoned Giles before leaving the visitor center. Hearing his voice, so full of warmth and eagerness to see me, instantly returned me to the realm of human connectedness. I hadn't realized that I had left it. Giles was thinking of me. Giles was waiting for me. I was ecstatic as I hung up the phone, and realized that I had been traveling in a kind of emotional semi-coma. For almost two months I had been on the road, probing deeper into unfamiliar territory, farther and farther from home, completely on my own. I had been moving among people, around people, beside people, but not *attached* to people. I was a stranger, a loner, wherever I landed. If trouble arose, I would be forced to turn to strangers for help. Of all my fears, this was the worst. People might be willing to help me, but, too, they might not. They could simply say "sorry," and move on down the road, leaving me stranded. Strangers are not obliged to shelter you. They bear no responsibility for your welfare; they are not kinfolk.

As the weeks had passed, I had gradually become inured to my solitary status, but it had taken its toll. Only after speaking to Giles did I realize the undercurrent of strain I had been bucking throughout my travels. This is why I was vulnerable to his obvious longing for me, in spite of ethical considerations regarding his marital status. He would have to deal with those. The need to be with someone who cared was too strong for me to resist, and I knew my conscience would be no match for the warmth of his arms.

Not long after crossing into Wisconsin, I found Wanoka Lake Campground in a national forest not far off Highway 2, the most inviting campground I had seen so far. Sunlight filtering through emerald green conifers and hardwoods suffused the place with soft warmth.

I backed my rig into a site surrounded by deep green shrubbery speckled with sunlight. I popped the top of my camper and unloaded my campstove, propane tank, and camp chair. The sky was blue and clear–no wind, no flies, no mosquitoes. Perfect, but where was Wanoka Lake? A lane leading away from my campsite seemed likely to lead me there, so I followed it. Before long a narrow band of brilliant cerulean blue appeared between the forest verges ahead of me. It looked so beautiful, the sparkling blue against the forest greens. As I continued on, the lake gradually widened before me, until, at the end of the path, I emerged onto its glistening, white, sandy beach. The lake was small and circular, with lambent light glinting on its surface. The path made a circuit around the lake, and I followed it, exulting in its perfection.

Had an especially pleasant run down forest service road 234, running through dappled light and green shadow. Led to another lake as beautiful as Wanoka. What a gorgeous place!

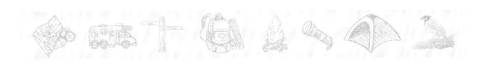

CHAPTER 9

Michigan: Giles Again

Wednesday, September 9, 1981

Lake Superior

*W*ent down to the lake for a last look before packing up and heading *east toward Ashland, Ironwood, and Marquette, Michigan. Stopped in Ironwood for breakfast. Passed into the eastern time zone—three hours later than California!*

Two hundred-forty miles to cover today. Too much driving. But I'm so eager to reach Port Huron where Giles will meet me.

I can't believe that I have really made it this far. The Great Lakes! To think, a few months ago, this was only a dream.

I marvel at the landscape, lakes everywhere, remains of the massive ice sheets which ravaged southward during the ice ages, gouging depressions in the earth, then filling them with meltwater as they retreated to their northerly bases.

My entire route today led through the lovely northern forests, their fall colors already showing. White birches and yellow quaking aspens glinted like sparks against the dark green of balsam fir and pine. Glorious red maples blazed among them, while the blue of Lake Superior, like frames of a filmstrip, threaded *flick, flick, flick,* in and out of the foliage.

At the end of my day's journey, I found Bay Furnace Campground, on the shores of Lake Superior. With few people here, I had my choice of campsites, and pulled into one with a view of the lake. Wooden steps led down a low bluff to a sandy beach edged by dark forests curving off into the distance. In the evening, I sat on the steps with my camera, awaiting one of the colorful sunsets Lake Superior is known for. Before long a pale rosiness appeared on the horizon and slowly deepened into a wide band of vermillion. Satisfied, I took my photo, then returned to the snug quarters of the greenhouse.

Expenses:	$11.65	gas
	4.00	breakfast
	3.00	campground

Thursday, September 10, 1981
Geography Lessons Observed

Awoke by the shores of Lake Superior, in no hurry to move. Took a photo of the sunrise. Ate a leisurely breakfast of beans, ham, scrambled eggs, toast, and two cups of coffee. Studied my maps to get the lay of the land.

I left at mid-morning continuing east along the narrowing land bridge separating Lake Superior from Lake Michigan, then on to the Straits of Mackinac, where Lake Michigan and Lake Huron pinch their waters together.

Driving along, I formulated a mental map of my surroundings: over my left shoulder, the Soo Locks, and beyond that, Canada; Great Lakes on all fronts, and ahead of me the soaring Mackinac Bridge across the straits, all geographic features of first magnitude, to my mind. It seemed as though the pages of my geography textbooks were flipping by me, each feature on the land connected to a photo I had marveled at, or a description I had studied. As I traveled, I addressed each familiar phenomenon like a family member: "Hello, Lake Superior. I know how you got there," and, "Why, here's the Straits of Mackinac. Yes, I do know how to correctly pronounce your name." And, "all you pretty little lakes, you're water-filled dents in the ground caused by blocks of melting glacial ice."

How richly gratifying, basking in my exceptional knowledge, smiling smugly to myself as I moved on down the road.

But my superiority complex soon faded into the usual anxiety about finding a campground for the night. I crossed into Michigan's Lower

Peninsula and drove to Wolverine, a small town hidden a few miles off the freeway. At a general store, I asked for directions to the State Forest campground where I planned to stay the night. It was not difficult to find, but it was deserted, and had a strange, inimical feel. There's no accounting for it; sometimes a campground just feels spooky. Here the trees seemed to lean in on me, watchful, as though poised to prevent my leaving. My uneasiness stayed with me all afternoon, and only intensified as the forest darkened. I tried starting a fire with pine kindling and starter fluid, but the kindling was wet and refused to ignite. After many attempts, I gave up and tromped away thinking, irrationally, it might flare up if I stopped crowding it—the "watched pot never boils" idea.

When I returned to my campsite, I continued to ignore my fire—let it do what it will, I don't care—and started preparing my supper. It was then that I saw two headlights approaching from down the dark road. Fear clutched at my chest, the fear of being alone in a spooky campground with unsavory people. The vehicle, a small camper, approached slowly and parked near me. I watched to see who the occupants were. Soon, a light came on inside the rig, and I could see an elderly man and woman. All the tension drained from my body. Their proximity and the glowing lights in their camper immediately comforted me. Perhaps, after all, they had wanted comfort, too, and had sought my small lights and, finally, my blazing campfire.

Friday, September 11, 1981

Frankenmuth, Michigan

During my year of preparations before leaving California, I had compiled a list of "must see" places on my journey. One of them was Frankenmuth, Michigan, which I had read about in a travel brochure. It was famous for Bronner's Christmas Store, touted as the world's largest such emporium, and the Bavarian Inn Restaurant, famous for its chicken dinners.

Michigan is shaped like a mitten, and Frankenmuth sits on the west side of the mitten's "thumb." From Wolverine I continued south then southeast through Saginaw, then south again to Frankenmuth. At the entrance to the local campground, I was horrified at the ten-dollar fee, and for a campground that was nothing more than a parking lot with huge RVs shoehorned side by side into narrow slots. However, I had no other choice, so I wedged my rig between two behemoth RVs and hunkered down.

Across the street the famous Bavarian Inn and Restaurant and its German-themed complex of gift shops and tourist attractions—the essence of consumerism gone wild in America—beckoned tourists to their doors. I sat grumping in my lowly camper, cantankerous, and disdainful of the ultra luxe motor homes boxing me in. The irony of visiting a place that represents what I deplore: greed, and what I don't have: money, did not escape me. I had already spent so much money, and now the only way I could enjoy this place was to spend more. What the hell was I doing here anyway?

I sank so deeply into my purple funk I actually began to feel physically sick. Then I remembered I hadn't eaten anything since morning, and my grouchiness was probably mostly due to hunger, since I am one of those people who begin to disintegrate when their blood sugar level drops. I looked across at the Bavarian Restaurant with its fanciful glockenspiel high up on the clock tower. Charming figurines depicting scenes from The Pied Piper of Hamelin danced in and out of little doors while music played. It was enchanting, and I smiled a bit in spite of my gloom. What difference would it make if I splurged a little more? A specialty chicken dinner at the Bavarian Restaurant would be just the ticket to turn my mood around.

At 5:30 that evening, I nervously joined the group lined up at the entrance to the restaurant. I hoped I was dressed well enough and didn't need a reservation. Inside, the dining room was already crowded with early diners. Several parties before me were seated and then it was my turn. "Table for one, please," I said hesitantly, expecting to hear, "Sorry, seating for parties of two or more only." But the hostess surveyed the hall, then led me to a table set for four, one place setting for me, and three conspicuously vacant. As she seated me I glanced around and saw that I was in the exact center of the dining room, entirely surrounded by happy families all of whom had an unimpeded view of the hapless, solo woman sitting under the blazing chandelier in the center of the room.

I might as well have been on a raised platform beneath a spotlight. Nearly paralyzed with self-consciousness, my eyes darted frantically around the room searching for a focal point, but no matter where I looked I was staring at diners. My hands felt large and neon and I could not find a place to rest them. Every movement of my body felt awkward and magnified. If only I had brought a book or map. Or even a tiny slip of paper to pretend I was writing something. I wanted desperately to flee, but it was too late. The waitress stood over me with a menu.

At least now I had something to focus on, and something to occupy my hands. In the time it took to scroll down the menu, I forgot about my embarrassment. Looking at all the tantalizing offerings, I had a sudden shift of sensibilities away from my psyche and toward my stomach. Tonight I was going to feast, onlookers be damned. I ordered the specialty chicken dinner, then sat back and sipped a stein of German beer while waiting for my meal.

It began with hot noodle soup accompanied by a basket of just-baked, fruit and nut breads. Next came a steaming plate piled high with breaded, freshly fried chicken flanked by savory sweet and sour red cabbage and warm, vinegary German potato salad. I ate like a linebacker and reached for more, abandoning myself to the meal, licking my fingers, and flaunting my gluttony for everyone to see. What I didn't eat was wrapped in foil and sent away with me. I had had no meal like it since leaving Oregon, and was not likely to have another for a long time. After dinner I waddled back to my camper and slipped contentedly into my sleeping bag.

What a swell place Frankenmuth is.

Expenses:	$12.16	dinner
	12.50	gas
	10.00	camp
	1.43	fudge, postcards

Saturday, September 12, 1981

Lingered in my camper this morning drinking coffee and munching granola bars. Walked a few blocks to Bronner's Christmas Store, basically a warehouse full of everything imaginable for Christmas. Mother would love it.

Left Frankenmuth after buying some sausage. It's a gray day and I'm down in the dumps again, probably because I've been driving every day and spending so much money. Feeling lonely. Everyone annoys me.

Sunday, September 13, 1981

I have arrived at Crazy Horse Campground in Port Huron at the easternmost edge of Michigan; another mile across the St. Lawrence Seaway, and you're in Canada.

This is where Giles and I have agreed to meet tomorrow. Today I will pass the time with errands, a few "household" chores, and a call to Ruth van Leer.

Ruth van Leer is my mother's first cousin. I had never met her, but throughout my childhood my mother had mentioned her from time to time. I knew only that she lived in Holyoke, Massachusetts. As a child I wasn't particularly interested in family history, but as an adult, I began to wonder about my mother's early life on the east coast, and about her relatives there. Before leaving Oregon, I had asked my mother about Ruth. Ruth had married a strange man named Mark, Mom said, and had two daughters, Susan and Sarah. Susan, only twenty-five years old, had recently succumbed to cancer. "Do you think Ruth would welcome a visit from me?" I had asked. "I think she would," Mom had answered, and she offered to help me get in touch with her.

The prospect of family awaiting my arrival on the other side of the continent would be motivation to keep going if my courage should fail, a beacon guiding me to a safe haven, a place to stop and be welcomed after weeks of solo wanderings.

I wrote to Ruth proposing the visit and waited for a reply. It came very soon. Ruth was overjoyed at the prospect of my visit, and encouraged me to stay as long as I liked, but a week at least. She said it would be like having another "chick" in the nest. It struck me that her grief over losing her daughter, so young and so recently, must be almost unbearable. I would be arriving in Holyoke in less than two weeks, now. It gladdened me to think there would be comfort for both of us in this meeting.

Monday, September 14, 1981

Giles

I awoke with butterflies in my stomach. Giles said he would meet me today. Would he really come? It seemed like a long shot to me. I was half convinced that his fervor for me would have diminished by now, and that he would not want to drive the 150 miles from Hamilton to see me again. But at 8:00 a.m. a small sedan pulled up at my campsite, and out stepped Giles.

How handsome he looked in his gray V-neck sweater, and how ecstatic I was to see him. We spent the whole wonderful day together.

Over breakfast Giles listened as I described my recent adventures. "You must write a book, dahling," he began. "Why don't you come live in Toronto and write there? I'll help you find a flat and I'll be there to help you."

"Giles, you're married," I countered. "Nothing could last between us. You would lose interest, or your wife would find out, and I would be stuck in Toronto, thousands of miles from my family. Besides, I can't afford to live in Toronto." Giles was a romantic, full of impractical ideas. He persisted, painting rosy pictures that held great allure for him, but offered little benefit to me.

"I'll pay your rent. You would love writing here."

"A kept woman, Giles?"

Giles had been free with his embraces and kisses, but not inclined to go further, a guilty conscience, probably, and rightly so, but a clear indication he was devoted to his wife, and that even if I had agreed, I wouldn't be "kept" for very long merely as a cuddly "friend."

At 6:00 p.m. Giles took me in his arms for a final farewell. I told him I would be crossing into Canada tomorrow to visit Pt. Pelee, a known birding hot spot, then on through southern Ontario to Niagara Falls. En route, I would probably stay at Courtcliffe Campground, not far from Hamilton. Giles said he would try to meet me there. Before he left, he pressed a 100-dollar bill into my hand. "Take it," he said. "It'll help you get back on your budget." Then he touched the end of my nose, got in his car, and drove away.

CHAPTER 10

Canada: Giles, Oh Giles!

Tuesday, September 15, 1981

I left Port Huron this morning after buying groceries, gas, and breakfast. My destination for today was Pt. Pelee, the southernmost point of Canada, and a premier destination for birders during spring and fall migration. To get there, I would have to drive through Detroit; there was no way to avoid it. So far on my trip, I had detoured around large urban areas, but now I had no choice. I would have to negotiate heavy traffic and find the right exits to get me into Canada.

The way to do it, I discovered, was to mentally gird my loins, enter a trance-like state, and plow through. It wasn't as bad as I thought it would be, except for nearly being creamed by a semi truck that did not yield to me when it entered the freeway.

I made my way through a series of exits and arrived at the bridge crossing into Canada sooner than I had expected. I had never driven across an international boundary before, and I was anxious, not knowing what to expect. The official at the border greeted me politely, if not warmly.

"Where are you coming from?"

"Oregon, originally."

"What's your destination?"

"Pt. Pelee."

"Are you carrying any weapons?"

"No, I just have this little can of pepper spray."

"Tear gas!" he exclaimed. "You can't bring that into Canada!"

"But, it's not tear gas, it's pepper spray, and it's the only protection I have."

The officer restated his directive and jerked his thumb over his shoulder toward a bay of parking spots where other vehicles had been diverted for inspection. "Pull over there!" he commanded. "We'll have to seize that and search your vehicle."

"Seize!" I sputtered. "You could just *ask* me for it. I'm not a criminal." The officer was not impressed, and I realized that perhaps I was being a little too sassy with Canadian authority, so I pulled off to the side. A dyspeptic customs official clambered into the greenhouse and began upturning cushions and poking into cabinets. Satisfied there was no contraband, he ordered me to relinquish my *weapon*, my lipstick-sized pepper spray. Thoroughly humiliated, I pulled the *weapon* from my purse and handed it to the custom's man, who recoiled at the sight of it.

"I can't touch that! You have to throw it in that garbage can yourself," he whined, as though a mere touch would trigger the spray and douse him in deadly contamination. I couldn't say what I wanted to, which was "give me a fucking break," so I walked to the garbage can and did as I was told, stripped of my protection, and stripped of my dignity. "You're free to go now," he said. As I climbed up into my cab, the customs man issued his last order. "Enjoy your stay in Canada," he called cheerily as I pulled away.

In fact, except for the incident at the border, I did find Canada to be pleasing. Produce stands, all of them tempting, appeared frequently along the road, and the houses all seemed cozy. I picked a spacious, uncrowded campground near Leamington and claimed my spot. It was early in the afternoon so I decided to drive into the park Instead of waiting until tomorrow.

Pt. Pelee National Park is the southernmost tip of Canada. It is a spit of land that projects south into Lake Erie, tapering to a string-width's curve of loose sand at its end. During migration, birds alight there in the thousands as a final feeding and resting point before continuing on across the lake, either north or south. As many as 75 species or more can be seen on a given day during peak migration periods.

I drove along a wooded, two-lane road at a leisurely 35 miles per hour (50 km), stopping at the marshview boardwalk. I walked the three-quarter-mile length of the floating boardwalk through a marsh of sedges, reeds, cattails and lily pads, stopping at the intermittent observation towers for far-reaching views. I had read that this was an exceptionally fine facility, and what I had seen so far confirmed it. Unfortunately, I was a bit too early in the season for the masses of birds I yearned to see, but, in spite of it, I did see many marsh wrens and red-winged blackbirds, and I also spotted a swamp sparrow, a first for me.

Later, I took a quick tour through the interpretive center, probably the finest of its type I had seen anywhere, with colorful, sophisticated displays of butterflies, birds, and other wildlife. Obviously the Canadians put a lot of money into their parks.

Back in camp I relaxed and took in my surroundings. The campground was large, and there were RVs, but it was a much pleasanter place than the campground in Port Huron. Even so, I was anxious to get back into national forest campgrounds, rather than spend money on lavish private places sporting recreation rooms, swimming pools, laundries, and other amenities that suck the coin out of your pocket.

How foolish of me to have envisioned myself staying at cheap forest service campgrounds throughout my trip. I had overlooked one simple, but salient point: there is a very large stretch of land between The West and The East. It's called The Great Plains. It's a grassland, not a forest. Hence, no *forest* service campgrounds, a particularly embarrassing oversight for a geographer.

Expenses:	$15.00	campground [two nights]
	13.50	gas
	10.50	groceries
	2. 15	ice
	1.00	toll bridge

Wednesday, September 16, 1981

After an early breakfast, drove out to the tip of Pt. Pelee. A blustery, gray day, but the Point was alive with gulls, common and Caspian terns, hawks, sanderlings, and millions of annoying flies.

A nature path near the interpretative center led into a dense thicket of shrubbery teeming with birds. I entered, but every time I raised my binoculars, mosquitoes congregated in clouds around my head, frustrating my efforts and driving me batty. I missed a lot of birds because of it, but managed to get a positive ID of a black and white warbler before charging half-crazed out of the mosquito thicket back to my car.

Back in the campground I met my next-door campmates, an older woman named Eleanor and her husband, very friendly birders from New York. I told her I had seen a black and white warbler, but no others so far. Eleanor had seen several other warblers including the Blackburnian and Chestnut-sided. I longed to see for myself these birds with such colorful, intriguing names.

I spent the rest of the rainy, gloomy day inside the greenhouse staring out the window. Over at Eleanor's campsite, she and her husband were chatting gaily with another couple. I longed to join them, to enter into their conviviality, but it seemed a tightly bound foursome, and my intrusion would be awkward. I had, after all, only just met them.

Thursday, September 17, 1981

This morning Eleanor came over to tell me she had spotted huge flocks of hawks. "Go get your binoculars and come with me," she ordered, her command suffusing me with the warmth of motherly love. To be wanted by someone, so far from home. Eleanor would never know how grateful I was to her, how easily I could have dissolved into tears by her kindness. We went "hawk gawking" around the campground and I discovered she was expert at hawk identification. She could distinguish a Sharp-shinned hawk from a Cooper's hawk at a glance, and most of the other hawks as well. Compared to Eleanor, I was a rank amateur.

When we returned, Eleanor's friends invited me to breakfast. They seemed to take a liking to me, welcoming me into their circle as though I had been one of them all along. I accepted, of course, but had to restrain myself from leaping and whooping into their campsite, revealing my neediness. We had birded and now breakfasted together; we were friends, but only for today.

Along the way, others, too, had taken me into their circle. We had sat by the fire and shared a bottle of wine, or had birded and hiked together, becoming close like old friends, camping compadres, vowing to stay in touch and meet again someday. Inevitably, though, we would part. I would arise in the morning and find them pulling up stakes, rolling up sleeping bags and folding tents, systematically separating their lives from mine. I would feel a knife blade twist in my chest as I watched them stowing things in the trunk of their car, preparing to leave, chattering happily about their next destination. "Come with us, Lynn," they would urge in my imagination. How could they leave without me? When all was packed, we would gather at their car and exchange warm hugs all around. "Take me, take me," my stifled inner child would cry out. But they would get into their car and slowly pull away, waving, not knowing that behind them they were dragging my heart, through the dirt and grit, like old shoes and tin cans rattling from the bumper at the end of a wedding.

I left after breakfast and took Highway 401 east toward Toronto. It was very stormy, dark clouds scudding across the sky and strong winds creating tense driving conditions. Luckily, I didn't have far to go. I found the road leading to Courtcliffe Campground, but as I approached, it felt less and less like a safe refuge. A long, gray road curved up to a strange stone house that looked more like a fortress, cold and forbidding, than a place to greet visitors. This must be the office, I guessed, although no sign said so. I knocked on the door, then, slowly opened it. A very old, feeble man sat, bare-chested, at a desk, reminding me of the strange man I had encountered at Mt. Hebo in Oregon. I recoiled at the sight of him, the affront of his naked torso. He did not greet me or speak. I wanted to turn away, but I had told Giles this is where I would be, and I didn't know where else to go. When I asked about camping, the grim office attendant assigned me a campsite and charged me $7.50, *without* electricity. That would cost a dollar-fifty more, plus 25¢ for a shower, he said. I begrudgingly paid the price, but did not spring for the extras.

I left the office and tried to follow the map the man had given me, but the roads throughout the campground were nothing more than muddy tracks leading randomly up a knoll. I couldn't tell which were official roads, and which were errant tracks leading nowhere. The campsites were barely more than patches of mud beneath the trees; I finally found my patch deep in the forest among the convoluted loops on the hill, and pulled in.

I faced a long, rainy afternoon confined to my camper, brooding over the likelihood of ever again seeing the sun at this time of year and at this latitude. I was bound for Massachusetts, and then Maine, but it was now mid-September, and it would be mid-autumn before I could turn south. In my mind's eye I pictured a national weather map for January with splotches of zip-a-tone snowflakes and zig-zag squiggles–blizzards and thunderstorms–covering the entire eastern seaboard. No doubt about it, Old Man Winter would find me stuck on the East Coast. So, where was I to go? What was I to do? I had not really devised a plan before I left, except to hole up somewhere if stalled by winter weather, perhaps even to stop and work temporarily in some interesting place. It seemed a romantic notion, back in July. Now, as winter loomed, I anxiously considered whether I should change my plans, skip New England, and hightail it into the Deep South. Then I remembered, on that national weather map of my mind's eye, I had seen zip-a-tone snowflakes over Florida, too.

Cold, gray gloom pressed in around me, seeping through the thin walls of my camper as I ruminated. Drooping conifers leaned in overhead snuffing out what little light the afternoon had to offer.

With no heat and no light, I sat under my sleeping bag, depressed and miserable, my fingers and toes tapering into icicles. I sat through the afternoon and into the evening gazing out into the pitiless gray, too cold to rouse myself and cook a meal, too cold, even, to strike the match that would bring to life the small circlet of blue flame on my stove, my only stopgap against the chill.

Far down on the highway cars sped by, bound for warm, well-lit places. Through a narrow slot between the black conifers, I watched the steady stream of approaching yellow and receding red as they passed by, on and on, oblivious to the desolate camper in the sepulchral fen north of them.

Then, breaking cadence, two yellow beams, like the eyes of an animal seeking a lair, slowed near the campground entrance. Or was it only a trick of light through the trees? But, no, the beams flared in the dark as the vehicle made a right angle turn onto the campground road. It pulled up beside the campground sign and paused a moment. "Don't come in here," I pleaded, fearing a carful of sociopaths intent on evil.

The vehicle moved slowly up toward the stone office. There it stopped again, briefly, then came on, looping back and forth through the unlit campground, probing, searching, advancing. "Please don't come up here, please, please." Halfway up the hill, the vehicle stopped once more, the yellow eyes shimmying with the pulse and pant of the engine. "Oh my god," I breathed, "Please let me be invisible."

The vehicle rolled forward again, its headlights sweeping through the trees with each turn. Suddenly, the beams caught me full on, pouring light into my camper and utterly exposing me within. Now the car moved faster, and with purpose, as though locked on to its target. Coming straight toward me.

The car pulled up to the greenhouse and stopped. I shrieked and bolted from under my sleeping bag to wrench open the camper door just as Giles stepped out of his car. "Giles! It's you!" I flung myself into his arms, mad with joy.

From the sodden, brown muck he stepped into my camper and instantly filled it with warmth. He carried a large paper bag from which he pulled a bottle of champagne and two champagne glasses. Before my disbelieving eyes, he reached again and again into the bag pulling out more surprises: smoked oysters, rye rolls, cold cuts, meat salad, gherkins, poupon mustard, and muffins. While I rummaged for my melmac plates and bowls, Giles opened jars and tins and set out a feast on my tiny table. Then, with a flourish, he uncorked the champagne and filled our glasses with bubbling bliss.

"Oh, Giles," I cried, "I can't believe you found me and brought all this. It's perfect, just perfect!"

He held me and kissed me as he always did, but nothing more. We dined by the light of a single utility candle. After our meal, he bundled me into his car and took me into Hamilton to show me his workplace. Later he returned me to my camper saying that he would try to come back again before I left tomorrow. When he was gone, I lay in my sleeping bag relishing the glorious Cinderella evening I had just experienced. Prince Charming had appeared and transformed the cold grip of this place into a glowing champagne banquet.

Friday, September 18, 1981

Giles did come back. He was here by 8:30 this morning. Over a cup of hot tea, he proposed a day trip to Toronto. "I'll take you to breakfast at my favorite restaurant. Then we'll go to the Eaton Centre, and I'll show you around."

"Giles," I said, fussing a little. "I feel guilty having you spend so much money on me." I did feel guilty, too. Not just because of the money, but because I knew he was neglecting his job and deceiving his wife.

"Remember, dahling," he replied, touching the end of my nose. "It's my company; I am the boss." About his wife he made no comment.

Even though I was excited at the prospect of spending the day with Giles in Toronto, I had some queasy misgivings. I was suspicious of his continuing largess, and wondered why he lavished such attention on me. I worried, too, about being seen with him in Toronto. The bitter pang of my own compromised ethics settled in my gut, yet I knew that I would not decline.

We spent the entire day together. As promised, Giles took me to the Eaton Centre where I goggled at the enormous, light-filled structure, peered through store windows, and rubbed (for luck) the left foot of Eaton's statue. At lunchtime, we went to a Mexican restaurant where we ate enchiladas and drank margaritas, easing into laid-back mellowness. I didn't ever want it to end, but ultimately the time came for me to return to my dismal campground. Giles drove me back and we parted shortly thereafter. He drove home to his unsuspecting wife, and I dragged myself into my sleeping bag for a night of tossing and turning.

Saturday, September 19, 1981

Slept until 9:30 this morning. Didn't mean to, but, in addition to my agitation over Giles, I was troubled by worse than normal menstrual pain.

Still cold, gray, and dreary. Dressed and hurried down to the office to pay for another night, although I do not relish the idea of being here a single moment longer.

Sunshine is what I need, but not likely to get for another month or two. Trying to prepare psychologically by reminding myself that at least I am not tent camping. I do have shelter.

Starting to fantasize about snug homes, wood-burning fireplaces, ovens, hot showers…

Disheveled and miserable, I made my way through the mire up to the bathroom. A few minutes later, when I stepped out, I nearly ran into Giles, who was standing just outside the door and had come looking for me. For the third day in a row he had driven from Hamilton to see me. It seemed strange. It obviously wasn't lust that motivated him. Was it possible he truly cared for me? We talked for a couple of hours and he asked me again to come to Toronto to live and work.

I loved being with him; he was so stimulating and attractive, but Toronto was so far away, so alien. And, damn, he was so married.

Before leaving, Giles promised he would try to come visit me in Maine, wherever I landed. For the third time, he drove away, and I was left to continue on, wondering if he really would pop up again.

CHAPTER 11

On to Maine

Sunday, September 20, 1981

I left Courtcliffe Campground and took the QEW highway through southern Ontario around the lake, through St. Catherine's, and on to Niagara Falls, where I was profoundly impressed by the spectacle. To stand at the brink of the falls and look down or up—a water's eye view—I felt minimized and very lonely. I could see why this was a traditional destination for honeymooners. If only I could be here with Giles. I missed him terribly.

I continued on southward, bypassing Buffalo and making my way to Highway 20 where I turned east and headed for Skyline Resort Campground near Alexander, a much nicer place than Courtcliffe. I went for a run then took a luxurious hot shower. Back in the greenhouse, I bundled into my parka and huddled under my sleeping bag, bracing for a predicted low temperature of 30 degrees. I read until about 10:00 then snuggled down to bed.

Expenses:	$14.40	gas
	8.50	campground
	2.45	beer
	2.00	Niagara Falls
	0.35	bridge

Monday, September 21, 1981

I awoke in a good mood this morning. Left about 11:00 after cooking myself a hearty breakfast, and continued on through upstate New York past cornfields and leas of yellow and purple wildflowers. My route skimmed the northern ends of the Finger Lakes, appearing on the map like chili peppers dangling from the string of Highway 20. I passed through the small villages of Avon, Bloomfield, Geneva, and Seneca Falls, all quaint with greeting-card charm and gorgeous old houses.

Just east of Seneca Falls I found Montezuma Wildlife Refuge, a marshland at the north end of Lake Cayuga. It had an up-to-date visitor center, observations towers, and an auto tour, which I decided to take. It was a pleasant diversion, but didn't yield many birds, only a female oldsquaw.

I decided to stay at nearby Cayuga Lake State Park for the night, a few miles south of the wildlife refuge. Although the campground was pretty, the dark and rain only gave it a sorrowful look. I didn't pop the top of my camper, hoping that would help to retain some heat. I was cold, and spent the rest of the day bored and huddled under my sleeping bag, pining for sunshine, hoping to see it again before winter sets in. Missing Giles.

Wednesday, September 23, 1981

Holyoke

Yesterday evening I pulled into a campground somewhere between Bridgewater and Richfield Springs. It was a large, wide-open, treeless place, with not a soul around. The entrance kiosk was closed, but I drove in anyway and selected a site close to the restrooms. I popped my camper top and waited for an attendant to come collect fees.

The place was eerily quiet, as though Earth had been depopulated. It was evident no one had seen me, and no one was going to appear. For all intents and purposes, the campground was defunct. After sitting for a long time, I put on my sweats and took a thirty-minute run around the campground. When I returned, I went into the restroom in the hopes it might be warmer in there. Strangely, the facility was sparkling clean, obviously recently attended to, with showers. On a whim, I turned on the hot water tap in the shower, and to my surprise, steaming hot water came pouring forth. Free hot water! I couldn't believe my luck. I stripped and stepped under the most luxurious stream of hot water I had ever felt. The heat tingled and melted into my skin as I let out a long sigh.

Back in my camper, darkness fell as I prepared a simple supper. Once I had eaten and cleaned up the dishes, there was nothing to do, so at 7:30, I tucked myself into my sleeping bag, thinking, who cares if this is ridiculously early to go to bed. I can do what I want.

Naturally, I awoke at an equally ridiculous hour the next morning, something like 4:30, well before dawn. Aha, I thought, if I can pull out of here now, I'll be leaving before anyone can come and collect a fee, and I'll get off with a free night of camping!

So, in the dark and stillness of a cold, damp morning I pulled out of the ghost campground and headed for Cooperstown, home of the Baseball Hall of Fame. It was still dark when I arrived, and the picturesque little town was asleep, all quiet and closed down. It was a spooky feeling, as though I was an alien out of sync with the normal lives of other people. I drove through the town's single stoplight and was relieved to find a coffee shop with lights on. I went in and ordered breakfast. Afterward, I strolled through the empty streets, visiting, from the outside only, Doubleday Field, Fennimore House, and Farmer's Museum. Just as the sky was beginning to lighten, I ended my unorthodox tour and returned to the highway.

Ruth van Leer was expecting me today. I wondered if she was filled with as much anxious anticipation as I was. In only a few hours, barring any difficulties, I would be at her house.

I drove to Albany, got on the turnpike and drove south to the Interstate 90 exit. From the interchange, I turned southeast and crossed into Massachusetts, arriving in Holyoke in the early afternoon. I pulled over to a curb and consulted the directions she had mailed me. I found the place easily, an old, white, two-story house with a narrow driveway. With sweaty palms and butterflies in my stomach, I pulled in, walked up the steps, and rang the doorbell.

The door opened, and there stood Ruth, a slightly mannish, short woman in her early 60s, wearing gray slacks and a white shirt, the flesh and blood personage of the phantom east coast cousin my mother had spoken of so many times.

"You must be Lynn," she said. I looked at this woman, my first cousin once removed, and felt instantly the "Coleman-ness" of her, my mother's side of the family. She gave me a quick hug and led me into the house. We sat in her dim living room and began talking, splicing the strands of our family history. We chatted the afternoon away until the light began to fade. Sitting across from Ruth I had the sensation at times that I was speaking to my own mother: the texture of her skin, the sensible black shoes and white socks, the puff on a cigarette. Ruth told me the tragic story of her daughter Susan's recent death, choking back her emotions. I guessed that she had never spoken of this to anyone, had kept it to herself as though her pride would not allow her to succumb to grief. I understood now why she had made reference to me as "another chick in the nest." While listening to Ruth tell her stories, I had removed my shoes and curled up in an easy chair. By evening I felt as "daughterly" toward Ruth as I did toward my own mother.

Giles called me tonight at Ruth's house. I was so thrilled.

I stayed with the van Leers for six days. Sarah, Ruth's daughter, my second cousin, came from Albany on the third day, and again I felt the relatedness as soon as she walked through the door. It was as though a sister I had never seen entered my life. Sarah, Ruth and I sat around the kitchen table drinking coffee and planning menus. I had sat like this with my own mother and sisters hundreds of times before. It was so shocking to have found another group of people three thousand miles away whose essence was so like my own family.

Ruth and Sarah took me on excursions around Holyoke, visiting colleges and other places of interest. They showed me the best places to shop for groceries, the safest places to run, the best bookstores. At home Ruth cooked a dinner of fresh scallops, corn scraped from the cob, and fresh lima beans in cream and butter. One night Sarah bought huge lobsters and cooked them for supper.

The night before I was to leave, Ruth worried that I didn't have warm enough outerwear for Maine. She poked around in closets and found an old down-filled snowsuit that she insisted I take along. There was nothing they wouldn't do for me, it seemed. I felt undeservedly pampered. I had found a haven, a home place of caring people, *family* people, who shored me up with love, guidance, food, supplies, and good wishes enough to launch me confidently onward toward Maine and Acadia National Park and whatever adventures awaited me there.

Tuesday, September 29, 1981

This morning I packed up my camper and went back in the house to say goodbye. Ruth and Sarah made me promise to come back again on my way south. I thanked them and hugged them, and tried, clumsily, to express the love I felt.

As I pulled away from Ruth's house, my two familiar companions, apprehension and excitement, hopped up into the passenger's seat beside me. It happened every time I embarked on a new leg of my journey; there they were, one holding me back like a frightened child tugging on my arm, the other luring me onward to undiscovered wonders.

From Holyoke I took Highway 202 northeast to Belchertown, then turned due north to the intersection with State Route 2. Here I turned east and continued across northern Massachusetts to Interstate 495, where I again turned northeast. The fall colors were asserting their dominance in the landscape now, vivid, brash, unlike any colors I had ever before seen in nature. There was no convenient place to stop for a photograph, but I knew there would be plenty more opportunities ahead.

At Lowell I converged with the Merrimack River and followed it past Lawrence, Haverhill and Merrimac. Just before the river bent south to empty out at Newburyport, I ditched the freeways and took the Elm Street cutoff across Interstate 95 and over to State Highway 1A at Salisbury. In two more miles I was at Salisbury Beach savoring my first glimpse of the Atlantic Ocean. In spite of the personal significance of this event, the waters of the Atlantic, gunmetal gray, looked exactly like the Pacific on a stormy day, except I was facing east instead of west. Still, as I drove, I kept murmuring, Wow, that's the Atlantic Ocean. Wow!

On the drive north to Portsmouth I tried to take in everything, peering and blinking in wonder at all the new sights. The town of Hampton, especially, seemed like a storybook place to me. The inns were freshly painted and trimmed in contrasting colors, a continuous parade of them, more like row houses or hotels than the rambling, ranch-style motels I was familiar with on the west coast. I drove along, rubbernecking and drooling at such unattainable luxury. I ached to stop and check in for an overnight, to flout my own tight-fisted budgetary constraints and go for it. But I didn't.

I pressed on. I wanted to stop at the approximate halfway point between Holyoke and Acadia National Park. I was less inclined to follow my whims and wander off my intended route now that winter was looming. I needed to visit Maine then turn south before too long.

I stopped at a campground near Saco, Maine, and took it as a kind of welcome to the region that the man in the office greeted me with a distinctive New England accent, the first I had heard, exactly as I had imagined. He even answered, "Ay-yup" when I asked him if the campground had showers. I backed into my designated spot with an ear-to-ear grin on my face. Yes, indeed, I was in New England.

Wednesday, September 30, 1981

On a map, Maine's coastline appears to have been severely roughed-up. Bitten, chewed, shredded and scraped, like wool coming off a carder, it is splayed into thin lengthwise strands of land alternating with equally elongated and abused inlets and bays.

Glaciers, of course, were the culprits. They left behind emaciated wisps and fragments, the thousands of islands and attenuated peninsulas that create the most highly indented coastline in the continental United States.

And another Maine phenomenon: although it is one of the most northerly states, its coastline doesn't run due north, but northeast, until around Bucksport. There it turns almost due east. So, to get to Mt. Desert Island from, say, Baxter State Park in the north, you go south (down) and east, hence, "Down East," the name applied to the stretch of coastal Maine extending from Bucksport and Bangor to Dennys Bay, the easternmost point of Maine. People who live there are "Downeasters."

I crossed many bridges as I slowly made my way north on Highway 1. The surrounding countryside glowed with color, corridors and arenas of flaming red and amber, rosy pinks, pale yellow, orange. The marsh grasses had turned to burnished rust, and the sky was an intense, crystalline blue.

At last I arrived at Ellsworth, only nine miles north of Mt. Desert Island, and before I knew it I was on the Trenton Bridge crossing the Mt. Desert Narrows separating the mainland from the island.

Acadia National Park covers roughly half of the island, but it is a patchwork park, not a continuous tract of land. Some patches are triangular or rectangular, and enclose features such as hills or ponds. Other parcels are larger, encircling glacially molded mountains or larger ponds. You drive in and out of government land as you tour the island.

I drove east on Highway 3 toward the resort town of Bar Harbor on the northeast side of the island. I was bound for Blackwoods Campground, the only one of two park campgrounds that remained open this late in the season. It was just off Route 3, about five miles south of Bar Harbor, which I would soon be passing through.

Bar Harbor is a famous resort area, but apparently the word "resort" hadn't registered with me when I had read about it, because a town packed with people and motels didn't come to mind. I had imagined it to be, had wanted it to be, a wild, remote, and rugged place on a windswept shore, with the charm of a rustic fishing village. And, of course, folks would come for those qualities, I figured, but not too many folks, and not too often.

It was nothing as I had imagined, and as I drove through town, I thumped the side of my head with the heel of my hand. "It's a *resort*, dummy," I said to myself. "Of course it will be crammed with people."

Established originally as a vacation place for the likes of the Vanderbilts and Astors, who built elaborate "cottages" in the area, the town was now a compact tourist village nestled against Frenchman Bay, full of restaurants, inns, and curio shops, and bustling with tourists. I drove slowly through town on the main drag, along with a cavalcade of enormous Class A motor homes clogging the narrow streets. Just as I would turn my head to get a glimpse of Frenchman Bay or an offshore island or an intriguing store front, a thirty foot Winnebago or Fleetwood would rumble up beside me, preempting my view with a pattern of bold, jagged lines and words like "Wilderness" or "Expedition." By the time the behemoth had passed, the object of my effort was far behind. Frustrated, I gave up on sightseeing for the moment, but made a note to come back another time, once I had gotten settled somewhere.

The sign at the entrance to Blackwoods Campground said, "minimum two nights, no refunds." I paid for two nights and was directed down a lane that led abruptly from sunny warmth into shadowy gray. The campground sat on a cold slab of granite, beneath the intertwining branches of imposing black spruce trees blotting out sunlight like a tarp of black canvas. There was an inexplicable pall of sadness about the place, as though the campground itself was lonely. Repelled by the gloom, I struggled with an impulse to turn and flee, but where would I go?

I found my site, pulled onto the gravel pad, and cut the engine. The campsite had no electrical hookups, so the small lamp I had brought along was useless. I had only candles to push back the darkness of night, now occurring earlier each day. Worry and dread consumed me. How would I stay warm in this dismal place? Should I leave? Forfeit my campground fee and go find a motel? What if I couldn't find one? Where else could I go? I felt shaky and nauseous. I was spiraling into despair, totally unable to cope and fighting back the rising panic in my breast.

I sat in a stupor in the back of my camper. Why was I feeling so out of control? I was safe. I had a warm sleeping bag. I had food. Food! That was it! I hadn't eaten anything since early that morning. This was all about low blood sugar. It had happened before. I should recognize it by now. Why else would such minor inconveniences throw me into such a tizzy?

I popped the top of the greenhouse and forced myself to prepare a supper of boiled potatoes and carrots and a fried hamburger patty. I ate like a starved person, and instantly felt my anxiety fade. A full meal, that's all it took to restore my equilibrium. I poured a glass of wine and lit a candle, my palliatives against darkness, and settled down to think and plan. It wasn't all that bad here. I could hack it for one or two nights. Since I was paid up for two, that would allow me all day tomorrow to explore the island at leisure, look for other accommodations, and contemplate my options. Who knew what doors might open when I went looking? Feeling better, I tucked into my downy sleeping bag.

Thursday, October 1, 1981

Smuggler's Den, a campground listed in my campground guide, sat just off route 102 north of the village of Southwest Harbor on the "quiet" side of the island. It had electricity and also featured weekend clambakes open to the public.

That's me for, I thought. It sounded like fun, and a good way to mingle with some real Downeasters. I itched to move to Smuggler's Den right away, but I was obligated for a two-night stay at Blackwoods. I recalled the sign that said "no returns." It was not my normal modus operandi to back out of a commitment, but I decided I would drive back and, gulp, ask for a refund on the second night.

Back at Blackwoods, I stated my case to the park ranger, making up some cockamamie excuse, and pleaded for a refund on my second night. He was clearly annoyed with me, but he gave in, refunded my money, and advised me sternly not to come back. I pulled away feeling a bit ashamed, but only for a few moments. The burst of sunlight at the campground's edge, and the open road before me soon took care of that.

Again on Highway 3, I continued west, cutting across two stubby knuckles of land pointing south across the water to the Cranberry Isles. Against a deep blue sky as clear as glass, the hardwoods seemed to throb with color. Pulses of red and yellow flared from the leaves like crayon outside the lines into the pellucid blue air. As I rounded Ox Hill, Highway 3 turned sharply south and ran down to Seal Harbor where the sudden appearance of glittering blue water delivered a punch of Technicolor. I continued along the shoreline, dazzled, to Northeast Harbor, where acrylic glints from the white sails of yachts at their moorages nearly blinded me.

My route now turned north and ran along the east side of Somes Sound, a drowned glacial trough, similar to a fiord, but without the sheer, steep walls. A long, narrow arm of the Atlantic Ocean, the sound cut deeply north through the center of Mt. Desert Island, bifurcating the southern two-thirds of it into two peninsulas resembling a lobster's claw. Now my views, filtered by green pines, reached across the water to the west shore.

I drove on around the northern curve of the sound and then turned south along the western flank. About a mile and a half north of the village of Southwest Harbor, I found the sign for Smuggler's Den, and turned in. The campground owners were friendly, but explained apologetically that their facility was closing for the season today. I had a fleeting moment of alarm as my options dwindled, but then I remembered; I had seen a sign for another campground a few miles back up the road. I was sure of it, it was posted high on a hill, but I couldn't remember the name, or if it was open.

I turned the greenhouse around and reversed course along Highway 3. Please be open, please be open, I chanted as I backtracked north. Yes, there it was, up on the hill: MUSETTI'S SOMES SOUND VIEW CAMPGROUND, next exit, Hall Quarry Road.

Hall Quarry Road was a narrow loop road bulging off the highway like a muscle on a flexed arm. It curved gently through a forest of hardwoods flaunting its autumn colors. It was like driving through an avenue of flame, which became more beautiful the farther I drove. As I approached the sound, I craned my head to see around the next curve, expecting to see the water at any moment. The campground had to be nearby, close to the water. It was Somes Sound *View* Campground after all.

I had no idea what the name Hall Quarry referred to, except, of course, I did know that a quarry was a pit from which rock was mined. I assumed the area was, or had been, a mining region, but I didn't give it much thought. It didn't occur to me that Hall Quarry might be something more than a mining pit. I was mainly concerned about finding the campground and wasn't expecting anything else.

Hall Quarry, it turned out, was more than just a defunct granite mining operation. It was also a sweet little village of about thirty houses and cottages strung along the eastern-most bend of Hall Quarry Road. It sat charmingly upon granitic outcroppings rising step-like from the sound in a series of handsome gray ledges and cliffs. The campground abutted the village and sloped gently down to the water's edge. I turned into the lane that led to a tiny entrance station. No one was there, but the sign said: *Campground Open, choose a site and someone will be around later to collect fees.*

I could hardly believe my good luck. The place was gorgeous almost beyond belief. I drove through the grounds. No one else was there. The campsites sat nestled randomly among a mixed wood of pine, birch, maple, and beech, radiant in hues of vermillion, gold, and yellow, and brilliantly underscored by the blue streak of nearby Somes Sound.

Each campsite had its own arbor of brightly colored trees and shrubbery. It was difficult to choose, but I finally selected one close to the entrance station. I backed into my site and turned off the ignition key. As the buzz and whir of engine and tire noise subsided in my head, the calming voices of nature began to emerge.

After a while I slid open the side door and stepped out into a frenzy of bird activity. Birds darted and swooped everywhere: warblers, redstarts, flickers, and sparrows. The trees and shrubs rang with birdsong. No wonder this place was known as a birding hotspot, and this was peak migration season, to boot. Rejoicing, I grabbed my binoculars from the greenhouse and did a quick survey of the birds in the immediate area. The action was dizzying. As soon as I would train my binoculars on a redstart, another warbler would pop into the scene, and before I could identify it, another would fly into my peripheral vision. I was swinging my binoculars wildly from one bird to another with one hand, while trying to flip through the pages of my field guide with the other. In the short distance between my site and the one next to me I saw American redstarts, black-throated green warblers, a yellow-shafted flicker, yellow-rumped warblers, and a warbler I couldn't identify, maybe a Nashville. I was in birder heaven. As long as the weather held I would stay here and identify every bird on the island. I figured that would be about a week. Little did I know that my time frame was about to change dramatically.

Very soon I was to meet Rudy Musetti. I had seen him pass through the campground earlier in his red pickup. I knew he must be the owner from the way he hurried around checking the restrooms and hauling out garbage bags. He had driven right by me without so much as a glance in my direction, but he hadn't stopped to collect my fees. He finished his business and drove away.

Guess he isn't too worried about his money, I thought. A few hours later, he was back. I saw his bright red truck turn down the driveway and make straight for my campsite. He parked in front of my camper, crosswise, like a gate.

I knew the instant he stepped from his truck he was a man to be wary of. He did not smile or call hello, but strode assertively into my space. I quickly slipped a sweatshirt on over my tank top and stepped out of my camper to intercept him. He barely nodded at me, but with the boldness of assumed entitlement, he stepped, uninvited, into my camper. He sat in the forward passenger seat, which was rotated inward to face the center of the van. I sat opposite him on the bench seat. Too close, I thought. This conversation should be happening outside.

From the moment he sat down I sensed he was on the make. He leaned forward, reducing the already too short distance between us to a few inches. His face bore a hard, unyielding expression. He looked to me like a man intent on having his own way. I went silently on guard, limiting my smiles, watching my body language. I wanted to keep the conversation neutral, and maximize the distance between us.

Rudy took control from the outset. He asked me a few perfunctory questions about my travels, but when I started to answer, his eyes wandered and he fidgeted, no doubt impatient to get through this obligatory foreplay.

I get it, I said to myself. He's not the least interested in my travels. He's probably not capable of being interested in anyone but himself. I gave up any attempt at conversation and waited to see what his next move would be.

Within a few minutes, as though I had asked him about his personal life, which I hadn't, Rudy divulged more information about himself than I wanted to hear. His name was Rudy Musetti, age 49, the campground owner, as I had suspected. He lived about a half mile back up Hall Quarry Road. He told me he was divorced and had four adult daughters. He revealed intimate details of his split with his wife, vilifying her while at the same time admitting that she had found him in bed with another woman. Rudy simply brushed off my observation that maybe his wife was justified in divorcing him. His sharing of these private matters with me, a stranger, was distasteful and made me feel uncomfortable. I knew very well this discussion of divorce and adultery was a maneuver meant to get me on the subject of sex, and, no doubt, on the fast track toward seduction.

Everything about Rudy spelled CAD. So, why, in spite of my aversion, was I taking stock of his physical attributes while he spoke? He wasn't handsome, but he was attractive. Hard muscled, barrel-chested. A pouty lower lip, and fine brown hair brushed softly to one side of his forehead.

It was his voice, though, that particularly fascinated me. Deep and sensual, it came with conviction from his forward leaning body. He had a strong New England accent, the "a's" drawn out and twisted into "aahr's," a disarming trait hard to ignore. While he spoke, he peered intently at me with a glint in his eye, as though trying to detect a scent of interest emanating from me.

Rudy owned three cottages in Hall Quarry, "camps" as they are called in this region. Two of them were further down the campground road on the shore of the sound. The third was on Hall Quarry Road across from the entrance to the campground. I had seen it when I drove in, a small, white, two-story cottage facing the sound. He offered to show me the shoreside camps. I deemed the invitation to be innocuous enough. At least, that's the way I worked it in my mind. We drove in his truck the short distance to the cottages and got out. As we stood on the deck of one cottage looking out over the water, a breeze passed across my shoulders and I shivered. Without a moment's hesitation, Rudy put his arms around me and brought me close into his arms. I had known him for less than twenty minutes. This man is bad news, I thought, not a man to get involved with.

I truly did not want to become involved with Rudy, but did I withdraw from him? No, I didn't. It just felt too damn good. Once again I faced the familiar approach-avoidance struggle between my desire for physical warmth and the more prudent behavior my conscience was pushing for. Rudy was quite willing to supply the physical part, and had no compunctions about it at all. When we returned to my campsite, he invited me to his house for a drink later. So much bait: a warm house, sociability, a cocktail, a sexy man. I couldn't resist in spite of my own internal warning system.

At his house later that evening, Rudy mixed me a rum and Coca-Cola, the drink of choice in Hall Quarry, apparently. It felt good to put my feet up in front of a blazing fireplace. For a while we enjoyed pleasant conversation, like friends, and I felt my wariness slacken a bit. Rudy talked about his camps and said he was busy getting them ready for the winter. What would that entail, I wondered, since those of us living in California's temperate climes, didn't "get ready for winter."

Rudy actually listened as I fretted about continuing my travels during winter, and then he threw me a curve ball.

"Why don't you stay here this winter, in the Hall Quarry camp?" The idea caught me off guard, pinning me to the back of my chair.

"Oh, I couldn't," I automatically blurted.

"Why not?" he said, drawing out the "o" to a string of nasal, flattened "a's.

"Well, I'm on a budget of only $400 a month, Rudy. I couldn't afford it. I don't have any winter clothes. I don't know how to drive in snow. I couldn't afford to heat the house." I was stacking up objections as fast as I could, but at the same time my mind began darting around among the possibilities.

"I'll only chaaahge you $200 a month." He said. "And I'll bring you a caaahrd of wood."

The offer did jive with my original notion of hunkering somewhere for a while, maybe take a temporary job. I relaxed a little and listened as Rudy continued.

"There's an oil furnace for backup heat if you run out of wood. Besides, you would be doing me a favor. I wouldn't have to close up the house."

"I don't know, Rudy," I said, doubtful.

"You wouldn't have to worry about traveling in winter," he argued.

The idea began to ferment a bit in my mind. "I'll think about it," I said.

It felt so good to laze by Rudy's fireplace, mellow with rum and Coke and now stoked by an exciting new twist to ponder regarding my future travel plans. I wanted it to stay like that, just friendly, no pressure. But it was getting late, and I wanted to return to my camper. As I was slipping into my jacket, Rudy pounced.

"Don't go," he said. "It's early."

I was standing in front of the fireplace. Rudy stood, walked over, and pulled me to him. "Stay all night with me," he wheedled.

"Rudy! No," I protested. "Jesus, we just met. Cool your jets."

"C'mon. Why naaaaht?" He drew out those o's and a's, whining like a spoiled child. But his arms were strong and held me tight against his barrel chest. Each time I pulled away, he pulled me back. He was a man who would not give up, a man captive to his own reeking biology. He breathed hot breath into my ear and began maneuvering me, half willing, half unwilling, into his bedroom.

I did spend the night with him and awoke in the morning to gaze across the bed at a rumpled, snoring stranger. Sex with Rudy had been a one-sided affair, all Rudy, and no Lynn, not that I was terribly surprised. I dressed quickly and hurried outside to cleanse myself in the fresh autumn air. Okay, I was weak this time, I allowed myself as I walked back to camp, but it does not have to happen again. Even if I do decide to spend the winter in Maine.

I spent the next morning wrangling with my concerns about moving into Rudy's cottage. The cost of rent and food was within my means. It was the heating that worried me. If Rudy's cord of wood didn't last the winter, I would have to buy more, or pay for oil heat, which was very expensive. I would have to find work to supplement my budget, and I had no idea what the job market would yield.

And then there was basic winter survival, about which I knew nothing. In my naivete, I regarded wintering in Maine, with its severe climate, as tantamount to wintering in Antarctica, dangerous, risky. I could get lost in a blizzard, or become housebound without food. I would be incommunicado with no telephone in the cottage, and there was no room in my already strained budget to have one installed. These were my fears, fantasies probably, but echoed by my mother when I called to tell her what I was considering.

There was also my worry about mobility. I was terrified of driving in snow and didn't know if my VW would hold up to the rigors. And what about winter clothes? I would need to buy boots, woolens, long underwear and who knew what else.

As I stewed, my gaze wandered up the lane to the little white cottage. It was tucked into a semicircle of beech, maple, and birch trees glowing red-orange and vermillion in the autumn sunlight. A platform bird feeder stood on a post in the green front yard. I saw myself stepping out into freshly fallen snow to fill the feeder with seed, luring redpolls, chickadees and blue jays closer for a good look. I pictured myself sitting snugly inside by the wood burning stove in the kitchen writing in my journal, sipping hot cider, and daily watching the forest colors deepen until the leaves began to drop and the first snowfall transformed the landscape to white. I could imagine a thin wisp of smoke rising from the chimney into the silence. My balance scale gently tipped from dreary to dreamy as these images began to mount.

There were other attractions, too. Hiking trails, all over the island, miles and miles of them. The trailhead for Acadia Mountain was only a short walk from the cottage door. I could walk there, hike to the summit, and return easily in a morning. And the old carriage roads once used by the wealthy, but now closed to motorized traffic, would be excellent running trails. And there were those tiny seaside towns dotting the island, waiting to be explored.

Well, maybe Rudy was right. It would be sensible to stay put for the winter, and in such a beautiful spot. My deliberations ended abruptly. I would accept Rudy's offer and spend the winter in Maine. Somehow I would make it work. It was, after all, the very kind of serendipitous experience I envisioned long ago when I first hatched my travel plan.

Rudy appeared around 2:00 and we made the deal. Later that afternoon we opened up the house. He put up storm windows and checked out the furnace and stove. Then he left and returned with a load of wood and a black and white television, a perk that would help me stave off loneliness and cabin fever in the months to come. We chucked wood from the back of his pickup into my driveway, and as I watched the pile grow, two questions I hadn't thought to ask broadsided me: Who's going to stack this wood? Who's going to split this wood?

Not Rudy. The last thing that came out of the back of his pickup was a wedge and a splitting maul. "You can borrow these for the winter," he graciously offered. For the *winter*? My questions were answered.

Finally, the house was ready for me to move in. Rudy had been all business while we were working, mostly ignoring me. I took it as a sign that he had lost interest and would leave quickly when we were finished. But, no. Once the chores were done, his focus zoomed right back to me. Far from being depleted by all his labors, Rudy had plenty of energy left for one more task. He came at me with a glint of clear intent in his eye, wrapped his arms around me, and tried to back me into the house. In spite of his fervor, this time I warded off his advances. But it became alarmingly clear to me that over the next few months I would be dealing with Rudy. He was my landlord and had access to the property, and he was a forceful, determined individual. My misgivings about staying rose again, not just because of Rudy's boldness, but also because of my own weakness. If I couldn't maintain neutrality with him, my winter sojourn could be a disaster.

Rudy climbed into the cab of his pickup and drove away, leaving me standing alone in the driveway. I walked across the road and down into the campground, loaded my camping gear into the greenhouse, and drove back up to the cottage, pulling up to the side door. Inside, the cottage smelled cold and musty.

This is a strange wrinkle, I said to myself. But it felt more like a knot than a wrinkle. I was supposed to be packing up and heading for the next campground. That was the plan. Camping for a year. Instead I was "uncamping," carrying armloads of dishes, clothing, and assorted gear into the house and stashing everything in drawers and closets. I walked through the rooms feeling curiously disoriented, off balance by the switch from my peripatetic ways. I felt a bit like a cheat, like I was weaseling out of a boast.

The last item I brought in from the camper was a 9 1/2 x 6 inch, blue spiral-bound notebook, my journal. I took it into the living room and sat in the worn, brown easy chair. For a while I looked through the front window toward the sound, a view I would come to love through all its permutations as fall turned to winter. Then I picked up my pen and wrote:

Friday, October 2, 1981

Today my journey ended, temporarily, on the opposite side of the continent from where I started. The route I have taken has led me to Rudy Musetti's cabin in Hall Quarry, Maine, where I will stay the winter until spring when the snow melts and I can continue south. I will keep a journal, but it will be an account of my life as a villager, not as a camper.

Who knows what this winter holds for me? I can only guess. Maybe Giles will manage to come visit, as he eagerly proposed in our last phone conversation. But I doubt it. Our paths converged at Yellowstone and again at Hamilton, by chance and by design. Now a much greater distance lies between us. It's a long way from Hamilton, Ontario to Mt. Desert Island, Maine. I know I must relegate Giles to the past, and rightly so. He is not attainable. Now I am ready to meet whatever comes my way. As I write this, my eagerness for new adventures is pushing aside my thoughts of Giles and my fears. The day is bright and warm. Soon I will go outside and see about this splitting maul and wedge business.

PART IV:

The Big Trip: Maine to California

March 12 - June 3, 1982

CHAPTER 12

Leaving Maine

Friday, March 12, 1982

Biddeford, Maine

I finished packing and cleaning this morning, a foggy, drizzly morning. At 11:00 a.m. I said goodbye to Jamie, Pat, and Arline and drove away from Hall Quarry with a heavy lump of sadness in my chest. Driving southwest down the coast, I stopped in Rockport at the offices of *Down East Magazine* to see if they had received my manuscript, "A Californian Down East," an essay I had written while staying in Hall Quarry. They searched through their stacks of manuscripts while I waited anxiously. Finally they found it and said that they were still looking it over. I gave them the address and phone number of my brother in Austin, Texas and resigned myself to a long wait before I would hear.

The weather still too cold for camping, I found a cheap hotel in Biddeford, cheap and crummy, where I checked in for the night. Lying in the squeaky bed I listened to the rain dripping from the eaves. The fog seemed to penetrate the stained, thin walls of my room. I was thinking of the view from my bedroom window in Hall Quarry. So many nights I had watched the snow falling, so many different kinds of snow I had never known: soft, fluffy snowflakes as big as tennis balls; frenzied flakes tumbling wildly, zigzagging and bouncing as they plummeted to the ground; and flakes tiny and hard as BBs that strafed the air in their descent.

Jamie Gonzales had trudged through that snow one day up to my back door. My downhill neighbor, he had seen me earlier struggling to shovel a path down my driveway. He came to offer sympathy and encouragement regarding snow chores. Wearing no hat to protect his thinly furred head from zero degree cold, he greeted me with unrestrained ebullience, his grin bright as January sunshine. In no time at all we were boon companions, whiling away many frigid winter hours playing Casino and Yahtze and harmonizing Dolly Parton tunes. The entire Gonzales family, mom Arline, sister Pat, and Pat's boyfriend George, welcomed me into their home, sharing hootenannies and baked bean suppers. Their friendship, and the friendship of many others, had generated affection and good cheer enough to warm the chilliest Down East nights.

In so many ways I had benefited from my months in Maine. I had worried I would not be able to go out jogging once snow and ice covered the ground. I saw myself sitting sluggishly around the house, snowbound, putting on weight. But it had not happened that way. I did go running, in rain and snow, and even at night. Often my runs occurred as the last event in a triathlon of daily chores. My journal entries often reflected that:

. . . raked leaves for two hours this morning, then split and stacked wood. Went for a three mile run this evening.

I got plenty of exercise, and splitting wood was not the least of it. Using Rudy's wedge and splitting maul, I set out to acquire the skill. The first time I tried, I placed a chunk of wood vertically on a stump and stood before it in what I supposed was a lumberjack stance. Sucking in my breath, I swung with all my might. The maul rebounded to the right and the wood shot to the ground, intact. Nothing had been split, including, luckily, no toes or shins. Again upending the wood, I spread my feet wide and stood holding the maul parallel to the ground, coaching myself—keep your eye on the wood and follow through. I raised the maul above my head and swung with abandon, as if to split the very ground beneath, putting all my one hundred ten pounds into the effort. With a sharp *craack*, the wood snapped apart into two neat pieces. I stared dumbstruck at the twin sticks. The thrill of power welled up within me and I whooped, all right! to an audience of squirrels and blue jays.

On days when my woodpile was stocked and I wasn't babysitting or housecleaning for the women who had hired me, I hiked the trails of Acadia National Park, sometimes with a friend, but more often alone. I hiked up mountains and granite cliffs, through forests and along shorelines. Some days I hiked or ran the carriage trails around lakes and through peaceful woods, silent but for the songs of birds deep within. I needn't have worried about falling out of shape. I expended hundreds if not thousands of calories daily and ate heartily in the evenings to compensate.

My days on Mt. Desert Island had been full of wonder, and I had accumulated memories enough to illuminate my reminiscences all the way back to California and for years to come.

Now as I lay in bed in Biddeford's chintziest motel, I grieved for what I had left behind. How could any experience lying before me compete with my beautiful winter in Maine? Tomorrow I would push on to Holyoke. I had promised Ruth I would stop back for a visit on my way to the Deep South.

Saturday, Sunday, March 13 - 14, 1982

I left at 7:00 a.m. this morning, stopping in Kennebunk for breakfast at a three-table place so small my knees nearly touched the only other customer. I ate fast and left in a hurry. There was no gawking at the landscape this time. It was a dreary, rainy day, and I wanted to arrive at the van Leer's in Holyoke before dark.

Monday, March 15, 1982

After twenty-four hours of home cooking and family togetherness, I waved goodbye to Ruth at 9:00 this morning. I took Interstate 91 south out of Holyoke, driving fast. That is, fast for me and for my doughty, but underpowered Volkswagen. I wanted to move quickly south to lessen the chances of being caught in any late season snowstorms.

The freeway paralleled the Connecticut River to the east, then shifted west of the river near Windsor Locks. As I approached Hartford, the usual anxiety about driving through large metropolitan areas revisited me. I figured Hartford, being the capital, would be a city of maybe a million or more people, and I wasn't relishing the idea of interacting with them on their highways. Hartford, in fact, was only a mid-sized city of less than 140,000 people, but I didn't know it. As I buzzed through it seemed to consist of a huddle of tall buildings, most of them presumably headquarters of insurance companies. High up on the side of one building, a familiar logo loomed out at me, the silhouette of a proud six-point stag, the famous Hartford symbol.

From Hartford, I changed over to Interstate 84, which took me southwest past New Britain, Waterbury, and on to Danbury near the border with New York. I drove hypnotically, allowing the landscape to pass by without much notice as I passed into southern New York. Near the town of Beacon I crossed the Hudson River and into Newburgh. Staying on Interstate 84 I pushed on to Port Jervis where the Delaware River and the border between New York and New Jersey all come together. Here I turned south along Pennsylvania Highway 209 following the Delaware River through the Delaware National Recreation Area. I was heading for Four Seasons Campground in the Pocono Mountains near Scotsrun.

Still some snow on the ground, but it has been melting fast. Temperature in the forties and some sunshine. It's a pleasant campground. There are many mobile homes here; they look permanent, but no one is around. Owner finally showed up and I registered. Went for a short run. Showered and ate a supper of cold roast beef, carrot sticks and bread. It's 6:35 p.m. and still not completely dark. I have my oil lamp lit; it is cozy inside my camper. Everything going well. Soon I'll be in the South.

CHAPTER 13

Down the Appalachians: Roads to Nowhere

There's something strange about the map of Pennsylvania. The south central portion bordered by Interstates 99 to the northwest and 81 to the southeast, looks like the cartographer went haywire, took a handful of pens and, in a fury, scraped them along the map in broad, sweeping arcs. It looks like a huge plug of land has pushed north into Pennsylvania shoving aside whatever was there while curving to the northeast. Every highway, road and river follows those curves, narrow and elongated, like taffy stretched to its thinnest.

At first glance I didn't recognize what it was; I truly thought something had gone amiss with either the cartography or the printing of the map, like maybe the map had slid off the presses before the ink had dried. Of course, that notion was ridiculous, so I shifted to a more scholarly view of the anomaly. What process would produce a corrugated topography like this?

Compression would do it. Millions of years of folding and crumpling of the earth's crust would jam the region into a series of long, narrow valleys and ridges. That's what did happen, in fact, in central Pennsylvania and farther south. This ridge and valley region is the northern extension of the Appalachians, ancient mountains tightly folded and deeply eroded by streams into a trellis-like drainage pattern. Short streams run down the flanks of the ridges into longer streams running the length of the valleys. And of course the maps of Virginia and West Virginia showed the same pattern.

Tomorrow I will drive into those mountains, cross the Appalachian Trail, and head for the Amish country.

Tuesday, March 16, 1982

I awoke to clear skies this morning and prepared for my day's journey into the Appalachians and the Pennsylvania Dutch country. Studying the map, I chose a route that passed through Reading on my way to Lancaster County, home of the Amish people. The name Reading, Pennsylvania was familiar to me from grade school geography, but I couldn't remember what it was noted for, if anything, so I raised my antennae for clues to its economy and character as I drove through.

The first clue was a complicated tangle of freeway interchanges and poorly signed exit ramps. They came up so fast I missed the ones I wanted, and found myself funneled down an off-ramp into a neighborhood that looked to be "crime central" of Reading. It was a mix of businesses with bars over the windows and shabby houses with peeling paint and garbage for yards.

Alarmed, I tried to backtrack as fast as I could, but although I knew the freeway entrance must be nearby, I could not find it. I drove down several streets searching for a way out, to no avail. Instead, I penetrated even more deeply into the squalid neighborhood where unsavory-looking men wearing defiant expressions planted themselves in the streets as though daring me to try and pass them.

Eventually I found a grocery store and pulled into the parking lot, hoping to get directions from someone inside. The appearance of the place offered little to reassure me. Heavily barred windows and a barred gate that could be pulled across the doors confirmed my suspicion that this was a high crime area. The parking lot was littered with cigarette butts and food-smeared paper wrappers. Dark, mean-looking men squatted in front of the store or leaned against the building openly drinking bottles of beer.

I did not want to get out of my van and walk into that store, but I would never find my way out of Reading without help. Instantly I took a giant leap of faith—I had no choice—and trusted that these men were not as surly as they looked, that some good would shine through their rough exteriors as I passed them. Maybe one of them might even smile.

I covered my binoculars and camera with my sleeping bag, slid out of my seat, and locked all the doors. Trying to appear nonchalant, but clutching my purse close to my body, I walked past the men, holding my breath against the smell of beer and smoke. No one spoke to me; only stared. The store was as tawdry inside as it was outside. Much of the merchandise was displayed behind locked cases, and slashes of fresh paint barely covered patches of graffiti on back walls and shelf ends. Customers and clerks alike wore grim, hostile expressions. The milk of human kindness was not in evidence here. I had the unnerving feeling that my gender, petite frame, and helpless look would not elicit one iota of sympathy from this lot.

Bucking up my courage, I strode up to an employee who looked like he might be a manager and asked how to get out of town. He didn't so much as slow down, but with a few points of his finger spat out some curt instructions and hurried away. I caught only a drift of what he said, but I did not have the courage to approach him again.

Back in my camper, I pulled out of the parking lot and tried to remember the direction he had pointed. I drove randomly down a few more streets looking for freeway overpasses in the distance. At last I found my way to an entrance ramp and, with a profound sigh of relief, pulled up on to the freeway and out of Mac the Knife-land as quickly as I could.

South of Reading the landscape became a gently rolling farmland. The road wound easily through the countryside and there was very little traffic. The tension from my Reading experience gradually drained away as I settled into a relaxed pace, relishing the scenery around me. Rounding a broad curve near the town of Honeybrook, I came up suddenly behind a small, gray and black, horse-drawn carriage with an orange and red triangle fixed to the rear of the cart. A bearded Amish man in black garb and a black hat was driving the rig, rolling slowly along at a one-horse pace. I slowed and pulled up behind him, keeping a respectful distance, charmed by the sight of this well-known emblem of the Amish lifestyle. He had appeared at the very moment I crossed the county border, right on cue, as though he had waited for a signal from some director of tourism to pull out onto the road for my benefit. I followed him until he found a wide spot, pulled his buggy over and signaled me to pass. He waved as I carefully pulled around him. A little farther on I saw another Amish man working his field with plows drawn by teams of four horses. He waved heartily at me as I passed.

In spite of my non-religious views, I felt an affinity for these easy-going, friendly people and their simple way of life. Without electricity or telephones in their homes, and without gasoline-powered vehicles, their lives must surely be less stressful and more community-oriented than most Americans. I admired them, and their ability to thrive as an enclave within the wider, mechanized, hustle-bustle world.

I found White Oak Campground near Quarryville, but in spite of its lovely name, it was deserted and dreary. Gray clouds hung over the region by now and threatened rain. Although I was tired and wanted to settle for the night, a wave of depression swept through me. Any passerby on the road could see the solitary, forlorn green camper in the wide-open campground, a sitting duck. Any passerby who wanted to could rob me, or worse, and I would be helpless. I unfolded my map and studied it for possible better options. There were no other campgrounds nearby and no towns, but Gettysburg was about seventy miles away, a bit more than an hour's drive. I tossed the map aside and decided, heck with staying here. I would make a dash for Gettysburg, and treat myself to a motel for the night. With luck I would outrun the rain. But I would have to get a move on. Daylight was waning fast, and the dark sky enfeebled what was left of it.

I yanked the pop-top down and slammed the latches shut, climbed into the driver's seat and hauled out, keeping a wary eye to the clouds. They waited until I reached the main road, then, like sadistic harridans, stooped and unleashed a terrific pelting of rain. Rain came so furiously water pooled in the road forcing me to slow down to avoid hydroplaning. My windshield wipers couldn't keep up with the downpour and I drove in a state of high tension straining to see the roadway. At last I could see the lights of Gettysburg shimmering ahead of me. I pulled into town at dusk. The light from the streetlamps glistened off the wet pavement, cheery and welcoming, as I drove through the small town looking for a motel. I found a Howard Johnson and checked in to a deluxe, but reasonably priced room where I flopped on the bed and closed my tired, burning eyes, glad to be off the road. Later, I went downstairs to the hotel's cozy bar and ordered a drink. Before long I was chatting with some friendly local folks who told me I shouldn't leave Gettysburg without taking the tour of the famous Civil War battleground.

Wednesday, March 17, 1982

Gettysburg Battlefield

I roused myself at 6:45 to a very foggy morning. I lingered in a hot shower, ate some cold cereal, and watched TV news. At 9:30 I packed up and drove to the tour center for the Gettysburg Battlefield tour scheduled for 10:00 a.m. I waited at the tour office for other tourists to appear, but at 10:00 I was still the only person waiting. An elderly man with a clipboard came through a door and greeted me. "You're the only guest today," he said. "Do you still want to take the tour?"

"Yes, I'm very interested in taking the tour," I said. He nodded politely and escorted me to the twelve-passenger touring van and invited me to sit wherever I wanted. When I chose to sit in the front next to him, he chuckled in an uncomfortable, self-conscious way, but opened the door for me. He seemed to be embarrassed to launch into his professional spiel with only one tourist on board. I was hoping he would dispense with the official script and just talk to me as we drove through the route.

Being a proper old gentleman, my guide responded to my occasional question, addressing me by my surname. At first it was "Mrs.", but then, seemingly unsure of my marital status, he switched to "Miss." Then back to "Mrs.", then "Miss" again. I could tell the poor fellow was obviously distressed about what to call me. "Please, just call me Lynn," I offered, but he couldn't do it, and eventually he stopped using a title altogether.

At the edge of the battlefield the guide reached over and switched on the tape deck. Solemn music issued forth, and then a man's deep, sonorous voice began…"Four score and seven years ago"…

I hadn't known what to expect, or how I would react to the tour, but the moment the famous speech began a deep awe fell over me. A lump hardened in my throat and tears stung in my eyes.

As my guide slowly drove through the hills surrounding Gettsyburg, the taped narration simulated the noise of the battle, the boom of cannon, the shouts of soldiers, and the moans of dying men. The armies of Robert E. Lee and George Meade, 172,000 men in all, fought here. The bodies of thousands of men had lain strewn about these very hills we were driving through. More men fought and died here than in any other battle in American history. I tried to imagine it. I tried to envision a front line of soldiers marching out from the shelter of trees into the open and into the direct fire of their enemy. I tried to picture the front line swaying "like wheat in the wind" as the enemy mowed them down.

Along the way, my guide stopped so that we could step out of the van. Looking around, I tried to picture this very spot covered with the bodies of thousands of men, dead or dying in agony. No doubt a body had lain exactly where I was standing, and no matter where I turned, bodies would have been scattered everywhere across the hills. It was nearly inconceivable. I wasn't just reading about this battle from some textbook in some distant school. I was actually here, where it happened. Never before had I felt the weight, the tragedy, of this battle, or any Civil War battle, or any battle anywhere, for that matter.

My bemusement at the awkwardness of my guide and the contrivance of taped narration gave way to respect as the tour continued. The gravity of what I was seeing humbled me profoundly and I remained silent, respectful, throughout the rest of the tour. Back at the tour office I thanked my guide for his special attention. I told him how much the tour had moved me, and that I thought being the sole guest had made it even more meaningful.

Across the street from the tour office, a restaurant, the Dutch Cupboard, beckoned to me. The façade was Pennsylvania "Deutsch" and so was the menu: bratwurst, red cabbage, vinegary hot potato salad, food to comfort the battle weary. Inside, the restaurant was quaint and colorful, reminiscent of the Bavarian Inn in Frankenmuth, Michigan. And the food was equally delicious.

After lunch, I returned to the greenhouse, made my way to the freeway, headed south, and soon crossed into Maryland. At Frederick I veered southwest, crossing the Potomac and grazing the border of Virginia before entering West Virginia and crossing the Potomac again at Harper's Ferry.

That I had traveled so far from Maine in so few days seemed unbelievable, such a sudden switch from the frigid snowscapes of Hall Quarry to the balmy pre-spring temperatures I was now experiencing. In spite of the warmth, it was still winter and I knew that snowstorms could occur along the Eastern Seaboard well into spring. Every mile I pushed south lessened the possibility of inclement weather, I thought.

Now, here I was on the threshold of the Shenandoah Valley with the Appalachians to the west and the Blue Ridge Mountains to the east. Shenandoah, such a lovely name, meaning something akin to "daughter of the stars." I would be camping in the valley tonight at Elizabeth Furnace Campground, providing it was open. At this time of year campgrounds were often still closed for the winter. But this one was supposed to be open year-round, at least according to my campground guide.

I found it west of the town of Front Royal at the north end of the George Washington National Forest. What a welcoming feeling to enter a national forest again, so reminiscent of the western forests I had left nine months ago. The familiar array of tidy campsites with floors of tamped leaves and pine needles, encircled by logs, and furnished with picnic tables and fire pits was like home at day's end, a place to unwind from the tensions of the road and exhale a deep sigh of relief.

The campground lay tented beneath a canopy of glowing green, the tender greens of early spring, lime, honeydew, clover. Even the air was green, green and smelling of earth, pungent and rich, trembling with a hint of the South's subtropical breath. Birds everywhere sensed it too, noisily singing out their joy and wild hope, darting endlessly among the trees in search of food and mates.

The thermometer dangling from my rear view mirror registered 65 degrees. I pulled off my jeans and changed into shorts and running shoes. After a few muscle-loosening stretches, I jogged off down the campground lane inhaling deeply the perfume of moisture and warmth wafting around me.

It's 7:30 p.m. and I still hear birds. Or is it frogs? Sounds like birds. Just stepped outside my camper. The stars seem even more brilliant here than they were in Maine, a continuous network illuminating the black sky. The air is still balmy, no need even for a light jacket. Nothing more to do. Bed.

Thursday, March 18, 1982

I awoke at 6:30 this morning after a fine night's sleep. The birds were already up and singing noisily. I stepped outside and took a little walk to acknowledge them: red-bellied woodpecker, Carolina chickadee, tufted titmouse, and eastern phoebe. The red-bellied woodpecker was a new bird for me, a lifer. He came close to camp and offered me a good view. No doubt he got an eyeful of me, too.

After breakfast of French toast, I broke camp and readied myself for the road. I continued deeper into lovely Appalachia to the town of Edinburgh, just off the freeway, where I found a laundromat and stopped to wash the pile of dirty clothes and towels accumulating in the back of my rig. While waiting, I studied my map of Virginia for a likely route east to the Blue Ridge Parkway. Running my finger south down the map along Interstate 81, I noticed the word *cavern* in two place names: *Shenandoah Caverns and Endless Caverns.*

My suspicions were aroused. That sounded like *karst* topography to me, a kind of landscape that develops in limestone or dolomite bedrock when acidic rainwater trickles downward through cracks. As the water percolates into the underworld it dissolves rock, which is carried off by underground rivers. Of course the rivers do their share of dissolving, too, until the rock is perforated with cavities. As more rock is eaten away, the cavities grow into caves and caverns. When a cavern grows so big the overlying rock is unsupported, the "roof" of the cavern collapses, creating a circular pit in the ground called a sinkhole, the most common feature of karst topography. Sinkholes have been known to swallow up cars, houses, parking lots, and more. Property owners must be wary. Living in a karst region gives new meaning to the adage, "build your house on a rock foundation."

I pulled out my United States geography text and turned to the discussion of karst topography. I found two photos of sinkholes and a map of the karst regions in the United States. Sure enough, the Shenandoah Valley was one of them, limestone and dolomite, rocks highly soluble in humid climates such as this. My route, Interstate 81, continued south right down the middle of the Shenandoah Valley, atop all those invisible, subterranean caverns, those sinkholes-in-waiting. May they wait until I was long past.

About eighty miles down the road a cutoff led to Buena Vista, a pretty little town in the Blue Ridge Mountains. At Buena Vista I drove up an access ramp onto the Blue Ridge Parkway and entered a world entirely different from the bustling freeway I had just left. The Parkway is a meandering two-lane road along the crest of the Blue Ridge Mountains, crisply striped and neatly maintained, like a private lane through a country estate, and it might as well have been, for I saw no other cars on my journey today. The Parkway allows you, no, forces you, to slow down. Not just your automobile speed, but your breathing, your pulse. The 45 MPH speed limit encourages dawdling, which is exactly what I did, stopping often to gaze and absorb the beauty of forests and the distant, rolling contours of the Appalachians.

I was looking for the first campground that wasn't still closed for the winter. I found it only fifteen miles into my drive, Otter Creek Campground on the James River, the lowest elevation on the Blue Ridge Parkway. Only one other camper was there, a young man by himself.

Set up camp and plopped into my camp chair with a beer. Yes, I feel the South speaking to me from down the road. It is cloudy, but warm and humid, like a steam bath. It feels so good. Makes the place seem friendly. Out of the corner of my eye I watch the young man busying himself at his campsite. Imagine! A young person traveling all alone in such a remote spot, and at this time of year!

Friday, March 19, 1982

I spent some time around camp this morning trying to photograph birds, one tufted titmouse in particular. But it wasn't going to happen. Birds don't hold still, and my patience usually runs out before I get an opportunity for a good shot. I gave it up and left camp at 10:30 a.m.

But, from the start, my drive today was plagued by uncertainty and tension. I had discovered from reading my campground guide that most of the campgrounds within a day's drive were closed, which meant I was driving "blind," not knowing where I was going to stay that night. This was counter to my usual game plan, and very unsettling.

Also, early into my drive my eyes began to feel gritty and burned from the strain of peering down the road. The discomfort worsened the longer I drove until even my eye sockets ached. On the outskirts of Roanoke I stopped for gas and a brief rest, but the tension had knotted me up too tight for relief. Back on the road, my eyes bothered me so much my vision became blurry, and the tension was giving me a headache. I was spiraling into that buzzing, disoriented condition I had experienced before on the road. My body was failing me and I realized I was incapable of coping. I had to get off the road.

Just then, I saw a sign ahead for a scenic attraction: Historic Mabry Mill. It was perfect timing. I couldn't have driven much further without being a danger to myself. I pulled off at the exit and drove into the parking lot.

The mill stood at the edge of a silver pond in a scene of perfect tranquility. Its barn-like architecture and massive water wheel against a background of bare tree branches lent a gray, stately aspect, and its reflection in the pond doubled the effect. A sweeping green lawn sloped gently upward away from the mill on all sides. Near the parking lot, a wedge of flagstone paving pointed toward the pond, adding an element of textural contrast. The place had been the subject of scores of paintings and photographs. And no wonder, the composition needed no arranging; it already looked like a painting or photograph, perfect as it was, and perfectly beautiful. Even an amateur photographer like me could not err with a setup like this.

At this time of year there were no other visitors. I had the place to myself, and I needed it. The serenity gave me a chance to decompress. As I walked through the grounds, my sense of geography slowly returned to me. I had been covering territory, but without understanding where I was in relation to anything else. I had been just a moving dot on a map, oriented to nothing, too anxious and upset to think about my surroundings. Now I had time to reconstruct my mental map of the Eastern Seaboard, and place myself in it. And not just the Eastern Seaboard, but the entire country. I wanted to keep that colorful physical map of the U.S.A. and Canada, with its deep green for low places, and brown for high places, right there in my mind's eye, as though suspended from the sun visor above the driver's side windshield.

I took a few photographs of the mill and grounds then returned to my camper where I sat for a while searching my maps for nearby campgrounds. There were many little tent symbols on the map indicating campgrounds on the Blue Ridge, but I doubted any would be open this early in the season. I feared getting back on the road without knowing where I would stop for the night. The way I was feeling I could not endure a marathon drive in search of lodgings. The map showed a small town, Hillsville, about twenty miles off the Parkway west of a place called Meadows of Dan. Maybe, being so close to the Parkway, it might have lodgings. I decided to take a chance and drive the twenty miles.

It was fortunate that Hillsville did have a motel, because by the time I checked in I was no longer *compos mentis*. Hunger, in addition to road weariness, was playing a role in my mental state. I had just enough presence of mind to recognize that I needed to eat, so I rummaged through my ice chest, quickly stuffing my mouth with anything I could find that would relieve the pangs.

Looking out from my motel room, I felt very much in strange surroundings. The usual view from urban motel rooms, buildings, signs, streets, traffic, was lacking. This motel, albeit located in a town, was decidedly rural. There was none of the accoutrement usually associated with a motel: no traffic, no noise, no restaurant, and no people about. From my window I saw only rolling hills and little of the nearby village. It felt odd, as though I had been quartered in some surreal, leftover set from the Twilight Zone. The place gave me an uneasy feeling of being watched by people in hiding. Was this one of those mythical Appalachian backwaters where people in tumbledown shacks spied at you with evil intent through crossed eyes?

Further down the road and across the fields I saw a high school with the faint trace of an oval track in the adjacent field. In spite of dark clouds piling up overhead, I put on my running clothes and jogged toward the track. A good run was what I needed to shake off the languor of sitting behind the wheel of my rig all day. But at the track I managed only twelve laps before fizzling. It was hard work, and I could tell my lung capacity had deteriorated. Nevertheless, as usual, running did the trick. By the end of three miles, my tension was gone. On the way back to the motel, I scolded myself, that's it, no more neglecting my running.

The clouds produced a few thunderstorms in the afternoon, although the day was very warm. There was no place to go, so I moped around the motel room pondering the next phase of my journey. I needed to come to a stop somewhere for a few days, maybe a week, to shake off the tedium of the daily camp-and-go regimen. It could be Charleston or Savannah, and I definitely planned to spend at least a week in the Everglades in Florida. But even Charleston, the closest of the three, was still several hundred miles away across the entire state of South Carolina. It looked like a few more long haul days were inevitable. Tomorrow I would start early and press on to Asheville, North Carolina.

Saturday, March 20, 1982

Today is the vernal equinox, the first day of spring, a day symbolically bright and blooming with promise, I hoped. But instead Nature chose to do her ironic best to thwart me.

I finished breakfast and was on the Blue Ridge Parkway by 8, looking forward to a grand drive after a good night's rest. I took the nearest entrance onto the Parkway and immediately rammed into an obliterating wall of fog, the thickest I had ever seen. Fog pressed against my windshield and side windows shrinking my visible world to the inside of my camper. Panicked, I hit the brakes and reflexively veered toward the side of the road, but it had disappeared. For an instant I thought of backing up, but I couldn't back down the on-ramp, even if I could see it. There was nothing I could do but keep going. I continued at a crawl, straining desperately to see the painted line at the edge of the road, but it was gone, too. I was like a blind woman feeling my way in darkness, sensing the road an inch at a time, praying I wouldn't drive off the pavement. At this speed, I was at risk of being rear ended by someone coming up behind me, but I was too terrified to go any faster. There was no way for me to judge distance, no approaching car with headlights to give me perspective.

Suddenly, out of the gloom before me the back end of a car loomed. My foot shot to the brake pedal as I braced for an impact, but it didn't come. It was only a nasty trick of the fog, compressing its droplets into the dark shape of a vehicle just to taunt me. I drove, barely creeping, for half an hour or more until, almost imperceptibly, the fog began to thin allowing me to accelerate and, blessedly, revealing the curves coming up before me. At last the sun's heat dissipated all traces of fog, and I gradually relaxed into the drive. But then, as I rounded a broad bend, a large imposing sign at the side of the road appeared bearing a message: *Road Closed.*

How could this be? There was no barricade across the road and no notice of road closure when I got on the Parkway. I wanted to reach Mt. Pisgah Campground south of Asheville, and the Parkway was the only direct route. All other roads on the map were narrow, winding, and very much out of the way.

I pulled over to the shoulder and stared beyond the sign down the road. It didn't look closed. It curved away smoothly and invitingly with no sign of construction: no orange pylons, no flaggers as far as I could see. Maybe the sign was left over from some past project and had been forgotten by the crew, I reasoned. But how odd that it didn't offer a detour or closure dates or any information that usually appears on an official sign. I lingered at the side of the road, indecision gnawing at me. My map was useless for pinpointing my position; the fog had obscured any road signs or side roads that I could have used as references points, and I didn't know how far I had already driven. I dreaded the thought of backtracking, not knowing how far I would have to drive and if I would hit the dense fog again. I had to do something, so I pulled back onto the road, drove past the *Road Closed* sign, and continued south toward Asheville.

A mile passed, then another and I began to breathe easier thinking I was correct in my assessment that the sign was a mistake. Ah, yes, I would make it to Asheville in good time, and under a clear sky, too. I drove three more miles, and then, about thirty yards ahead, I saw it, a barricade spanning the width of the road and posted with a large black and white sign. I slowed, cringing, and approached: *Road Closed.* That was all, no recommended alternate route or any other advisory. Again I peered down the road and saw nothing to prevent me from continuing, but the barricade made an emphatic statement–no passage! It was the end of the line for me. Sitting there, stunned, a scene from Alice in Wonderland flashed back to me. Alice is walking down a path in a dark forest when a strange creature with a whisk-broom mouth comes whisking toward her, sweeping away the path as it approaches. When it reaches her feet, it pauses, then coldly steps around her and continues sweeping away the path she had just walked, leaving her lost and helpless standing on her remaining small square of path.

I was Alice, stranded on a patch of road, my forward movement stymied and no visible means of egress. I had no option but to turn around and retrace my route, which, I fervently hoped, had not disappeared in the fog or by the cruel misdeeds of some strange broom-mouth creature.

Again, studying my map, I saw U.S. Highway 21, fourteen miles south of the Virginia border. It led down off the Parkway and connected with a couple of twisting state highways leading to Wilkesboro. From there U.S. Highway 421 would take me back up to the Parkway. But had I already passed Highway 21? Had I even come to it yet? Because of the fog, I didn't know, and the only way I could find out was to turn around, drive north again, and hope to find it. With this option, I could end up back in Virginia, forced to repeat my morning's journey, a prospect I found intolerable. Another problem was that I didn't know if this circuitous detour off the Parkway would return me to it beyond whatever obstacle had caused the closure. If not, I would have to backtrack again and endure another long and tiresome detour.

Luckily, I did find Highway 21 and exited the Parkway. Peering through the windshield, I searched for highway signs indicating my route. I passed side roads that could have been the ones I was seeking, but they were not marked, and again uncertainty churned in my gut. Impulsively, I took the next road I came to that seemed to head downhill. It was narrow and winding, and I fretted that it would peter out or turn into a rutted dirt track leading to nowhere. I didn't know if I was on the road to Wilkesboro, or the road to hell. To calm myself I sighed deeply and gave myself a pep talk. Buck up, Lynn, and stop with the worrying. Big girls don't freak out like this.

Eventually I did find a signpost directing me to Wilkesboro, and at long last I finally got back on the Parkway, only to pull up behind an elderly couple tootling along the scenic byway at twenty miles per hour. I followed them, cursing, unable to pass, one hundred miles to Asheville and twenty miles beyond to Mt. Pisgah Campground. According to the information in my tour book, the campground was open year round, but, guess what? That's right. It was closed.

Tired, hungry, and on the edge of hysteria, I pulled off to the side of the road and sat, inert, unable even to think. I rummaged through my ice chest for a snack and gobbled it down, but the strain was too great for food to assuage. The Parkway with its closed campgrounds and tight curves had gotten the best of me. My nerves were shattered. I knew I should rest, but I was too tense and too fearful of being caught on the road after dark to linger long enough to regain my composure. I had to find a way out, a place to collapse. Consulting my map I saw that Interstate 26 intersected the Parkway near Asheville and led down to Columbia, South Carolina and the coastal plain. I'd had enough of scenic byways and the freeway looked good to me now. There was bound to be lodging along the freeway.

But would there be? Studying the map further, I saw that all the towns within the first fifty miles of the Parkway were small, as indicated by a tiny circle, and off the freeway. Would there be any lodgings in such tiny places? I could not abide the thought of even one single, fruitless mile off the freeway in search of a refuge.

Returning to my map, I noticed some of the town names were printed in red. Then it dawned on me. Of course, red print means something. "Ah, Lynn, goose!" a voice in my head scolded. "Read your map legend."

I scrutinized the legend in the bottom corner of the map looking for the meaning. There it was at the bottom, printed in red:

Community names printed in red have lodging and dining facilities that can be located by checking the AAA TourBook.

Hendersonville was only eighteen miles down the freeway, and its name was printed in red! I would find lodging there, and whatever came first, fleabag motel or white trash trailer park, I didn't care, that's where I would rest my head tonight.

I hurried on to the freeway and headed for Hendersonville, but after only a few miles I saw a sign for a campground, South Mills River Campground. Although six miles off the freeway, it would be cheaper than a motel, and the prospect of saving a few dollars was just enough motivation, barely, for the detour.

What I found was a small collection of rusting trailers randomly scattered among piles of brush and junk, obviously permanent dwellings. A girl with stringy blond hair and a tattered dress sat on an upturned pail beside one trailer. I rolled down my window and asked her if there was a vacant space. She stared blankly at me as if she didn't understand English, then got up and ambled over, a vacuous look on her face. Her eyes seemed not to focus, each appearing to gaze vaguely in a different direction—shades of *Deliverance*. Yet the girl spoke genially and directed me to a motel in Hendersonville.

In one last push, I arrived in Hendersonville and pulled into the first motel I saw, the Dutch Inn, a gaudy, blue, barn-shaped structure. It was run down and chintzy, but I didn't care. I checked in and with a sigh of gratitude threw myself on the squeaking, sagging bed.

CHAPTER 14

The Carolinas and Georgia: Dobermans and Desperation

Sunday, March 21, 1982

The Blue Ridge Parkway and the Piedmont were now behind me as I eased down from the uplands of South Carolina onto the Coastal Plain. I could tell I was in the South. The sun was shining and it was warm and slightly muggy. An occasional squashed possum lay beside the road; in the West it is usually skunks. Gas prices were the lowest I had encountered so far, $1.15 per gallon, an indication of the South's vitiated economy, perhaps. Low gas prices were all right with me. I liked this aspect of the South.

Dreher Island State Recreation Area lay adjacent to Lake Murray only thirty miles from Columbia, the capital city. I was fearful that the place would be a dump, unattractive and under-maintained as some recreation areas are. Not Dreher Island, though. The large campground was woodsy and fragrant with the essence of loblolly pine, the balmy air exuding a hint of the South's geniality.

For the first time in many months I stripped off my sweatshirt and slid into a short-sleeved t-shirt, kicked off my shoes and socks and wiggled into sandals. With a cold beer in hand, I slumped into my camp chair to soak up the eighty-degree warmth. For an hour, I luxuriated in the headiness, listening to the squawking of common grackles and thanking my lucky stars that the horrors of the last two days were over.

Later, when the drowsiness of the beer had worn off, I changed into my running shorts and shoes and set off down the road leading away from the campground, relishing the idea of a good, long, sweaty run to exorcise any unpleasant residua from the last two days of anguished driving. As always when I ran in unfamiliar places, I kept a watchful eye for anything that might pose a threat: traffic speeding around blind corners, unsavory characters, and especially dogs on the loose—I had been chased and bitten by dogs before. But, this bucolic setting seemed to present no problems as I ran by groves of trees and occasional farmhouses. Ahead of me a long, high hedge paralleled the road, separating it from a large house atop a knoll. A sweeping lawn fanned upward from the hedge to the house. Wary of what might be hidden behind the barrier, I skirted widely away to the opposite side of the road, keeping a sharp lookout until I left it behind me.

I continued on through open country for another mile, then, turned back toward the campground, running easily and dropping my guard, knowing the way was clear. Ahead of me I saw the dark green hedge again, but I would not have to avoid it now. I cruised along at a good clip, almost brushing the hedge as I ran. Just as I cleared the last shrub I heard it. Growling. Not low, warning growls, but growls of killer intent. I jerked to a halt and looked up. Two black Doberman pincers were charging full speed downhill at me, and I knew I was going to be attacked. In the heart-stopping second before they reached me I listened for a command from the owner, "Stay!" but it didn't come. I was helpless, with nowhere to go and no one around. I couldn't outrun the dogs, and running would only make them more savage. They were almost on me when I turned to face them.

"Bad dog!" I shouted, brandishing my index finger at them like a stick. "Bad dog. Go home!" I braced for the assault and the tearing of teeth into my flesh. No one would hear my screams; no one would see. But the dogs faltered. I stood my ground and scolded, slapping my hands together angrily, stomping my foot, sick with fear, and praying the dogs would yield to my display of authority, praying they had heard these words before from their master. "Bad dog! Go home!" The dogs crouched low, growling, tails pressed down. I took a tentative step backward, facing the dogs, assailing them with continued abuse while slowly taking backward steps. They stayed. My heart thumped like thunder in my chest as ever so slowly I widened the distance between them and me, all the time haranguing, scolding. The instinct to run almost overwhelmed me, but I restrained myself, eyeing my adversaries, never turning my back, until I was a safe distance and they were almost out of my sight. Then I turned and sprinted away as fast as I could.

Back in the campground I sat quaking at my near brush with death. Was that being overly dramatic? No, it wasn't. Two angry Dobermans could easily have finished me off. At the very least, I would have been badly mauled. I had had no other recourse but to face them down. It was only by pure chance that the dogs had responded to my bravado.

Park ranger named Tommy chatted with me a while. Told him about my encounter with the dogs. Used park telephone to call Mother and Susan. Thunder and lightning in the evening. And rain. Delightful.

Monday, March 22, 1982:

Charleston and Cap'n Blackie

Last night's storm freshened the greenery in camp this morning. Lingering water droplets sparkled in the sunlight along tree branches. While I cooked my breakfast, two eastern bluebirds darted in close enough for me to get a good look, so lovely with their soft, cottony blue breasts bright in the morning sun.

Today I would arrive in Charleston, on my list of places to see since the inception of my dream, and one of the few sizeable cities I had planned to visit. It was a beautiful city, so said the brochures and tour books, with expansive green lawns and magnificent shade trees. I had great expectations and mounting excitement as I packed up and prepared to leave.

At the gas and grocery store near the park entrance, I stopped for supplies before starting out. It was only 120 miles to Charleston, and I was looking forward to a pleasant drive and new sights.

It is always good advice to subject your expectations to scrutiny, sift a bit of rationality over them to minimize potential disappointment. I had not done this before I arrived in Charleston. I had expected to encounter the broad lawns and famous shade trees as soon as I reached the outskirts. This was not the case. Instead, the streets leading to the Visitor Information Center had an inimical feel, lined with run-down, sleazy storefronts and boxy, wooden, two-story residences slumped with age and roughened with curls of peeling paint. I pulled into the first parking spot I could find on Meeting Street with the intention of walking to the Visitor Information Center. It was an uncomfortable walk past clusters of vagrant men muttering scurrilous comments at me as I made my way toward Market Street. But I passed safely to the tourist center where I made a reservation for a carriage tour tomorrow. I wasn't going to give up on Charleston on the basis of one walk down Meeting Street. Tomorrow I would surely be more favorably impressed.

There was a campground near Charleston I had read about in my campground guide, Cap'n Blackie's it was called. A large ad in the guide gave the impression it was a safe, well-managed place, a good base for my stay in Charleston. The name itself evinced images of an amiable old sea-faring guy retired from the sea and now running a campground for tourists. I was optimistic. Cap'n Blackie's was between Charleston and Folly Beach, a small town on an offshore barrier island a few miles south of Charleston. I hurried back to my camper and followed the directions in my guide to Cap'n Blackie's.

Cap'n Blackie's Campground was the exact opposite of what I had envisioned. A weedy, dirt track led to the campground "office," a tiny, battered trailer with a screen door hanging from its hinges. The trailer sat amid the owner's eclectic junk collection. As I approached, a man appeared in the doorway, scratching at his belly, which protruded from the bottom of a once white, sleeveless undershirt. A mat of black chest hair spilled over the edge of its scoop neck, and his chin was covered with black stubble. Beyond Cap'n Blackie's trailer, I saw a hodge-podge of small, dilapidated trailers scattered among the weeds and brush piles, each with its own junk collection, occupied not by tourists, obviously, but by members of the seamier side of humanity.

"Lookin' for a site?" he asked.

No, no, no, I thought. I was stricken with horror, but unable to think of a way to extricate myself from this place. No words came to me that would suffice. I couldn't make myself say, Um, I think I've made a mistake. I just couldn't. I was stuck. In a kind of daze, I stepped into Blackie's rancid-smelling trailer just long enough to pay the fee. He pointed to my designated weed patch and stepped back into his hole. I drove into the midst of the other trailer dwellers, feeling their voyeuristic eyes on me. As before in Reading, Pennsylvania, when I had found myself in a slum, I tried to quash my dread, tried to convince myself I would be all right here, but disgust rose unchecked within me. I backed into my spot and turned off the engine, then climbed into the back and drew the curtains on my windows, but not before seeing a shifty-looking man staring at me from the adjacent site. In spite of my attempts to buoy my spirits, despair threatened to consume me.

If I had to stay the night at Cap'n Blackie's, I would; I had no choice. But I sure as hell did not intend to sit there with curtains drawn and the doors locked for the remainder of the day. As quickly as I had thrown the curtains closed, I threw them back open. I reached up and slammed the pop-top down and latched it.

Wedging myself between the two front seats, I squeezed into the driver's seat and drove back down the dirt lane away from the cesspool of a campground. I turned south on the highway and drove toward the ocean. There was very little traffic. I found a place to park along the road and walked toward Folly Beach, breathing in the fresh, salt air. The street grid ended at the shoreline, truncated by a long boardwalk lined with crab shacks, curio shops, cafes, and surfing shops. Folly Beach, I knew, was a favorite vacation spot, especially for surfers, but today the place was nearly deserted, too early for the summer hordes.

For an hour or two I strolled along the boardwalk and beach, stopping to bird, or just sit in the sand gazing at the Atlantic. Finally, I began slowly walking back to my camper, dawdling to kill time. This time I walked on the opposite side of the road, which is probably why I had missed the tidy little RV park I now saw about a half block ahead. Trim and tidy with its neatly arranged rows of campers and its tiny office building painted in crisp gray and white.

Oh no, how could I have missed this? I fretted. The sign at the office said *open*, and I could see there were several vacant spaces. I must stay here, I thought, even though I had already paid for my space at Cap'n Blackie's. I ran the remainder of the way back to my camper, quickly hatching out an excuse for getting a refund.

I drove back to Cap'n Blackie's, nervous about asking for a refund. When I muttered something lame about how I'd changed my mind and decided to drive on south into Georgia, he saw right through me. "You worried about them men down by you, they won't hurtcha."

"Oh, no, it's not that," I lied. "I just want to be moving along." He cocked a gimlet eye at me but begrudgingly returned my money. I left as fast as I could and returned to the sweet little RV park out on the quiet highway. I snugged myself into one of the spic and span little spaces and set up my rig, relieved, and telling myself that sometimes exigencies of daily travel justify a little white lie. No harm done to Cap'n Blackie. He would do just fine without me.

Tuesday, March 23, 1982

I woke up to a breezy, pleasant day in the 60s, perfect temperature for a jog around Folly Beach before returning to Charleston for my tour. By mid-morning I was back at the tourist center, stepping up into a horse-drawn carriage for the Charleston Historic Tour. It seemed such luxury to be carted around and tended to by someone other than myself. I settled back expecting to feast my eyes on the grand homes and elegant gardens I had read about. But I saw little of them and was disappointed until I realized I was on the wrong tour for residential Charleston. For that I should have booked the Home and Garden Walking Tour.

But antiquity is fascinating too, although it often wears a tattered façade, as it did in Old Town Charleston. However, in spite of my mild disappointment, the romance of Charleston's past soon cast its spell over me. Charleston, or Charles Towne, as it was originally called, was the only walled English city in North America, the wall in place by 1712. Charleston's European history dates to well before pre-revolutionary times, and even though I knew European colonization of the New World began as early as the 15th century, the information took me by surprise. Growing up on the west coast, *historic* to me meant mostly events dating from the mid-19th century, around the time of the gold rush, or a little before. Now, actually seeing and touching buildings in use since revolutionary and pre-revolutionary times gave me a fresh appreciation of our nation's history.

On the tour, I was particularly intrigued by The Powder Magazine, a small brick building built in 1713 for storing loose gunpowder. With three-foot thick walls at its base, tapering to two feet near the ceiling, the arsenal was designed to implode in case of an explosion, and because it never did explode, it exists today as the oldest surviving public building in the Carolinas.

When the tour was over, I continued on my own, walking into the residential area I had missed while riding in the carriage. At my leisure, I ambled down shady streets admiring the stately homes and peering through iron gates into lush, hidden gardens. After a few hours, I felt I had seen a reasonable sampling of Charleston and, tired, I returned to my camper and drove back to Folly Beach.

Wednesday, March 24, 1982

I was up at 6:45 this morning feeling the urge to push on. But first, I had missions to accomplish in Folly Beach: gas, ice, groceries, and, finally breakfast. I left Folly Beach at last, and immediately got lost, requiring me to backtrack until I was on the right route again. I drove non-stop to the Georgia state line where I stopped at the Visitor Center. A very helpful, pleasant girl loaded me up with maps and brochures describing places to explore and camp in Georgia, including Skidaway Island State Park, where I was bound.

Skidaway Island borders the Skidaway narrows, part of the Intracoastal Waterway that threads through the barrier islands along the Eastern Seaboard. I was interested in the formation of these islands and eager to see in reality the textbook examples of this type of coastal topography.

To get there I would pass through Savannah on Highway 204, also known as Abercorn Street. My plan was to establish myself at the park campground and return later to tour Savannah. I followed Abercorn Street at a leisurely pace, taking in as much of Savannah, primarily the outskirts, as I could. Toward the southern end of Savannah, the road was lined with a mix of small, plain residences and forlorn looking commercial establishments seemingly rooted in the vegetation growing up around them, the kinds of places old timers would remember from their youth, but the younger set would mostly ignore.

Gradually the city thinned and gave way to rural Georgia. I was on the edge of town when I heard a loud *snap!* in the vicinity of my left foot.

I hit the brake with my right foot and steered, slowing, to the side of the road. As I stepped with my left foot to disengage the clutch, the pedal collapsed, lifeless, against the floorboard and did not spring back. There was no way to shift into any gear, forward or backward. I was broken down and stranded.

As much as I feared mechanical breakdown, I feared having to ask strangers for help even more. But this I would have to do. I locked my camper and started walking back toward town, not daring to hope anyone would care about helping me. Down the road I saw a service station with what looked like a red telephone booth in front of it. As I neared I could see that it was. But what if the phone was out of order, then I would have to go into the service station and approach someone, probably a surly, not-to-be-bothered mechanic, and ask to use the phone.

But the phone did work, and with shaking hands I called the number on my Triple A card. A host of crazy worries crowded into my mind as I dialed: The number might be wrong. My card might not be honored in Georgia. I might not be able to hear the operator. The operator might be snippy or hostile. I might be too nervous to explain where I was.

To my great relief, and surprise, my call went through swiftly and a helpful dispatcher said a tow truck would be on the way soon. She was right. Within a few minutes a tow truck pulled up behind me. I explained the problem to the driver. "Sounds like a broken clutch cable to me," he said as he winched my woebegone greenhouse to his truck.

In short order my camper and I were delivered to the nearest Volkswagen service center in Savannah where two friendly mechanics assured me they could repair the problem right away. While I sat in the waiting room I wondered about this profound fear I have of asking strangers for help. I thought of Blanche DuBois in *Streetcar Named Desire*. "I have always depended on the kindness of strangers," she cooed. Apparently it was no problem for Blanche, but, then, she was delusional. I was sane, or so I thought. So where did this fear come from?

Answers to questions like this are not easily extracted. It's easier simply to shrug, and say, "I don't know," and leave the explanation festering somewhere in the dungeon of one's psyche. But I had time on my hands, waiting for repairs to my vehicle, as good a time as any for a session of self-analysis.

"Get in touch with your feelings," was the pop psychology of the day. Good idea, I thought, but it wouldn't work unless I could be unflinchingly honest with myself, probing into that submerged emotional territory.

I closed my eyes, and concentrated on "getting in touch" with the fear I had experienced as I walked toward the service station. It was relatively easy to recreate the feeling, but what was the basis for it? That was the hard part. I struggled to reach that bottom world where I believed the source of the problem lay, but nothing resounded. It seemed as though a barrier existed between my ego and my id preventing me from penetrating deeper. I was only treading water, only skimming the surface.

I propped my bent elbow on the wooden armrest and pressed my forehead into the palm of my hand, as if to squeeze out the answer from behind my compressed eyelids. I kept trying, peeling back layers, closing in, until, finally, like a bell sounding in my head, the answer popped out and resonated with truth.

It was the fear of being ignored, dismissed, or brushed aside as though I were invisible. But where did this come from? Now the answers came tumbling forth, easily, like a scroll loosed from its ties. It arose from a profound sense of unworthiness, a pervading view of myself as a cipher, not worthy of attention or notice. It was a self-view that had been with me, I was surprised to realize, most of my life and had been the lens through which I viewed the world and the people in my environment. As I had walked from my disabled camper toward the service station this was the expectation and fear I had carried with me, that I would be ignored—by the telephone operator, by the men at the service station, and by anyone I would need help from. But where did this self-view come from and why was it so intense? I looked for answers by traveling backward into my childhood.

Two, I was, or younger. I was standing in my crib gently rattling the slats and whimpering. Awake from my nap, fretful, I wanted to get out of that dark, cold room. A band of light from the living room shone under the bottom of the door and I could smell the faint aroma of bacon and green beans cooking. My sisters would be huddled around the oil-burning stove playing with dolls or tea sets. I heard my mother's voice rise occasionally above their shrieks and laugher, but she did not come. She was busy. Six kids, endless loads of laundry, and three meals a day to prepare. Too busy to come to the aid of her forgotten fifth child crying in the darkened front bedroom. I waited for an eternity, neglected, but not daring to kick or cry harder, comprehending, even at that early age, that I was not important enough for Mother to come running. This was the earliest episode I could bring to mind that was significant in the embryonic development of my self-concept: I am of little consequence.

Another episode came to me. It was the winter of 1949. I was six years old and in the first grade. At the close of each school day I was to cross the street at the corner of the school where the crossing guards were on duty, and walk the two blocks home. Two blocks seemed like a lot of open ground to cover, a long stretch where scary things could happen. It would have been too much for my timid heart had I not been able to see from the school grounds my father's corner grocery store and the roof of our house behind it, beacons to safety.

On this day in early winter, it had begun to snow in the morning, and by the close of the school day there were two or three inches on the ground. It would be the first time I would walk home in snow. My hooded red wool coat hanging from a hook in the classroom would be welcome today. I buttoned up and stepped out into the white wonderland, pulling the hood over my head. The snow crunched under my shoes as I walked to the corner and waited with the other children for the crossing guards to extend their flags across the intersection so we could cross. As I stepped onto the curb on the opposite side of the street, I heard taunts from boys behind me. "Little Red, Little Red!" they jeered. I didn't turn to look, but quickened my pace. Suddenly, a group of boys were at my flanks like a pack of wolves, scooping up snowballs and hurling them at me. I tried to run away from them, but they persisted, laughing and pelting me. They didn't stop until I reached the end of the block when finally they tired of their game and left me. But I was sobbing when I reached our grocery store where my mother stood in front waiting for me.

"What's wrong?" she asked when she saw the tears.

"Some boys threw snow balls at me," I said between sobs. I was only six and couldn't make her understand, couldn't verbalize my feelings. It wasn't just the snowballs that terrified me. The boys had lain in waiting, ambushed me, and pursued me with intent to harm. I was terrified knowing I had to walk those blocks again tomorrow. I wanted my mother to hug me, to tell me she would walk with me, to comfort and assure me that it would not happen again. But she didn't.

"Well, never mind," she said and turned to walk to the house.

Something critical happened on that snowy day when she said, "Never mind." My mother had conveyed a message. It was the same message she had sent when I was two, awake in my crib longing for her, wanting to be attended to. When I needed her protection and her reassurance she hadn't understood the depth of my fear, or if she had, minimized it. And once again, another piece of my developing self-concept was emplaced: I am not important. I am not deserving. It had neither a negative nor a positive charge, because, of course, I was not conscious of it. It just was.

Reflecting back on these incidents, I did not fault my mother. She had done the best she knew how. In so many ways she was an extraordinary woman and the rock in our family. Her stoicism in emotional matters effloresced into strengths in others. She was at the helm in domestic affairs, preparing three meals a day, every day for thirty years until all her children had left home. She sewed skirts, frocks, blouses and wedding dresses for five girls. She filled the house with music from old phonograph records, everything from Verdi operas to the silly songs of Spike Jones. At Christmas she baked hundreds of cookies for family and friends and saw to it that the Christmas tree was amply underlain with presents for us on Christmas morning.

She provided all this yet remained, for the most part, emotionally distant and uninvolved in our personal lives. She admitted as much to me later when I was a teen-ager. "We had a 'laissez-faire' attitude toward child-rearing, I suppose. We didn't want you kids to get a swelled head." In a thousand subtle ways she insured that we did not, and the end result was that each of us, especially the women, exhibits to some degree today, the negative effects of her aloofness.

The VW service manager approached me from across the waiting room. "You're all set," he smiled. He handed me the keys to my camper. I returned his smile, thanked him, and stepped up into the driver's seat.

Back on the road, heading once again for Skidaway, I brought my thoughts to a conclusion.

To appeal to a stranger when I needed help would be to risk being dismissed, rejected, diminished. And if that happened, it would confirm what I had subconsciously believed about myself, the self-image I had acquired in childhood and carted around throughout my life, the image I had, unknowingly, been supplanting for the last nine months traveling alone through the country, managing on my own, chipping away little by little at the old persona, rebuilding a new self-image of confidence and worthiness. I could not afford to allow rejection to undermine what I was building.

That was my fear, and now that it was out in the light, I knew this new understanding would pave a smoother way for me. What was I if not capable? I had dealt with loneliness, rainsqualls, windstorms, bums, and now mechanical breakdown. And I would deal with whatever awaited me down the road.

Here I am at Skidaway State Park, lush and gorgeous with Spanish moss-draped oaks and deep green pines. My only disappointment is the weather—rainy and dismal. I have yearned so long for sunshine. Now I am in the deep South and still no sun. The ranger said it's supposed to clear up tonight, though. Oh, I hope so.

Thursday, March 25, 1982

The ranger's prediction didn't pan out. It was still gray and overcast when I woke up this morning. I was out of bed at 6:30 and into Savannah by 10:00. Unlike my entrance into Charleston, my drive into historic Savannah was relaxed and stunningly beautiful with its multitude of garden-like squares. There was little traffic as I drove into town on Abercorn Street to Reynolds Square where I found a parking spot nearby. Historic River Street was only a few blocks away.

It was hard to believe I was in a downtown area. From where I began my walking tour, I saw mostly large parks, Savannah's famous "squares" shaded by magnificent oak trees and filled with azaleas, each square dominated by an ornate monument to its namesake. In such genteel surroundings, I felt none of the tension I had experienced in Charleston. I strolled along the streets stopping often to relax on a park bench or to gaze up at the facades of the many Georgian houses nearby.

Making my way toward River Street, I became aware of the one obstacle to complete enjoyment of my tour: gnats. Or midges. I don't know what they call them here. There were millions of them, so tiny they seemed to float, gathering in my hair, attacking my eyes and nose so relentlessly I couldn't blink or blow them away fast enough. I would rather have contended with rain and cold. At 11:15 I could take them no more and went into a tavern on River Street in search of a respite from the little buggers, which I found in the form of a whiskey sour and a sandwich.

After lunch I wandered down Bull and Abercorn Streets away from the river. The sun came out and chased away the bugs, allowing me to fully enjoy the beauty of Savannah unbesieged.

After my self-guided tour I drove back to camp and did some sightseeing there, too. While ambling along a nature trail, a pileated woodpecker, the largest woodpecker in North America, flew directly across my path and landed on the trunk of a nearby tree staying long enough for me to get a photo. This was my first sighting of a pileated woodpecker, astonishing birds because of their large size and also because of their similarity to the extinct ivory-billed woodpecker.

CHAPTER 15

The Sunshine State: Enter Greg

Friday, March 26, 1982

Across the border at the Florida welcome center I was offered samples of fresh orange and grapefruit juice, both of which I gratefully chugged. Anything free. After loading up with brochures and maps, I drove on through Jacksonville to a KOA—that's *Kampground of America* with a "K"—a few miles south. It was a windy day, but sunny, and I was glad for it. The KOA was spread over a well-maintained, expansive green lawn, where I lazed in the glorious sun. Some travelers camped nearby told me about St. Augustine, our nation's oldest city, established in 1565 by the Spanish. It sounded like a fascinating place to visit, and since I had no other plans for tomorrow, I decided to make it my next stop on the way to Melbourne, where Russelle and Verenice Bailey, parents of my brother's wife, lived. I had never met them, but wanted to pay a courtesy call since it was unlikely I would have met them otherwise. Also, it would be a tribute to my sister-in-law who was a friend as well as a relative.

Saturday, March 27, 1982

Early this morning I made my way to Highway 1 and drove the thirty miles southeast to St. Augustine on the coast, intrigued by the idea of a town 400 years old, much older than our country. I parked my car some distance from the Castillo de San Marcos, the 300 year-old Spanish fort and St. Augustine's oldest structure. A long paved sidewalk led to the fort through a broad, green lawn that extended to a concrete seawall at ocean's edge. I approached, looking up at the scabby gray and white stone walls, stained and peeling with antiquity.

Wandering around the inner courtyard, I examined the gun deck and cannons facing outward through crenels in the battlements. The fort first came under fire in 1702 when the British tried in vain to breach the walls. They tried again and again, but, although they succeeded in burning the city, they never breached the walls of the fort.

Not too many folks visiting the fort today, perfectly all right with me. I lingered in the inner courtyard half doped up by the warm sun on my back as I leaned over the battlements and gazed out to sea, trying to grasp the reality that St. Augustine was here long before the American Revolution. The history lessons I had learned as a child in school on America's "young" side were no substitute for actually standing on these masonry walls constructed so long ago when Florida belonged to Spain. What was it like then? I tried hard to imagine it.

Melbourne, Florida is a popular retirement community. That's why the Bailey's had moved here. I found my way to their house without too much difficulty, arriving at 2:00 p.m. after a long haul down Route 1 at the virtual brink of the continent. Verenice and Russelle welcomed me warmly. Russelle, who suffered from advanced Parkinson's Disease, was subdued in his greeting, but Verenice took me in hand right away, declaring that I was hungry—though I declared that I was not. She sat me down at her table and fed me a huge lunch, insisting that I take seconds. Then she said, "You're tired from your trip. You go rest. Sleep for an hour and a half then I will wake you and we will get ready to go to dinner."

Given a choice, which I wasn't, I would have kicked off my shoes, curled up on the couch and enjoyed a get-acquainted chat with the Baileys, perhaps over a cup of coffee. But Verenice had more of a management style of hospitality. She was steady on track with her plans, no fudging, and I couldn't help but feel her efforts were causing her some stress.

Although I felt naughty about it, I railed, inwardly, at having my free will curtailed, even temporarily. I had always hated that. But even while the hackles were rising on the back of my neck, I was searching for the internal strength and wisdom to weather this visit gracefully. Verenice was giving me her best. She was a lovely, gracious woman doing her utmost to entertain her daughter's sister-in-law. The Baileys were treating me like a beloved, long-time friend. If our visit was to be successful, I had better shuck my negative attitude and behave myself. So I went to the guest room as I was bade, and lay on the bed for an hour and a half.

The evening played out exactly as Verenice had planned. She and I struggled to maintain a lively conversation at dinner. Even though I addressed several comments to Russelle, he was somber and spoke very little. I did not know then that deadpan expressions and slow, quiet speech are typical symptoms of Parkinson's disease. I was aware that I felt sorry for him, and as dinner progressed, I began to understand the strain that Verenice must be enduring.

Sunday, March 28, 1982

I woke up feeling cheery this morning. I was in Florida—in fact about two-thirds down the length of it—the Sunshine State. It would be blue skies from here on, I was sure. I got out of bed at 7:00. Verenice and I chatted while she prepared a hearty breakfast for me, insisting I needed the fortification. At nine o'clock I bade the Baileys a warm farewell at their front door. But instead of walking out into a morning of bright sunshine, I walked out to dark clouds, rain, and a vigorous wind.

I had a one hundred mile drive ahead of me to Jonathan Dickenson State Park on the coast, due east of Lake Okeechobee. The rain increased steadily as I drove until it was pounding harder than I had ever seen, even in western Oregon. I drove the entire distance clutching the steering wheel and trying to peer through sheets of water running down the windshield. At times the pavement disappeared under the deluge and I feared being washed away. At last I found the state park and pulled in hungry and very irritable. I turned off the engine and listened to the rain drumming on the roof of the cab. The cold and damp seeped through the camper walls, carrying desolation and loneliness. I was utterly alone. What I needed now more than anything was connection with another human being. I threw my rain jacket over my head and dashed out into the pouring rain to a pay telephone and called my mother. She sounded worried when I described the storm I had driven through, but

I reassured her I was all right. She was comforted thinking I had found shelter for the night, and I was comforted knowing she was thinking about me and cared.

Monday, March 29, 1982

There was no shelter at Dickenson State Park last night. I was awakened by rain and wind that had intensified into a major subtropical storm. I cowered in my sleeping bag terrified by the buffeting of my camper in the wind. Powerful gusts slammed against the sides rocking me back and forth. Was I about to be swept away? I didn't know. Was this a hurricane? Should I try to seek shelter? I didn't know what to do or where to find help. There were no other campers, so I couldn't take my cue from the actions of others. I rode out the night awake and fearful as a landlubber in a ship tossing on a stormy sea.

This morning I slid back the camper door and found my rig standing in several inches of water. It was still raining and the trees were swaying wildly. I had no way of knowing if I was in the best place or worst place for weathering this storm. And I did not know if it would get worse. I had to find shelter somewhere, or someone who could tell me what to do.

I hastily broke camp and climbed into the driver's seat, shifted into low and, holding my breath, slowly pulled forward through the water, testing my brakes as I advanced. When I emerged onto Highway 1, I saw what the tail end of a tropical storm looks like. The ravaged roadway was strewn with palm branches, boards, and garbage. Floodwater pooled across the roadbed, but there was no telling how deep it was. I knew it was dangerous to drive through floodwater, but I had no other choice, so I kept going. I managed to make my way to a gas station. As soon as I stepped down from my seat, the wind-driven rain lashed at me. By the time I filled my gas tank I was soaked. Farther along the highway I saw a McDonald's with the lights on. It seemed an unlikely refuge from the gusting wind with its large glass walls, but there were people inside. I hoped that they were Floridians, accustomed to, and unruffled by, storms like this.

I never thought a McDonald's would feel cozy, but this one did. I was so relieved to be inside in warmth and light. The few people who were there seemed not to pay much attention to the storm. I took heart from this and relaxed with my fast-food breakfast, gaping out at palm fronds streaming backward from the tops of trees like hair blowing back from a face.

In no hurry to leave the relative security of McDonald's, I studied my map for the likeliest route to the Everglades. A short connector road, Highway 706 led to Interstate 95 three miles to the west. That's what I wanted. No more back roads until I was clear of this storm.

I found the connecting road easily and turned west, but in less than a quarter of a mile I came to a sign: Road Closed. Flooded.

There was nothing to do but turn around and go back to Highway 1. All the roads would be flooded, I was sure. There would be no way for me to get out of here. Back on 1, I pulled into the McDonald's parking lot and consulted my map again. If I could make it a few more miles south to West Palm Beach, I could catch the main highway going west from there to Belle Glade at the southeast corner of Lake Okeechobee. If I couldn't get through, I could at least return to West Palm Beach and perhaps find an RV park there.

This time the road was open. I made it to Belle Glade without too much trouble and turned south onto Route 27, a narrow, two-lane road paralleling a canal through the swampland of Broward County. What followed was twenty-five miles of driving hell. The rain had stopped, but the wind, now coming at me from the southeast, caught the sides of my narrow camper and tossed it around like a paper boat. Truck after truck passed me coming from the south, each one sucking me into its flank then, *whomp!* hurtling me back across my lane as it passed. With each truck passing, my camper swerved out of control for a few terrifying moments as I wrenched the steering wheel to pull back into my lane. No one had ever told me about the VW's notorious instability in high winds.

Finally the wind subsided and driving became less frightening. I turned on my radio and twisted the dial until I found a news and weather station. I was hoping to find out about last night's storm. The newscaster said Palm Beach County was hardest hit—exactly where I had camped— and six inches of rain had fallen in twelve hours accompanied by gusts of hurricane force. Well, that's good, I thought. At least I wasn't scared out of my wits for nothing.

With the storm behind me I felt the familiar delight of travel well up in me again. The Everglades were just ahead. I had always regarded them as a kind of storybook place, as inaccessible to me as a night in a five-star Paris hotel or a cruise in the Caribbean. Yet in less than an hour I would be there.

I drove south to Homestead, then southwest to the park entrance station and directly to the Long Pine Key campground. I was worried it might be full, but there was no need. At this time of year there were plenty of empty campsites. It was luxury just to drive around the loop and leisurely scope out each one. They were large, each with a lawn and a picnic table.

I picked the one I thought was best and pulled in. The day was slightly humid and warm as I lifted the pop-top and set up camp. I made myself a sandwich and sat in the warmth thinking about all the new birds I would see. The Everglades was a birding hotspot, one of the few places in the U. S. where birders could see tropical species such as the endangered Everglades kite, anhinga, roseate spoonbill, and short-tailed hawk, to name a few.

After lunch I wandered around the campground in search of Everglades bird specialties and found a common yellowthroat, a small, bright yellow warbler with a black mask across the face, and a rufous-sided towhee, nothing unusual but always a pleasure to see. I also encountered lots of mosquitoes, but Cutter's took care of them.

This evening I was sitting by my picnic table writing in my journal when something moved into the edge of my vision. I looked up and saw a rufous-sided towhee hop out of the bushes into the open. I watched as he came closer. When he got to the picnic table, he hopped onto the bench, then up to the top. He was so close to me and so brazen. It seemed like he wanted to be friends. I got up and went to my camper, fetched my bag of birdseed and sat on the camper floor in the open doorway. I sprinkled some seed near my foot and waited. But not long. The towhee hopped right over and up onto my step-stool within inches of my hand. I thought he might hop onto my finger if I extended it. He was so tiny, so sweet. I could have scooped him up in my hands and kissed his feathery little face if he would have allowed it. Unquestionably, moments like these have brought me the greatest joy on this trip. And tonight I saw my first firefly.

Tuesday, March 30, 1982

Up early today and at the nearby Anhinga Trail by 7:30. Much of the trail is an elevated walkway overlooking Taylor Slough, a main channel that brings water into the park. At this hour there were few people on the walk. Sunlight, warmth, and the rich fecundity of green plant life—this was the perfect spot for viewing wildlife. A strange, dark, gangly bird, similar to a cormorant, stood in the shallow water with its wings spread. I recognized it as an anhinga, sometimes called snakebird because of its long, sinuous neck. I saw one swimming underwater with only its beak and upper neck projecting like a periscope above the surface. I saw a purple gallinule, common moorhen, black vulture, green heron, palm warbler, and a smooth-billed ani, species I had never seen before. And to top off the morning, an alligator rose above the water and lingered long enough for me to sense his *gravitas*.

Back in camp I brewed a cup of coffee and began studying my bird books, reading about the birds I had seen already, and the birds I hoped to see during my stay. I knew high season for birds was winter, but late March was also likely to be productive. Every now and then I would glance up to scan the bushes and trees for something interesting, and, indeed, I saw something.

A man. Dark-haired, medium build, and holding binoculars to his eyes. He was standing close to some nearby bushes peering intently into them. Obviously a birder. I watched him for a while, but he didn't notice me. He was stocky, but not fat, pleasant looking, but not handsome, about my age, perhaps a little older. I wondered if he were finding birds I had overlooked. When he came within earshot, I spoke.

"Hello. What are you finding?" He looked at me as though he didn't understand what I was asking and didn't want to be bothered.

"Birds," I said, and held up my binoculars and bird book. He smiled as I moseyed over to where he was standing. He told me what he had seen around camp, and I told him what I had seen at the Anhinga Trail. We introduced ourselves. He was Greg, on vacation from Fresno, California, forty-one years old, and single.

Well, I'll be damned, I thought. This one is legit, *and* he's a birder. My visit to the Everglades might turn out to be richer than I thought.

We walked together awhile, scanning nearby shrubs and trees. He had come to the Everglades specifically for birding. He mentioned several other places in southern Florida he wanted to bird, all of them places I planned to go as well. Greg had plans for the rest of the morning, but before he left I invited him to come back later to share his sightings with me.

For the rest of the morning I stayed around camp relishing the pleasant surroundings. At midday I set up my camp stove on the picnic table and retrieved a two-pack of veal patties from my ice chest, thinking a veal patty sandwich would be a tasty lunch. I placed the Styrofoam tray on the picnic table, slit the plastic wrap and put one patty in the frying pan. As I looked down to turn the gas burner on, I heard a *whoosh* sound above me. I looked up just as a hawk swooped in and landed on a tree branch overhanging the edge of my campsite.

It was a red-shouldered hawk. I stood watching him, transfixed by its boldness and strange behavior. Hawks just don't come that close to humans. But then I recalled the little towhee that came to my camper yesterday, as tame as a house pet. Well, that's to be expected in a national park, I guess. Like bears in Yellowstone.

The hawk sat perfectly still, his dark eyes peering down at me. When it appeared he was content to remain perched there, I turned my attention back to my veal patty, now sizzling in the frying pan. Two seconds after lowering my eyes, I heard three powerful wingbeats and felt a concussion of air. The hawk came at me, claws thrust forward. I shrieked as his talons tightened around the veal patty sizzling in my frying pan. I felt the wind of his wings on my face as he lifted off, the veal patty skewered on his talon. He lighted a few feet away on the grass and tore into his catch. Frozen from the shock, I stood staring at the bird then remembered the other veal patty on the table inches from me. In a flash I grabbed it, foam tray and all, and threw it at the hawk.

That's when I heard the laughter. Loud guffawing. Greg was coming through the bushes, laughing his head off. I stood there sputtering, embarrassed, but still eyeing the hawk. I had felt the bird's amazing power at close range. I had seen the talons gripping the veal. I understood the damage they could do. Greg could laugh all he wanted.

He finally stopped laughing and raised his camera to photograph the hawk as it continued devouring the veal. Now convinced the hawk would not attack me, I grabbed my camera, too. We both got several shots of the feasting bird. Finally the hawk flew off, and I was faced with scrounging through my stores for a meatless lunch.

In the evening Greg and I went back to the Anhinga Trail. He proved a very good birder and being with him sharpened my skills. Later we drove into Homestead to do errands and have dinner. Back in camp we sat and talked and shared a bottle of wine. Then we went for a late night walk. That night Greg moved his tent to the campsite next to mine.

Wednesday, March 31, 1982

Greg and I decided to spend the day birding together. In high spirits, we drove out Highway 41, the Tamiami Trail. We stopped at the Shark Valley viewing area just off the highway. I was so happy to be birding with someone who, like me, had the patience to pursue an elusive northern parula or little blue heron, someone who understood the excitement of seeing a bird species for the first time, a "lifer." Together we saw beautiful birds we had never seen before: limpkins, white ibises, glossy ibises, little blue herons, roseate spoonbills, Everglade kites, swallow-tailed kites, great-tailed grackles, and wood storks. We were wildly celebratory on our way back to camp, popping tab tops off two cans of beer and sneaking swigs as we drove.

We knew where we were heading, although the words were not spoken. The casual, but emotionally charged shoulder bumps whenever we spotted a new bird spoke more loudly than words. Greg slept with me that night. By the time we fell asleep we had decided to travel together for the remainder of his vacation.

Thursday, April 1, 1982

Greg and I lingered in bed until almost 10:00 this morning cuddling, kissing, cooing. Over coffee and breakfast we agreed that we needed to have a conversation about our expectations for traveling together, a "pre-travel agreement." We agreed that we each valued our independence, that we did not want to impinge on each other's freedom, and that a healthy relationship must maintain these ideals. We were being mature, responsible adults.

And since we were independent, mature, responsible adults, Greg decided to go off on his own today, birding near the Flamingo Visitor Center, while I elected to go to Homestead to do laundry and other errands.

Back in camp I settled in the back seat of my camper, pencil poised over my journal, pondering Greg's entrance into my life. I scribbled a list of reasons he was a good prospect for a permanent alliance. He was single, educated, and about my age. We were compatible, at least so far. He was a birder. He had a sense of humor. He would make a good mate, I deduced, and at age 39, I should be thinking about settling down with someone.

Certainly I had made mistakes in the past, but I was older now, and wiser. My first marriage failed because, even at age twenty-two, I was a babe, completely ignorant about love and the sacrifices necessary to make a marriage work. Having fallen from good standing at the university, I did not know what to do with myself. When my husband-to-be proposed, my problem was solved. I would get married and be a wife. Soon after my first marriage ended, I married again, and for the same reason—to obviate the terror of facing an empty future. Now I would become the wife of a university professor. At the moment I said, "I do," however, I knew I was not in love and was making a mistake, but I didn't have the courage to stop it. In the next moment I was saying to myself, "Well, too late now. I'll just have to make the best of it."

But that was long ago and now I had a better understanding of the compromises a successful relationship demanded. I could do it. I didn't want to be alone for the rest of my life. It was true that I had some misgivings about traveling with Greg; perhaps I had been too hasty. I had only known him for a couple of days, but it wasn't marriage after all, just travel. If things went wrong we could go separate ways, nothing lost.

Yes, I had made a convincing list of the pros, stacking up all the glowing indicators of a good match. But I had not made a list of the cons. How could I, having known him for only three days? That list would have been equally conclusive, though, had I known him better. There were plenty of reasons why a relationship with Greg might not succeed, some of which I would soon discover, others that would not be revealed to me until much later, until I had traveled much farther down the route.

I closed my journal and changed into my running clothes. As I jogged down the campground road I saw Greg driving toward me. He grinned at me through the windshield and stopped. I leaned through the lowered window and kissed the man I had, through rigorous intellectual deliberation, determined to be the "right one."

Friday, April 2, 1982

Greg and I got up at 9:00 a.m. and puttered around camp trying to get organized for departure. But the forces of new romance worked against us. With so much to talk about, and so much kissing to be done, we accomplished almost nothing else. What we needed, we decided, was a mandate. Twenty minutes of silence. No talking at all. It was the only way we would complete our tasks. We shook on it then began organizing and packing, clamping our hands over our mouths and squelching giggles whenever the urge to talk threatened.

At last Greg transferred his gear to my camper and we drove away from Long Pine Key campground. I followed him to the Miami airport where he returned his rental car. We lunched at a Denny's then fled Miami. As the metropolis fell behind, we headed west on the Everglades Parkway, sky high and happy to be together, heading for a KOA near Corkscrew Swamp, a wildlife sanctuary south of Fort Myers.

Saturday, April 3, 1982

We hung around the KOA until 2:30 in the afternoon doing nothing but laughing, loving, and talking. Eventually we drove to Corkscrew Swamp and walked along the two mile elevated boardwalk through the oldest virgin bald cypress forest in North America. We had the boardwalk to ourselves as we ambled through the somber forest. The cypress, thick at the waterline where knobby "knees" and buttresses supported them, tapered upward into slender spires with mottled gray and white trunks. Draperies of moss, lichen, and ferns hung from the branches. As we rounded a turn in the walkway, I saw a phenomenon I had seen only in photos in physical geography textbooks, a strangler fig. Strangler figs are trees, but they look and behave like vines, the kind Tarzan loved to swing through the jungle on. I was astonished to see this subtropical species here until I remembered, I *am* in the subtropics. Greg was duly impressed as I explained how the tree germinates in the tops of other trees then sends its viney fingers downward, spreading and grasping until it completely surrounds its host tree in a thick, choking network of vines, often "strangling" it to death.

Somewhere off in the dim interior of the swamp came the loud *who-cooks-for-you* hoots of a barred owl. Determined to find it, Greg went crashing off through the cypress and sawgrass, and disappeared for several minutes. I waited on the boardwalk, marveling at Greg's devotion to his hobby. He returned covered in cobwebs and bleeding from scratches inflicted by the sharp blades of sawgrass. This bordered on obsessive, I thought. I loved birding, too, but I did have my limits where personal safety was concerned.

After Corkscrew Swamp, we drove to Fort Myers Beach on the Gulf Coast. We stopped at a Holiday Inn and asked for a room, but they were booked up. They would be happy, however, to locate a room for us at another motel for $70. We declined, but I was worried we wouldn't find a cheaper room in this ritzy resort area, or any room at all. Greg didn't worry about things like that, but I did. I feared being stranded at night with no place to stay. That's why I had always studied my maps and campground guides each morning before leaving camp. I knew where I would be each night, and planned my route so that I would arrive well before dark. Greg was just the opposite. Nightfall was not a worry to him. If there was a bird to see or another place to visit, he kept going. I wasn't happy about it, but then, this proclivity of his was an opportunity to test my new resolve to be more flexible. I tried to hide my concern as we went off to find another motel. Luckily, we found one soon for $51, which was still a little steep, but what the heck, we were on vacation, so, devil take the cost, especially if it's not mine. We celebrated with champagne and lovemaking.

Sunday, April 4, 1982

"Ding" Darling National Wildlife Refuge is a birding hotspot that attracts serious birders. It occupies much of Sanibel Island not far off shore from Fort Myers Beach. I could foresee a full day of birding ahead, so, as gently as I could, I suggested that we secure a campsite before visiting the refuge. To my relief, Greg agreed. We found a campground in Fort Myers, reserved a site, then drove across the causeway to Sanibel and spent a carefree morning driving and walking through the refuge. Our efforts yielded roseate spoonbills, a reddish egret, and all species of herons including the yellow-crowned night heron. As the morning hours passed, lunch was not mentioned, and by late afternoon we had not eaten. I had noticed the sapping of my energy and enthusiasm, and began to feel dizzy and disoriented by mid afternoon. I told Greg I was hungry and needed to eat. But even mentioning it I felt like a nag and a bad sport. Obviously birding was the greater good, and eating would interrupt the fun.

"We'll go eat pretty soon," he said, and drove on to the next birding spot. I would have accommodated almost any of Greg's preferences for the sake of our relationship, but with that dismissal he came very close to detonating a buried land mine. Indignation flared in me, all the more potent for my efforts to contain it.

How dare you, Greg! I wanted to scream. How dare you treat me like that! Who gave you permission to be in charge? Oh how I wanted to lash out at him, kick him, pound him. But I didn't. Instead, dutifully, I birded for another hour, seething with anger at his lack of consideration and falling deeper into the debilitating depression that comes with low blood sugar. Finally, my distress was too great to ignore and I told him again that I had to eat, that I couldn't function any longer. His face registered annoyance, but he complied.

We found a restaurant, The Oyster Shell, and ordered bowls of fish soup. Tension pounded in my temples as we waited. Two opposing factions of my persona were sounding off against each other in my head. First Person: *You're being a pain in the ass. He's probably sorry he agreed to travel with you.* Second Person: *How dare he ignore you when you are so clearly in distress? As if you committed a sin because you were about to faint from hunger.*

As I ate the hot broth and succulent chunks of fish I felt vitality flow back into my body and I managed a smile. Greg smiled back and said that he would give me a soothing rub down when we got back to camp.

That's what I needed, he said. To him, my crankiness was a simple matter of hunger, but even when the soup bowls were empty and all the bread and salad was gone, I sensed something still amiss. Some nearly imperceptible, unhealthy thing wriggled like a restless worm inside my gut. Much later I realized I was stifling the same rage I had felt when Verenice Bailey had exerted control over me. Greg had done the same thing. He had overridden my will. He had trampled on me with his condescension and, in the interest of compromise, and for fear of losing him, I had allowed it.

Monday, April 5, 1982

Greg and I spent the day at our Fort Myers campground doing laundry and other tasks. I had gotten over my disgruntlement of last night's incident, but when Greg went off for a run I had time to do a survey of the greenhouse. One tidy, organized person made the interior livable. There were enough cubbyholes and drawers for my clothes and gear. With my bedding rolled up behind the rear bench seat, the center section of the camper served well as a tiny living room. But now two people shared the same space, and the newcomer was not a tidy, organized person. Greg had deposited his clothes in the center of the floor. His backpack and bags covered the bench seat, and his bird books, spotting scope, and binoculars were strewn on all the other exposed surfaces. Folding, stacking, and organizing were not part of his daily regimen.

He was sloppy and careless, and it bugged me. I resented seeing my little home in such disarray, but even more I resented the imposition on my orderly way of life. Once again I felt conflicted. Should I talk to him about it, or suck it up? Was I overly organized, too fussy? By the time Greg came panting back from his run, I was smiling sweetly but gritting my teeth against my annoyance, compromising once again.

Compromise. It had become a *leitmotif* in my dealings with Greg. But what were the rules of compromise anyway? It was so perplexing. Do you take turns? Do it your way this time and my way next time? Keep score and things will work out? In reality what I thought was compromise had been, in fact, acquiescence. I was simply going along with Greg's plan. I didn't know how to play the game of Give and Take, and in my attempts I was beginning to notice something unpleasant jabbing at my insides, truths that I didn't want to acknowledge. Right or wrong, I wasn't interested in playing the game. Compromise didn't feel good to me. I liked having things my own way. It's what I was used to. But, like the night so long ago when I had said, for the second time, "I do," I pushed aside the indicators of disaster and reminded myself, "but aren't we so very in love?"

Tuesday, April 6, 1982

We left Fort Myers heading north on Interstate 75. At Harbour Heights the freeway crooked northwest then west and ran straight for the Gulf of Mexico. We drove until we were gazing at the flour-fine, white sand beaches and aquamarine waters of the Gulf Coast. Here was paradise, dazzling and pristine as though angels themselves were the groundskeepers. I had never seen water so clear, so deeply blue-green, and only a few inches deep as far out as I could see—a friendly and benign tropical heaven utterly irresistible to an inveterate wader like me.

My frequent exclamations of, "It's so clean. It looks so tidy," began to annoy Greg. "Do you only like nature when it looks clean and tidy?" he growled.

"Of course not, Greg," I said, "but you have to understand I have never seen any landscape like this, and I can't help it. It does look clean and tidy." I tried to stop my gushing, but I was thinking, so, he's as annoyed by my fondness for "clean and tidy" as I am by his sloppiness. Well, tough. He knows he's a slob and he's just pissed because he's farther from godliness than I am.

I kept my comments to myself as we approached Fort Desoto Park on Mullet Key south of St. Petersburg. The crossing to the key was difficult for me, though, because we had to drive a long causeway across a vast expanse of that thrillingly gorgeous turquoise water. I kept my head turned away from Greg and looked out my side window, murmuring softly over and over, "Wow, wow! It's so clean. It's so tidy."

We birded along the beaches of Mullet Key looking for American oystercatchers and magnificent frigatebirds. In late afternoon we turned back toward St. Petersburg and went looking for the KOA listed in my campground guide. After taking an unplanned detour down a wrong road, we finally found the campground. The last available site was a

184

"Kamping Kabin," basically a miniature barn. I was so tired I crossed my fingers that Greg would approve in spite of its commercial, Disney World cuteness. I heaved a sigh of relief when he said, "It's kind of cute." We cooked our supper inside the "Kabin" but slept in the camper.

Wednesday, April 7, 1982

From Florida's Gulf Coast we drove inland and north to Ocala National Forest where we hoped to find red cockaded woodpeckers and summer tanagers. By 3:00 in the afternoon I began thinking about finding a camping spot. It was that old dread of being stuck without a place to bed down for the night that nagged at me. Such foresight was lacking in Greg, though, and unless I had the backbone to press the issue, we would be birding by starlight. It was just getting dark when I mustered the nerve to insist that we move on to the campground.

Just as I had feared, we arrived too late and found the campground full, including the overflow sites. I sat fuming in the passenger seat as we drove away. I hated this feeling of vagrancy. Being settled in a campground by mid-afternoon was the one daily constant that lent a sense of security and routine to my otherwise random wanderings, and now Greg was depriving me of that. We left the campground not knowing where to go. But soon we found a side road, more of a dirt track, really, and drove down it until it petered out in a grove of trees.

"We'll camp here tonight," Greg said.

"Greg, this might be private property," I objected.

"No one's going to see us," he countered. He had no idea, and wouldn't have understood if I told him, how humiliated and ashamed I would feel if we were discovered and run off by the owner or by police. Or worse.

But I could see there was no other choice, so we popped the top and set up camp. Later, after a simple supper, a full moon emerged above the horizon and we went for a walk. I felt better once I had eaten, and by bedtime Greg and I were tender lovers again.

Thursday, April 8, 1982

First thing out of bed, Greg slung his binoculars over his shoulder and walked off into the woods to bird. I stayed around camp and cooked my breakfast, watching gray clouds thickening overhead. I decided to venture out and do a little birding on my own unencumbered by Greg's marathon birding style.

Walking among the trees, I saw a flicker of a small bird darting low through the leaves. He's behaving like a warbler, I thought. My heart quickened at the prospect of seeing a new bird. I waited, staring into the trees, waiting for the bird to move again so I could pinpoint his location. I slowly shifted positions to see through different configurations of branch and foliage. Then a soft flutter, and the bird flitted to another twig. I caught a fleeting glimpse of blue-gray. Blue-gray? That could be a northern parula, maybe. I had never seen one, but I knew its field marks from hours of studying my field guide. Then I saw him and heard him, too, the buzzy trill of his song ending in the *zip* note described in the bird book. Such a beautiful bird with its blue-gray back, yellow breast and striking white wing bars. I was exultant and proud to have identified it, and, in the dark pit of my evil little heart, hoped that Greg had not seen it. On my way back to camp I found another blue-gray specialty, the tiny blue-gray gnatcatcher, as tiny as the parula and every bit as captivating. Two new birds in only an hour of birding. So much for Greg's marathon style.

Greg was impressed with my finds, and he had not seen the northern parula. We birded together in the afternoon in an unsuccessful search for summer tanagers. The clouds that had been mustering all afternoon now clotted into fearsome thunderheads. We made it back to the camper just as a furious storm hit. The hardest downpour I had ever experienced, harder than the rain at Dickenson State Park, beat down on us as we cowered within the flimsy tin walls of the greenhouse. Waterfalls of rain cascaded from the troughs around the upper edges of the camper. Lightning flashed close by through the trees and I told Greg I thought we should get out there. If we found ourselves stranded by floodwater no one would know we were there.

Then a flash and a sharp bang like a gun firing made us both jump. Lightning had struck a nearby tree. My heart beat wildly as I realized the danger. "Let's get out of here," I yelled. To my relief, Greg didn't protest. We drove out of the woods through torrents of water, but made it only as far as Ocala, about twenty miles away. Rain and flooded roads prevented us from driving any farther. We inched through water nearly up to the camper floor in search of lodging. I feared all the motels would be full with people seeking refuge, but luckily we found a room right away at a Travel Lodge. After checking in, we went for dinner at a nearby Chinese restaurant where the waiter told us a tornado had touched down close to where we had been camped.

Friday, April 9, 1982

In the morning things looked brighter. Standing water was everywhere, but the sun was shining. Our bright mood faded over breakfast, though. This was the day Greg was to return to Fresno. After breakfast, I drove him to a car rental office where he picked up a car for the drive back to the Miami airport. Although we parted on loving terms, I confess a light-heartedness returned to me as I stepped up into my familiar place behind the steering wheel of my beloved camper, solely mine. I was on my own once again, freewheeling and calling all the shots.

I drove north toward Gainsville, stopping at a bank for a cash advance on my credit card. From Gainsville I drove northwest on Highway 27 toward Newport in the Florida panhandle, destination St. Marks Wildlife Refuge on Apalachee Bay, south of Tallahassee.

It was a good day's drive, not too tiring and no more rain. I set up camp and immediately saw my first summer tanager. After all the searching for this bird with Greg, here I had seen one with no effort at all. Later I went for a run down the campground road and saw hundreds of swallows, but couldn't tell which species. It had been a good day with good birding. And, loving thoughts of Greg were gradually replacing my anger and resentment of the previous eight days.

Saturday, April 10, 1982

Drat. Rain started in the middle of the night and continued into the morning. So disappointing, but I went birding anyway. I walked for an hour through the refuge finding more summer tanagers, Carolina chickadees, and swallow-tailed kites. In mid morning I left St. Marks and drove toward Tallahassee to link up with Interstate 10, a major east-west, cross-continent freeway. From Tallahassee I drove west all the way to Mobile, Alabama, about 250 miles under cloudy, rainy skies, thinking about Greg the entire way.

In the afternoon I registered at a private campground just off the interstate, bought propane, ate supper, and washed some clothes. I hadn't really seen much of Florida's scenery today. My mind was occupied with thoughts of Greg. I wanted to be with him again, and I didn't want to wait until July, when my journey would end. I missed his loving, his companionship.

I didn't want to admit it, but the nature of my journey was shifting. Until I had reached the Everglades I had no thoughts of my return home, wherever that was. I was content with my roving, exploratory ways, in no hurry to finish up. Now a restlessness was hectoring me. I wanted to hurry on. Much to my chagrin, my desire to explore was ebbing. Ahead of me lay the states of the Gulf Coast—Alabama, Mississippi, Louisiana, but I sensed that I would see little of them. I knew I would feel like a quitter and a fraud to pass up so much of interest, but my longing to reunite with Greg consumed me.

Before we parted in Ocala, Greg and I had talked about meeting again in Arizona sometime in mid-May. We both wanted to bird in the Chiricahua Mountains in southeast Arizona where we hoped to find the rare coppery-tailed trogon. Birders from all over the United States traveled to the Chiricahuas to see this beautiful emerald green and red bird whose habitat spilled over from Mexico into Arizona's extreme southern haunts.

By mid-May, though, I would be traveling with my sister Susan. Long before I left Oregon she and I had planned to meet in Austin, Texas where our brother lives, and then travel and camp together for a month. It was an exciting prospect for both of us. She had lived in Eugene all her life and was ready for a change. Now she wanted to leave Eugene's perpetual rain and relocate. "I want to live somewhere where there isn't any mold or mildew," she had said. We would be traveling through the arid Southwest where she would have plenty of mildew-free places to scout.

For me, it meant a jolly time with my sister, singing, laughing and generally horsing around. We had always been like that. Now I had to hit her, gently, with the news that Greg might be joining us for some of that time. But I would wait until I arrived in Austin to phone her and break the news.

CHAPTER 16

Fast Track to Texas: Enter Susan

Sunday, April 11, 1982

I breezed through Alabama, Mississippi and Louisiana today, 350 miles, longing for Greg the whole way. What little I saw of the swamps and bayous was more beautiful and extensive than I had imagined, especially Henderson Swamp between Baton Rouge and Lafayette. Along the way several bridges rose gracefully above the waterways giving me a good view, but there were no places to stop for photos. I pressed on to Vinton, Louisiana and arrived at a KOA by 3:00. Tomorrow, I would arrive at Aransas National Wildlife Refuge on the Gulf Coast in Texas, where I hoped to bird and take a rest from driving for a few days.

Monday, April 12, 1982

I'd had about enough of KOAs for a while, and was looking forward to camping at Goose Island State Park, near Aransas National Wildlife Refuge, which, according to Greg, who had been there, had a very nice campground. It was a long drive from Vinton, so I set out early. I crossed into Texas and drove through Beaumont and Houston, stopping several times along the way for gas and supplies and simply to rest from the persistent, hard wind that battered me the entire drive. At Victoria I turned south and made for the Gulf Coast.

Goose Island State Park lay at the tip of a peninsula jutting gulf-ward between Copano Bay and St. Charles Bay, north of the city of Rockport. Birders all over America knew about this place, the place to go for viewing whooping cranes on their wintering ground. I planned to visit Aransas tomorrow, but for today I would stay put at Goose Island and rest.

Just as Greg said, the campground was beautiful, lush and humid. I backed into a spot and set up camp. Birds were everywhere: cardinals, catbirds, warblers. I saw my first hooded warbler and scissor-tailed flycatcher, two thrilling encounters. The scissor-tailed flycatcher was easy to identify; there's no other bird of its size in the United States with such long slender tail feathers like his. But the hooded warbler took a little more work. It meant getting out my field guide and studying the field marks. The male is yellow like several other warblers but, unlike the others, he wears a jet-black balaclava with a large opening in front revealing a wash of sunshine yellow across his face. That's a giveaway for an adult bird. But if its an immature bird, it looks a lot like other immature warblers, so the birder has to rule out similar species that would not be found in swamps or moist woodlands like the hooded. There's also the bird's song, different from other warblers, to consider. The challenge and gratification of identifying a bird species is part of the joy of the game, as if the sheer joy of seeing such beautiful creatures in their natural environment wasn't enough.

In need of exercise after my long drive, I changed into my jogging togs and ran out of the campground onto the fishing pier. Later, after supper, a company of fireflies gathered outside my camper windows blinking their tiny taillights on and off, doing their best to entertain me. In appreciation, I reciprocated by serenading them with their anthem…*Glow little glow-worm, fly of fire, Glow like an incandescent wire, Glow for the female of the species, Turn on the AC and the DC…*

Expenses:	$21.75	gas
	15.00	Goose Island St. Park [3 nights]
	12.83	groceries and supplies

Tuesday, April 13, 1982

Awoke at 6:30 to a warm, muggy morning and a barrage of birdsong. I stepped out of my camper for a quick look around and immediately found a white-eyed vireo, my first. My birding friends back in California were right, the gulf coast of Texas is a hotspot for adding life birds.

I returned to my campsite and set up my cookstove on the picnic table. The aroma of frying bacon attracted the attention of a cheeky squirrel. First he hopped up on the bench and then onto the tabletop, very cute until the little thief tried to grab my bacon from the frying pan, reminding me of the marauding red-shouldered hawk at the Everglades, except squirrels don't have talons. I shooed him away and thought, there's an irony here. We create parks and wildlife refuges partly to preserve habitat for birds and animals, then we crowd these places with people who inadvertently (or deliberately) subvert their natural diet with table scraps and other avian and faunal junk food that is harmful to them in the long run. In truth, even in places where we mean to protect wildlife, it's inevitably humans who prevail.

At 8:45 a.m. I left for Aransas National Wildlife Refuge across St. Charles Bay from Goose Island. I stopped first at the visitor center to pick up a map of the refuge and talk to the staff birder about the best places to bird.

I walked the Heron Flats Trail first and found a northern waterthrush, another new bird for me. On the way back I stopped at the main observation tower near the entrance to the refuge and looked for whooping cranes. But there was not a one in sight. Nor were there any other people on the tower, a sure sign that I was too late in the season for cranes. They had already returned to their breeding grounds in the north.

Next I tried the Big Tree Trail, twice, but the mosquitoes drove me back each time, in spite of two applications of insect repellent. Defeated, I headed back to camp, stopping for a bag of ice and a coke to quench my thirst. Back in camp I basked in the sun for a while, and then went for a run. After supper and dish washing I went up to the bathrooms for a hot shower. Refreshed, I sat outside long enough to see a female hooded warbler that hopped out of the shrubs to see what was going on. Soon after that the mosquitoes drove me back inside my camper. This is perfect habitat for them, warm and humid. It will be a relief to be out of the humid southeast and into the arid southwest. Out of mosquito land. And it won't be long, either. Soon I will cross the 100th meridian, the unofficial geographic boundary between the humid East and the arid West.

Wednesday, April 14, 1982

I was out birding by 6:30 this morning. On my way to the restroom I saw three life birds, three new species in about as many minutes. Any birder would be ecstatic about that. I saw a red-eyed vireo, blue-winged warbler, and Inca dove, their names alone having the ring of something precious or sacred. Would any non-birder believe I had just seen a bright yellow bird with blue wings? Probably not. Three years ago I would not have believed it, either. Except for blue jays or maybe meadowlarks, most birds to me were just LBB's, Little Brown Birds. But that changed in 1980 in California when I saw a notice on a bulletin board inviting interested people to help establish a new chapter of the Audubon Society. No birding experience necessary, the notice said. I made a phone call, and voila! I became a founding member of the Los Padres Audubon Society. I went out almost every weekend with my new birding friends, and my learning curve shot up dramatically. Birding was another way for me to enjoy and appreciate the natural world, the perfect adjunct to my geographic training. And being an excitable kind of person, each time I saw a new species, it gave me a chance to jump, whoop, gush, and carry on.

But on this cloudy, muggy morning, my birding was cut short as once again the mosquitoes forced me to remain inside the greenhouse most of the day reading and studying maps. My mood turned as gray as the clouds, thinking about Greg and missing him. I had to get out of the camper, move around or I would go berserk. At last, drenched in repellent, I braved the mosquitoes and went for a walk down to the ocean. Later, after a late lunch, I shook off the last of my ennui with a long run through the campground.

Thursday, April 15, 1982

Here on the Gulf Coast of Texas I was about 220 miles from my brother's home in Austin, which is where I would be tonight. This morning I left Goose Island around 7:30 and went to Rockport for breakfast. Over coffee I studied *A Birder's Guide to the Texas Coast*, by James A. Lane.

Lane's guides were well known to birders for detailing exact directions to the best places to see specific species.

After breakfast I backtracked to Farm Road 1781, following Lane's directions into the pasturelands southeast of town. The birding was excellent, just as Lane had said, but when I arrived at the ponds he described, I couldn't get close enough to see the hundreds of ducks, geese, and sandpipers swimming and wading there. Frustrated, I tried another farm road and lucked out with some glossy ibises and black-necked stilts.

By late morning I had had enough of back road birding and wanted to move on to Austin. I hadn't seen my brother Tony and his wife since our father died in 1979. I arrived in Austin at 3:00, and called Tony at the University of Texas where he was a professor of Bible Studies. He gave me directions to his house and said he would meet me there soon.

Not long after our reunion, Tony suggested we go for a run. He was a marathoner and I had run many 10K races and one half-marathon, but never an entire marathon. With Tony I knew I had a grueling run ahead of me, and dreaded it, but having a bit of a competitive nature, I agreed. We changed into our running shorts and headed for his favorite trail. As I had predicted, it was a hard workout for me in Austin's heat and humidity. We were running about an 8:24 minute per mile pace, normally an easy pace for me. But today with the sweat pouring off me it was all I could do to keep going. About half way through the run Tony glanced over at me and said, "You have a smooth, even stride." I beamed at the praise. We ran a few more steps and then he added, "It really hacks me off." In spite of my fatigue I gave a snort of laughter and galloped on to the finish in smooth, even strides.

Monday, April 19, 1982

Today was hot, about 91 degrees with humidity about the same. In the afternoon Tony said, "Ready for a run?" I wasn't ready. I wanted to stay inside where the environment was air-conditioned. It was too damn hot to be out in the heat, and for sure it was dangerous to be running, but I was too prideful to say no. I knew I was in good shape, so I told myself I didn't need to worry.

We started out at a fast pace, and from the outset I doubted I could sustain it for five miles. Half way through the run I was struggling to keep up with Tony, stealing glances at his feet, which always seemed to be a half stride ahead of me. I was sweating profusely and feeling sick. I didn't think I could make it, but I kept running, even though I knew it was dangerous to keep up the pace in that heat. But, curse my pride, I couldn't bring myself to tell Tony I needed to slow down. I kept thinking, don't be a fool, Lynn, slow down. I felt light-headed but there was only one more mile to go. I kept pushing and at last we crossed the finish line.

"You set a blistering pace, brother," I panted. "I came close to telling you to slow down back there, but I was too proud."

"Me?" he said. "I thought you were setting the pace. I almost told you I had to slow down."

Tuesday, April 20, 1982

It was a strange day with lightning and thunder, but warm. Tony came home at 3:00 and we decided to run the grueling seven-mile course around Austin's Town Lake. We set a brisk pace from the beginning and lapsed into an easy rhythm, both of us feeling light and strong. With one mile to go we picked up the pace and sprinted for the finish line. Just before crossing, Tony reached out and took my hand so that we crossed together, like duel winners in a race. Tony checked his watch and announced, "Six minutes and fifty-five seconds for the last mile." We were jubilant. I had never run any distance at a sub-seven minute pace, and we had done it after already running six miles. For both of us it had been one of those rare "runner's high" kinds of run.

After six days with Tony and Barbara, visiting, shopping, and gearing up, I was ready for my return to the road. The night before my departure, I called Susan to make final arrangements for meeting her in San Antonio on May 1. She would be joining me for the next month of my travels.

I missed Greg terribly. He had sent me flowers and letters telling me he was eager to rejoin me in May and ready to take a chance on a relationship. But lately thoughts of another man had entered my mind.

Pete had been my sweetheart in graduate school in Sacramento, California. Now he was a professor of geography at Southwest Texas State

University at San Marcos. I had thought of him as I passed through San Marcos on my way to Austin, and had been reminiscing about our lives together in the mid-70s. I hadn't treated him well, and thought it would be good to see him, try to set things right. I placed a call to him from Tony's house, but had only gotten his answering machine. To my surprise, he returned my call the next day and suggested we meet on Wednesday when I would be passing back through San Marcos on my way to Corpus Christi. I noticed my heartbeat quicken a little at the thought of seeing him again.

Wednesday, April 21, 1982

This morning I said goodbye to Tony and Barbara and drove south to San Marcos. I found the campus of Southwest Texas State University and the building that housed the geography department. Pete was in his office. He sat at his desk, a shambling guy in jeans and a T-shirt, shaggy brown hair. I felt an involuntary fluttering in my chest at the sight of him, and a momentary pang of lost possibilities.

We had lived together in graduate school and had roamed the back roads of northern California, studying volcanic formations in the foothills, mapping Pleistocene lakebeds, examining fault lines, chipping bits of serpentine rock from mountainsides. We were an ace team of field geographers.

Pete took me to lunch at his favorite barbeque place and ordered up two Shiner beers, a favorite Texas brew. As we sat at the table across from each other I flashed back to the countless times we had sat together in Sacramento taverns, drinking beer, talking geography. I remembered sitting beside him in geomorphology class, sneaking my hand up his thigh when the lights were turned off for a movie. I remembered the passionate mornings we never got out of bed, the lovemaking lingering and uncorrupted by lurid outside influences. I remembered the betrayals and lies and the pain I had caused him.

Now sitting across from Pete, sipping beers, he showed no bitterness or rancor. The angry outbursts and bitter accusations of the past were gone. We filled in the years since our graduate school days, listening respectfully to each other, our words softened by an ineffable sweetness. He had gotten his PhD from Arizona State University and had taken his first teaching position at San Marcos. He asked me about my travels and unabashedly expressed his admiration for my undertaking. We were kind to each other and I felt close to him. An unspoken question seemed to shimmer in the space between us: Could this once precious love be reclaimed? I wanted to reach out and take his hands in mine, to stroke his face and tell him with my fingers all that I felt, my enduring fondness, my sorrow for our lost love, my shame for the ugly things I had done to him, but I could not bring forth the acts of contrition. I could not own up to the cheating and the lies I had told. Not yet. I felt a throb of sorrow for what I had given up, the missed chance to spend the rest of our lives together. But it didn't matter. I could not have married Pete or any man.

Pete had proposed marriage once, in a funny way. "Would you like to grow old together?" he had asked. His question had fallen on me like a cage of cold steel bars. I had been married and divorced twice before I had turned twenty-seven, and the mere thought of marrying again terrified me. I had blasted him, cruelly, with my answer, NO!

Marriage meant entrapment. It meant once again consigning myself to a place and a role not of my own design. It's what I had done in every relationship I had had so far, followed a man to his destiny, instead of forging my own. At the time of Pete's quirky proposal I was about to finish my Master's degree, a major achievement in my life, and a monumental step toward building self-respect. In spite of Pete's love for me, I could not revert to my old ways. I had to continue along my own path to self-fulfillment. I tried valiantly to explain to him why I felt so strongly, why our marriage would be a disaster, but my words came out venomous and rough, making me sound shrewish and hard-hearted. Pete derided me for it, but I was too overwrought to find the kinder words, words that would make him understand I was thinking about his wellbeing as much as my own. As a result, he only saw me as a bull-headed feminist. It was only one of many hurts I inflicted on him.

I *had* become a feminist, literally at the turn of a page, in the summer of 1969. I was living with my second husband in Sacramento, and the book that opened my eyes was Betty Friedan's *Feminine Mystique*. I had read only the first few pages when I gave a startled gasp of recognition. She had pointed a literary finger at me and stated the cause of my failure in matters of love and marriage. I had been living my life in the slipstream of someone else's, some man, a husband or boyfriend, always trying to scoop out a niche for myself in his wake while he pursued his goals. It had never made me happy, and ultimately I had left every one of them, never sure why or what I was running to or away from.

Friedan explained it. I was one of the millions of women in the 1950s and 1960s who suffered from what she called the *feminine mystique*, the prevalent societal belief that women need look no further than marriage and child-rearing to fulfill themselves. While men were free to find their identity in any way they wanted, women had no identity other than that of wife and mother.

Many women of that era were unable to see themselves beyond the age of twenty-one. They had no image of their own future. They did not see themselves as individuals free to develop their own potential. By the time a woman was 18, or 21, or 25, if she wasn't married she was faced with a terrifying void—what was she to become? She had not been conditioned to think about that. Once a woman was married, her life's work was to be a wife, and she no longer had to think about it.

Friedan believed that the culture of the 50s and 60s did not permit women "to accept or gratify their basic need to grow and fulfill their potentialities as human beings." She saw women who were caught in the feminine mystique as being stunted in their growth, in a state of arrested development.

Betty Friedan was talking about me. I could have been the paradigm for her thesis. At age 22 when my boyfriend at the time asked me to marry him, I had recently been placed on academic probation at the university where I was floundering as a theater major. I was facing the void Friedan had described. When my boyfriend popped the question, the little girl inside of me clapped her hands and exclaimed, "Goody, goody, I'm an adult. I can get married." My life was all settled. I would become a wife. No matter that I scarcely knew my husband-to-be. No matter that I had no skills for housewifery or cohabitation, and no matter that I had no idea what love was. That marriage ended two rocky years later, and I was soon on to the next one, the one I could have avoided if I hadn't been so cowardly when I stood in front of the minister.

One day soon after Pete had finished his Master's degree I watched him drive away to Arizona to pursue his doctorate. My heart was breaking, but I could not go with him. I could not follow again a man who was following his dream. I had to find my own way and bear the loneliness already engulfing me. And so, I rejected the man who loved me. I stood, destitute of hope, destitute of spirit, watching as his car disappeared around the corner.

Now we were reunited at a Texas barbeque joint, and I was aching with shame for the pain I had caused him, but unable to express it. I didn't know then that thirty years later I would have another chance. Over mugs of beer once again, I would sob out my remorse and watch him wave it off with a flip of his hand and tell me, "I was hurt, Lynn, but I didn't hate." Our love was rekindled that night so many years later, a night of perfect bliss and redemption, but only one night. It was too late for us. Pete had found his mate, but I would be left with a profound emptiness and sorrow over a love that could never find its time.

Now after lunch Pete walked me back to my camper. We talked a little longer, hugged, kissed quickly, and parted. I thought about him all the way to Lake Corpus Christi. It had made me so happy to see him.

But what about Greg? Wasn't I in love with him? Hadn't he dominated my thoughts since Florida? I was passionate about Greg, no doubt about that, but I had been wildly in and out of love with many men. Love was an enigma to me. How could I tell when I had found the real thing? I had asked my mother that question when I was a teenager. Her answer: You'll know when the right one comes along.

By what signal, I wondered. Bells, whistles, telegram? Even as a teenager I suspected my mother's folk wisdom was bogus. Now in middle age, I was convinced. In spite of having felt deep passion many times, I hadn't heard the clang of any bell proclaiming, "right one" for Greg or any other man. I was still in the dark, cynical as ever, having never received the "signal."

And now here I was consumed with thoughts of Pete. The events at lunch replayed in my mind as I drove. Enough time had passed to ease the old bitterness and pain between Pete and me. I could easily have settled back into his arms, and it would have been as though we had never parted.

I had longed to touch him, stroke his hair, but I didn't have the right. My heart had ached with tenderness, with yearning, and with sorrow as I gazed at him across the table. Love was simmering between us. It was tapping on my shoulder, nudging. "Psst! Ahem! Hear that bell?" it was saying. "*This* is it." But I was still tone-deaf.

It was almost dark when I arrived at Lake Corpus Christi State Park, but I wasn't too anxious about it. The campground was welcoming with its broad lawns and well-kept facilities. I pulled into the first site I came to, set up my camper, and fixed a hurry-up supper. Before turning in for the night, I stepped outside for a look around. A common nighthawk flittered in the darkening blue sky. Smiling at the familiar sight, I returned to my camper and snuggled into bed, the downy wrap of my sleeping bag gradually becoming Pete's warm arms around me as I eased into sleep.

Thursday, April 22, 1982

I awoke at 6:00 this morning to drizzling rain and wind, a particularly disheartening sight considering the late spring date and the fact that I was in southern Texas. I had thought it would be all sunny skies and warmth in my journey through the southern states, but now I was obliged to adjust my expectations.

I grudgingly slipped out of bed and dressed in warm clothes and a rain jacket. With my binoculars draped over my shoulder, I walked to the office to pay my campground fee. On the way back I walked a side trail and spotted a bird I had never seen, an olive sparrow. The olive sparrow is non-descript, not a bird to exclaim over, except that it is a Mexican species, common in the United States only in southernmost Texas. For a novice birder like me, the joy in finding the olive sparrow was more than the mere sighting. From Lane's book I already knew they were common here, and I had studied their field marks, habitat and appearance, so even though I had never seen one before, I identified it right away. I got an A on that bird test. I was proud of that.

Rain forced me to stay inside my camper all the dreary morning grousing about the weather and bored out of my mind. At noon I cooked steak, mushrooms, and carrots for lunch. Eventually the rain stopped, but a cold wind blew, and dark clouds still hung overhead. I couldn't stand being cooped up any longer, so I grabbed my binoculars and went for a long walk. I saw the same regional bird specialties I had seen before, but my spirits soared when I spotted a golden-fronted woodpecker and a white-winged dove, two more beautiful life birds for my list. I also saw a hawk I couldn't identify, maybe a Cooper's, and a sparrow-like bird that completely stumped me. D+ for those two.

Such gloomy weather. Oh, for the sun! There's a limit to how much birding a person can do on such a day. But at least there are no mosquitoes here. Think I'll go for a run to shake off the blues.

Believe I'll head up the Rio Grande to Falcon Dam tomorrow instead of heading down the gulf coast for Laguna Atascosa. Maybe the weather will be better.

Friday, April 23, 1982

Damn lousy weather. It was still cold, windy, and drizzling rain when I awoke at 7:10 this morning. I gulped a light breakfast, packed up, and by 8:15 I was fleeing the doldrums of perpetual gray and heading for sunnier climes, I hoped.

From Lake Corpus Christi I turned southwest and headed straight for the Rio Grande. In the town of Alice, thirty miles down the road, I stopped for a breakfast of biscuits and coffee. Driving on through Alice, Benavides, and Hebbronville, I was astounded by the numbers of hawks perched on telephone poles and fence posts, hawks every which way I looked. I saw half a dozen bay-winged hawks, elegant, strikingly marked birds with large, chestnut-colored wing patches and white bands at the base and tip of their long tails. In flight they are flashes of white, black, and ruddy red.

Besides hawks there were thousands of other birds, too. So many I couldn't pass up the chance to stop and look. I pulled over onto the shoulder, climbed down from the cab, and darted across the road. Far away across the roadside fence, two large, strange-looking birds were winging low over the ground in broad circles. I swung my binoculars up for a look and caught my breath: black and white with large crested heads and large white patches on the ends of their wings. What luck. Crested caracaras, they were, tropical falcons of southern Texas that resemble vultures. I would not likely see these birds again, so I watched a long time while passengers in cars zooming by no doubt wondered why on earth anyone would want to gaze through binoculars out across the empty Texas plains.

I continued on toward the town of Zapata on the Rio Grande. Zapata is nearly astride the 100th meridian, the unofficial geographical boundary between the humid East and the arid West. I had crossed it traveling east on September 5 last year, heading for the wet side of the country. Now I was on the return route and eagerly looking for signs of the arid West that I loved. I had had enough rain and mosquitoes and humidity. I was longing for the cactus and sage and desert that suited my nature, and with each westward mile the landscape obliged me with the appearance of thorn bush, mesquite, and prickly pear.

The Rio Grande lay ahead of me and I was riding high in the driver's seat in anticipation of it. It was a famous river, a river of western legend and romance, and also the border with Mexico. I could stand on the east bank and look across into another country, a country of vaqueros and ranchos, of mission bells, and dark-eyed senoritas dancing in bright skirts.

It also meant birds, subtropical species that spill across from Mexico into the United States only in this part of Texas. Birders in the thousands come specifically to Falcon State Park and Falcon Dam for a glimpse of the brilliantly colored green jay and the rare green kingfisher.

I arrived at Falcon State Park at 2:00 p.m. The park butted up against Falcon Dam, built in 1953 to back up the water of the Rio Grande and create a man-made lake, Falcon Reservoir. The dam is the last major barrier on the Rio Grande before the river reaches the Gulf of Mexico. My California friends had told me that Falcon Reservoir is beautiful, but it's not. It's ugly, as all man-made lakes are. Dun-colored rings at the shoreline, devoid of vegetation, mark past high and low water levels, and dead, brown tips of drowned trees breach the water's surface beseechingly as though in a last, desperate plea for mercy from the rising waters.

After settling into a campsite, I walked around the campground and along the lake's edge and saw my first neotropical cormorant. In the evening I sat outside the greenhouse and nursed a beer. In spite of drizzling rain, the temperature was warm and there was a roof over the picnic table, so I could sit outside and be comfortable. What a difference it made not to be confined to the camper.

Before bedtime I took another walk, thinking of many things, including Greg. And Pete. And the journey I had undertaken alone over the last nine months. Only one more week alone, then Susan would join me.

Saturday, April 24, 1982

I arose early this morning and fixed a breakfast of Vienna sausage, scrambled eggs, cheese Danish and coffee. Outside the camper, grackles surrounded me, thrashing around on the ground and in the trees, squeaking and screaming. I amused myself by trying to find the perfect description for the clamor these birds make. I closed my eyes, listening, and it came to me: an army bushwhacking through a shoulder-deep forest of wadded newspaper swinging tennis racquets. *Whack, whack.* That was it. I had never heard such noisy birds.

I left camp at 9:15 to go bird at the base of Falcon Dam. I tried to follow my map but took a wrong turn and got lost, ending up instead at the border control station, panicked that I would not be allowed to turn around and be waved on into Mexico. I explained to the border guard where I wanted to go and why. He was courteous and gave me directions to the dam. No doubt I was not the first birder he had straightened out.

I drove to the base of the spillway and parked. From there I began walking downriver. Other birders wandered quietly along the banks weaving through the shrubbery, all of them probably redhots, I thought sardonically, assuming that only the most skillful ace birders would make the trip to this backwater just to pick up a few tropical rarities for their life lists. One birder from Austin stopped to chat. I asked if he had seen any ladder-backed woodpeckers. He smiled condescendingly, no doubt sizing me up for the amateur I was, and said, "Heavens no, dear, there are no ladder-backs here except in winter." He passed on by and I continued downstream. Within ten minutes I spotted three ladder-backed woodpeckers. To verify, I fingered through my field guide to make sure I wasn't looking at the similar Nuttall's woodpecker. Nope. Nuttall's are West Coast birds, and ladder-backed are year-round residents along the Rio Grande, emphasis on year-round. Ha! I thought. So much for red-hots. I lifted my head, smiling smugly, and went on to a splendid morning of birding. I saw a ringed kingfisher, three tropical kingbirds, an altimira oriole, and black-crested titmouse, all of them lifers. But the green kingfisher and green jay, the two "prize" birds still eluded me today.

Back in camp I stopped at headquarters and tried to call both Greg and Mother, but couldn't reach either one. Later I napped then went for a run. After supper I sat outside with a beer and listened to entertainment provided by the couple in the camper next to mine. The "Bickersons," as I referred to them, screeched insults and accusations at each other at a volume suitable for the hearing impaired. The program continued for an hour until the imprecations finally waned and the lights went out. In peace, I retired to my chamber.

Sunday, April 25, 1982

Coming out of the restroom this morning I saw my first plain chachalaca, a large, comical-looking, chicken-like bird with a loud voice. *Cha Cha Lac* he shouts–yes, shouts–over and over. The novelty wears off pretty quickly.

I tried to call Greg again, and this time I reached him. I told him about all the birds I had found at Falcon Dam yesterday. He congratulated me and praised my birding skills. I told him I was going back to the dam and wouldn't give up until I had seen the green jay and green kingfisher.

Oh how I wanted to see the green jay. Who wouldn't, after seeing his picture in the field guide. A truly tropical species, he is a spectacle of color with a crown and nape of iridescent sky blue. The sides of his head and his throat are glossy black. His back is grass green, and his underparts a pale, lime green. His tail is dark blue-green with yellow edgings.

The green jay is a fairly common resident of the lower Rio Grande Valley, but if you want to see him in the United States, you have to travel to southern Texas. That and his gorgeous appearance make him a "target" bird for serious birders.

I was vigilant in scanning the brush along the river, and it didn't take long. I heard his *cheh-cheh-cheh* notes first and looked toward the sound. There he was perched in a small tree at riverside, waiting for me, colors flashing like a gaudy Christmas tree ornament. I couldn't wait to call Greg and tell him. Now for the green kingfisher, I chortled, relishing the challenge. Unlike the green jay, he is uncommon and difficult to see, the smallest of all North American kingfishers. The male has a rich, dark green head, back, and tail and a wide white band around his neck. Beneath a chestnut upper breast his white belly is speckled with dark green spots. To find him, your best bet is to use your ears more than your eyes at first, and listen for a faint, but sharp *tick, tick* or a squeaky *cheep*.

Again I was successful. I heard the distinctive call, then scanned with my binoculars, and there he was, just as if he was posing for the field guide photo. Now my mission was complete and I hurried back to camp to call Greg.

After my call, I began breaking camp. The day was still young and I had seen all that I wanted at Falcon Dam. Another birding hotspot awaited me sixty miles downriver, Bentsen Rio Grande Valley State Park near McAllen. I drove down the valley through the communities of Roma and Rio Grande City, glancing frequently out the right passenger window across the low plains of the Rio Grande Valley to the purple-gray outlines of the distant Sierra Madre in Mexico.

I arrived at Bentsen Rio Grande and pulled into the campground. Soon after I settled into a campsite I took a short walk around the grounds. It was easy to see that this was birder heaven. Folks with binoculars hanging from their necks were leafing through bird books, and spotting scopes had been set up around the perimeter of the campground trained on some elusive bird in the bushes or trees. Here and there field guides, open and face down, lay at the ready on picnic tables.

It didn't take long for me to get in the swing of things. The couple camped next to me introduced themselves, Stauffer and Eleanor, birders from the East. We took to each other immediately and went off birding, scoring more chachalacas and green jays.

Word spread throughout camp that a well-known birding tour group, WINGS, was in the area and would be conducting an evening birdwalk. When I heard their leader was Rich Stallcup, I perked up. Rich was a friend of Greg's birding buddies back in California, and was known to be a good guy. Even though I was not a paying customer, I knew he wouldn't mind if I tagged along on his tour, especially if I dropped the names of a few California birder redhots.

At dusk the group assembled, our mission, common pauraques, birds related to nighthawks and whip-poor-wills. They cross into the United States from Mexico only in southern Texas. This strange bird has a tiny bill that looks as though it couldn't accommodate anything larger than a mosquito, but at dusk as it flits about in search of insects, the entire front of its face opens into an enormous maw.

Our group hoped to find them on the ground along the camp road, but before we set out, Rich had a birding tip for us. "Listen for the pauraque's call, a low *pur* note followed by a descending *wheeer*," he explained. "Try this technique. Cup your hands behind your ears and bend them slightly forward as you walk." Rich demonstrated while I tried to blend in with the shadows. Lagging behind I watched the dusky group of obedient birders, hands behind their ears, elbows jutting, slowly scanning from side to side like human sonar as they moved down the road.

Monday, April 26, 1982

During the night I started my period and woke up this morning with cramps and achiness. I drug myself out of bed and went to the restroom. Movement in the shrubs along the path caught my attention and when I investigated I found three painted buntings, two males and one female. *Painted* is the right word for these birds with a purple head, red breast and belly, and green back. More life birds for me.

Back at my camper I noticed the Millers were not at their campsite, off birding, no doubt. Just as well for me, since I felt too lousy to be in company with new friends. While I was hanging around close to camp, Rey the park superintendent came by and stopped to chat. I told him about the painted buntings I had seen that morning and that I especially wanted to see a groove-billed ani. "I think I know where you can find them," he said and offered to drive me around in search of one. We found no anis on that pass-through, but I did see a bronzed cowbird, not a bad runner-up.

Later, I wandered along the nature trail near the park entrance and spotted my first yellow-billed cuckoo. That evening I reported my find to the Millers who invited me to go riding with them in search of the still unseen common pauraque. We were successful, but with the intensity of my cramps and pain I was too miserable to enthuse. Finally the Millers returned me very tired and achy to my camper. I swallowed a couple of aspirin and collapsed into bed.

Tuesday, April 27, 1982

This morning the Millers came to say goodbye. Their vacation was over and they were going home. I planned to drive a few more miles downstream to Santa Ana Wildlife Refuge for a morning of birding. Santa Ana, another refuge in the string of wildlife refuges along the lower Rio Grande, was accessed, appropriately, along Green Jay Road in Alamo. At Santa Ana I walked around Willow Lake and found least grebes, black-bellied whistling ducks, and, to my surprise, Wilson's phalaropes. I heard a noise like a screech owl, but it turned out to be a loud toad.

I hadn't found any groove-billed anis, which were supposed to be at Santa Ana, so I went back to headquarters and talked to the superintendent. He drew me a map and told me exactly where to look for them. After trudging for what seemed like miles across brushy fields, I was about to give it up when I spotted two chunky black birds with pendulous tails in a bush, anis certainly. Quickly I swung my binoculars up and focused on the bird's beak. Sure enough, there were the distinctive grooves that distinguished them from smooth-billed anis, clinching the identification.

Too tired and achy for more birding, I trudged back to my camper and returned to camp at Bentsen Rio Grande, now nearly deserted. The rest of the day I pined around the campground feeling lonely and depressed; at night a thunder and lightning storm raged overhead to rub it in.

Wednesday, April 28, 1982

I was underway at 2:00 p.m. heading inland away from the Rio Grande through Harlingen and on to Rio Hondo where I found a campground close to Laguna Atascosa National Wildlife Refuge on the Gulf Coast, almost as far south in Texas as you can get. I arrived in late afternoon and stayed around camp doing laundry and journal writing.

Thursday, April 29, 1982

I spent all day walking the Paisano Path in Laguna Atascosa where I saw birds galore, and many of them new to me. A brilliant scarlet tanager with ebony wings perched on a tree limb long enough for me to get a few photos, one of the few bird photography successes of my journey.

Later I was sitting near the refuge headquarters when I saw two plump warblers with golden yellow heads and underparts, and blue-gray wings. Prothonotary warblers, I gasped. I had never seen one before. I grabbed my field guide to double check the description of their song and call note, then listened for the loud, ringing *zweet*, confirming the identification. As usual, I felt the thrill of putting together the puzzle pieces of bird identification—habitat, appearance, behavior, and song—to score a correct sighting.

Back in camp I gathered my toiletry bag and towel and walked to the restroom for a shower. As I was toweling off, I felt a burning sensation on my lower legs. I looked down to see a band of lurid, red welts encircling my ankles like bracelets. Chiggers! All the time I had been traipsing after groove-billed anis at Santa Ana, the little devils had been feasting, unbeknownst to me, at my sock lines. Now they itched and burned like sin, driving me nearly to distraction. Give me mosquitoes anytime over these nasty little varmints of the Texas woodlands.

Friday, April 30, 1982

Here I sit once again at Lake Corpus Christi State Park. This is my jumping off point for the San Antonio airport where my sister Susan will arrive tomorrow evening. She is joining me for the next month of my travels; this will be my last night of solo camping for a while.

How will Mother fare in Eugene if Susan moves away? I am worried about her, she will be lonely. I am lonely, too. I miss Greg and I'm anxious about the next phase of my trip and my uncertain future.

I called Tony to tell him when Susan would arrive at San Antonio. He said he would drive down to meet me at the airport, then take us to dinner before we all returned to his home in Austin. As I hung up the phone, a burden like a heavy backpack seemed to slough off my shoulders. Tony had taken charge of events and for the next few days I would be a pampered guest, relieved of the daily driving, decision-making, map reading, and stress of travel in unfamiliar places.

Saturday, May 1, 1982

It rained all night and was still sprinkling when I woke, but there were some glimmers of sunshine. After breakfast I packed up and was ready to go by 10 a.m., way too early. I would have had plenty of time for a long run, but now there was nothing to do but leave.

I drove north, stopping for gas and a rest, even though I had less than one hundred miles to go. It was early afternoon when I pulled into the San Antonio airport. I wandered the corridors and airport grounds until 4:30 when Tony appeared. At 5:00 Susan's plane landed. Tony whisked us away to the top of the Tower of the Americas where we dined high above the city in the tower's rotating restaurant. After dinner we walked along San Antonio's famous River Walk for an hour before Tony took us to my car and led us back to Austin.

Susan and I had much to catch up on. We spent our time in Austin visiting with Tony and Barbara, planning for our trip, and talking, talking, talking. Susan was not going to return to Eugene, she thought, and I, too, had an uncertain future before me. We had always relied on each other to lend a sympathetic ear and to offer advice, sometimes sound, often not so sound. But for now, we both anticipated a lively time together for the next few weeks.

Tuesday, May 4, 1982

Susan and I got started around 11:15 this morning. We drove west through Fredericksburg and Junction, then on to Sonora where we turned south toward the Rio Grande. We were heading for Amistad National Recreation Area at the confluence of the Rio Grande and Devils Rivers. The Rio Grande seemed like an old friend to me when we pulled into our primitive campsite, but for Susan this was new territory, and I wondered if she would react with the same sense of awe as I had on my first sighting.

Wednesday, May 5, 1982

This morning we left camp and drove a few miles downstream to Del Rio for breakfast and a bit of shopping. We browsed through the local Cornet where Susan bought a camp shirt and a blanket. Then we drove back past Amistad and continued on along Highway 90 toward Marathon. At the confluence of the Pecos and the Rio Grande, we pulled off at a paved vista point and walked to the brink of the canyon. A short distance downstream the broad Pecos joined the Rio Grande. I snapped a photo of Susan gazing over the retaining wall, then gazed awhile myself. Just before climbing back into the camper, I scanned the opposite shore with my binoculars on the off chance Pecos Bill might be over there roping a tornado with his rattlesnake lasso.

On we went out into the west Texas desert, leaving the Pecos Canyon behind and crossing the mesas of the Stockton Plateau. Texas bluebonnets spread the fields with blue, and ocotillos appeared along the road, their delicate red-tipped fronds welcoming me back to the West.

Before us and to the southwest rose the sharply outlined mountains of the Texas Basin and Range province. To the north, white cumulus clouds quickly gained height above invisible thermals rising from the heated plain. I watched with a skeptical eye knowing what they could become. Soon, as I suspected, the clouds darkened and merged into a wall of black thunderheads, and I knew we were in for a cloudburst. As we watched, awestruck and fearful, lightning flashed and the clouds let loose with a colossal deluge. But to the south the sky was clear blue. We sent out our most fervent wishes for the storm to retreat, but to our horror the black ceiling edged nearer and nearer until it was directly above us. We had to make it to the town of Marathon fifty miles ahead before we could turn south and be free of it. The storm battered us as we cowered in our seats and prayed to Thor for it to back off. But it dogged us, its leading edge perfectly aligned with the long axis of the greenhouse as we ran for Marathon.

It was a hair-raising ride, and we were plenty happy when we reached Marathon and pointed our nose southward into the blue. Glancing in the rear view mirror I watched the black clouds fall back like exhausted runners as we pulled away from the storm. Ahead in the distance the blue-gray Chisos Mountains loomed above the horizon beckoning to us.

Because it was late afternoon, Susan and I decided to stop at a private campground sixteen miles south of Marathon and continue on to Big Bend early in the morning. We found the campground on the wide-open plain, surrounded by nothing but blue sky, sage, and scrub. A few small, scattered mobile homes had the look of permanent fixtures, but no one was afoot when we pulled in. I stepped from the camper and looked out across the shimmering empty miles to the mountains. Silence, broken only by the tinkling note of a black-throated sparrow, lay poised over the desert like held breath. The light, that inexplicably rarefied, white desert sunlight, tingled on my skin melting me into a rapture of pure surrender. The desert had pulled me into its sway. Susan seemed to feel the magic, too. We stood, transfixed, heeding the desert's mandate: slow down, listen, watch, be silent.

We roused ourselves and began exploring the grounds. The place was vibrant with birds, probably brought down by the storm. "Look, Susan!" I exclaimed, "curve-billed thrashers." I swung my binoculars around calling out the names of warblers, kingbirds, and flycatchers, hoping to spark a little avian interest in my sister. There was no way she could escape it if she was to travel with me for a month.

That evening we sat in the camper sipping beer and looking out at the mountains. A small black and white dog crept close and sat shyly at our open door. Clearly, she wanted to join us, but not having been invited, she sat politely and waited. "Come on in, dog," I said. "It's all right." She cocked her head, but wasn't sure. "It's OK. You can come in," I repeated. This time she understood. In one graceful leap she was inside and onto my lap where she curled into a ball and waited to be loved. The three of us sat quietly together until the rosy skeins of sunset intertwined with the last dark remnants of the afternoon storm.

Thursday, May 6, 1982

After breakfast we left under cloudy skies, but as we approached Big Bend the sun reappeared. The Chisos Mountains rose before us with ocotillo, prickly pear and cholla cactus dotting their broad alluvial fans. We stopped at the visitor center at Panther Junction and bought books, brochures, and maps. From there we drove deep into the park to Rio Grande Village adjacent to the river for our first night of camping.

The campground was large and pretty with a green lawn and shade trees. We found a pleasant site on the edge near a nature trail and set up camp. Once settled, we walked the short trail up to a ridge overlooking the Rio Grande and across into Mexico. Below us the gray-green river curved sluggishly around a broad, sandy point bar. We looked down on a small farmstead across the river consisting of a few raggedly rectangular fields abutting river's edge. Beyond it laid the squat adobe buildings of the sleepy village of Boquillas. The scene was like a stage set, still and lifeless, until animated by a farmer who appeared at the wings and slowly led a burro laden with a bundle of sticks across center stage. Through the river proscenium we gazed a hundred years into the past. I glanced at Susan to share our wordless awe, but I could see she was deep in thought. I didn't know what she was thinking, but I was glad something was going on. Otherwise, travel would be meaningless.

Back in camp Susan and I prepared for a restful day in the sun. Susan changed into a bright fuchsia bathing suit and sat at our picnic table soaking up rays. She is petite, but buxom, and with her short, curly blonde hair she is an eye-catcher. She is also in good shape, and so am I, and I don't mind saying that even though we're a couple of post-spring chicks, we both look younger than our years. I put on shorts and a skimpy tank top and puttered around camp. It was inevitable that we would attract attention.

It came in the form of a fellow named Gordon, from the adjacent campsite, who smiled broadly at us across the lawn and wandered over to strike up a conversation. He was down from Santa Fe on vacation. He asked where we were from and I gave him a brief rundown of my journey explaining that Susan had only recently joined me. We passed the afternoon hanging around camp together and quickly became friends. Being part of the fine arts, fine dining set in Santa Fe, Gordon liked to cook. He pulled a small, box-shaped metal contraption out of his car trunk and set it up on his picnic table.

"What is that?" We asked.

"It's a propane camp broiler," he explained. "I'll broil us some hamburgers for dinner tonight if you want."

"We'll make beans and salad," Susan offered, and it was a deal.

Susan continued soaking up the sun for an hour. Having lived in western Oregon all her life, sunshine was a luxury, and moderation in tanning wasn't part of her outlook. I assigned myself burn monitor and spoke up when her skin began to redden.

"Susan, you need to get out of the sun and put your shirt on. You're burning." She came inside the greenhouse and slathered herself with cooling cream. Then she slipped into her new blue shirt—the one she bought in Del Rio—to cover the sunburn. Gordon wandered by and we waved him over to join us. He ducked in through the door and sat on the bench seat while Susan and I began rattling pots and pans in the tiny galley. We had laid out salt and pepper and condiments on our cutting board-sized table along with a box of Ohio Blue Tip Matches. Gordon watched as we prepared food, idly turning the matchbox in his hands. Susan had one of those matches in her hand at the moment and was about to light the stove when Gordon read dramatically from the side of the box, "Big… Blue…Tips." Susan's mouth dropped open as she quickly glanced down at her plentiful bosom partially covered by the blue blouse. Then she looked up and realized Gordon had been reading the matchbox. A split second of silence elapsed and, then, as if on cue, we all burst into laughter. "Big Blue Tips" became our byword and slogan from then on.

Sunday, May 9, 1982

Around midmorning Susan and I drove the Boquillas Canyon spur road and hiked the 1.4-mile trail into the magnificent canyon. The trail climbed up to a cliff overlooking the Rio Grande then descended down to the river. We walked downstream along a broad beach gazing up at the dramatically tilted and soaring limestone cliffs, bright in the morning sun. The canyon narrowed until the cliffs squeezed up against the river, ending our forward movement. We lingered for a while peering across the river at the *bocas*—caves—at the base of the cliffs, then turned and slowly hiked back up the trail.

Today was our last day at the Rio Grande Village Campground. We planned to move into the high Chisos Basin this afternoon and camp there for a couple of days. We loaded up our gear, said goodbye to Gordon, and drove back to Panther Junction. Along the way, Susan and I figured out a plan for meeting our respective boyfriends in Arizona. I had already told her that Greg would be joining us for a visit to the Chiricahua Mountains. I had thought she would be upset by this plan, but instead, she hatched the idea of inviting her current boyfriend, Denny, to fly in from Eugene and join us—a foursome for a week.

From Panther Junction we drove up into the mile high Chisos Basin to the campground. It, too, was spectacular, surrounded by the peaks of the Chisos Mountains. We settled in and went to bed early in anticipation of a long hiking day tomorrow.

Monday, May 10, 1982

I had read about the Chisos Mountains and the hike up to Boot Springs. It was one of the few places a birder could see the Colima Warbler, probably Big Bend's most famous bird, since it is found nowhere else in the United States. I had studied the bird's picture and the description of its song in my field guide and knew its habitat. I would have to work to see it, though. The round trip to Boot Springs was a rugged ten miles.

Early this morning I loaded my daypack and started up the trail. Susan elected to take a shorter hike to a different spot, so we agreed to meet back in camp later. My hike led through a beautiful juniper, oak, and pine forest. My guidebook described a particular ridge along the trail and advised looking and listening for the warbler in oak trees there. I had just crossed over the ridge when I saw movement in the oaks and heard the call I had memorized. There they were, right where the book had said, easy to spot and easy to identify, the rare Colima warbler. I cheered, *sotto voce*, of course, and gave myself a mental pat on the back. I deserved this one.

I continued on until I saw the famous "boot" rock formation jutting above the mountainside. At Boot Springs I rested before heading back down the trail. It was a long, knee-jarring, downhill jaunt. My legs and feet ached by the end of it, but I made it back to camp with no blisters.

Susan would be waiting for me, and I was looking forward to sharing stories about our hikes. She was in camp, but not alone. Across from her, slumped in my camp chair, was a strange man, a park maintenance man she had just met. She introduced me, but he didn't bother to stand or even straighten up in my chair, let alone smile or say hello. Rude, I thought as I shot him an ice cube glance. His behavior reminded me of Tom at Yakima State Park, surly and inappropriate for a park employee. I wanted him to get the hell out of my chair and out of our campsite. I was tired and resented his intrusion into our space, and I was angry with Susan for inviting him in.

I stepped into my camper and fumed. There was no place to go and now I couldn't even have a private talk with my sister. Eventually she stepped into the camper and started gathering her toiletries. I knew she felt my anger.

"I'm going to go take a shower at his cabin."

Don't be a fool, I wanted to yell at her, but I didn't say a word. How could I protest her going off with this stranger when I had done the very same thing with Marty the ranger at Organ Pipe Cactus National Monument? Without knowing him at all I had gone to his trailer to take a shower. But, then, Marty was goofy and clueless and I had judged him to be harmless. And I was right—that time. But I was wrong about Tom at Yakima State Park, dangerously wrong. Now I was worried for Susan's safety.

Susan was gone a long time. I was becoming frantic, and thought about going after her. But I didn't know where the cabin was, and didn't even know the man's name. To my great relief she finally returned to camp, unmolested, around dinnertime. We never discussed the incident, but I sensed she realized how alarmed I had been. Now that Mr. Park Maintenance Man was out of the picture, the tension eased between us.

Tuesday, May 11, 1982

After breakfast we packed up and drove from the Chisos Basin to the historic adobe village of Castolon in the southwest part of the park. Just beyond Castolon at river's edge we entered Cottonwood Campground where we planned to spend the night. We pulled into a large, open site and set up camp under a cloudy blanket of warm, muggy air.

As I tried to set up camp, lank strands of overlong hair kept falling into my eyes, driving me to profanity. Susan responded by setting up a camp chair and fetching the scissors from a drawer. "The Cottonwood Beauty Salon is open," she declared, and gave me a much-needed haircut.

Later, at twilight, we walked the deserted road to the old adobe store at the village of Castolon. The sun setting on the horizon cast a soft pink glow over the desert. We assessed the scant offerings at the store and bought a few odds and ends before starting back to camp. Stars began to speckle the clearing sky as we two small beings walked along the darkening road. The birds had long since gone silent, but night held off for one last song. We put our voices together in two-part harmony and sang: *With someone like you, A pal good and true, I'd like to leave it all behind and go and find, Some place that's known, to God alone, Just a spot to call our own . . .*

Wednesday, May 12 – Thursday, May 13, 1982

We left Big Bend this morning and headed north on Highway 118 passing through the tiny town of Study Butte and on into the immense open desert where, save for the strip of pavement below us, no trace of human occupation was readily evident. These were the wide, wild open spaces of Texas, for sure, and the Texans had a right to brag. Big. That is the word for this country.

Off to our right and ahead of us the rounded and furrowed Christmas Mountains rose out of a flatland of scrub. Farther on we could see the jagged and nearly vertical walls of the Corazones Peaks, formed from an ancient mass of molten rock that cooled and solidified below Earth's surface then slowly pushed upward through the overlying rocks.

As we drove through the limpid morning light, I fell, once again, under the desert's spell. I could have lingered for weeks, months, drinking in the desert sunrises and sunsets, the multitude of colors and shapes, even the intense heat and the thunderstorms. Perhaps I would return someday and try out the life of a desert rat, but for now we were pushing on to Fort Davis State Park where we would camp tonight.

From Fort Davis, it was another 150 miles to Guadalupe Mountains National Park on the border with New Mexico. We left early in the morning and started out, taking a side trip to the McDonald Observatory for a quick tour of the facility and a look at the giant telescope.

Back on the road, we zigzagged up over mile-high Guadalupe Pass and arrived at the national park in the afternoon. At Pine Springs Campground we chose a site among junipers and oaks. According to the brochure we picked up at the visitor's center, this was a very windy place, subject to occasional gusts of one hundred miles per hour. We found out for ourselves that evening when the winds rose into violent furies that battered the camper. Our tin can walls seemed small protection against the onslaught. I sought out the ranger and asked him if he thought it was safe to lift our pop-top. He said he thought we would be all right, but we should use "common sense." To me common sense meant batten down the pop-top and take on ballast, but the pop-top was Susan's sleeping berth, so it had to stay up. As for ballast, we could only hope that our combined weight of two hundred thirty pounds would be enough to keep us upright.

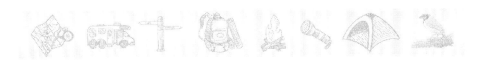

CHAPTER 17

Desert Southwest: Beginning of the End

Friday, May 14 - Saturday, May 15, 1982

The wind had died down by morning. After breakfast we left the Guadalupe Mountains and continued across the border into New Mexico, through Carlsbad and Artesia. At Artesia we turned west on Highway 82 heading toward the Sacramento Mountains in south central New Mexico where we planned to camp. We arrived at the campground in the early afternoon and were glad to find it empty. At well over eight thousand feet in elevation, the cool Ponderosa pine forest was a stark contrast to the temperature and vegetation of the desert. I built a fire and we made foil packet dinners of chicken, potatoes, carrots and onions. In the evening we huddled by the campfire watching the stars until bedtime.

I arose at 6:15 the next morning and built another fire, although it was not as cold as I had expected, only 47°. Sipping coffee and tuning in to the sights and sounds of the mountain morning, I heard the trilling whistle of a broad-tailed hummingbird. Looking up I saw a rosy-throated male streaking toward the ground performing his U-shaped courtship display. From a great height he plunged, wings whistling, almost to the ground, then, in a flash, he zipped skyward and plunged again, all to impress a female. Sitting there agog, I was definitely one female who was impressed.

When Susan woke I made breakfast of ham and eggs and campfire toast. For some reason I was feeling irritable, wanting to be alone. There seemed to be tension between us, maybe too much togetherness. But whatever it was, we both ignored it and spent a lazy day around camp. Later we worked off some of the discord with a long combination walk-run.

| Expenses: | $6.20 | gas, camp, ice, coke |

Sunday, May 16, 1982

Came down from the Sacramento Mountains this morning and stopped for breakfast in "Fat Cottonwood," aka Alamogordo.

On to White Sands National Monument and an hour's romp through the dunes.

Pushed on to Deming and checked in to a KOA. A fellow in the rec room challenged me to a game of pool. I beat him. Hah!

Called Greg and made plans to meet him in Tucson in five days.

Monday, May 17, 1982

From Deming we veered northwest on Highway 180 toward Silver City. We were on our way to Gila Cliff Dwellings National Monument near the confluence of the west and middle forks of the Gila River. Another geographic landmark, the Continental Divide, began blipping enticingly on my geographer's radar as we drove higher into the mountains. The Continental Divide, running the length of the Rockies along its crest, separates the waters flowing west and emptying, eventually, into the Pacific Ocean, from the waters flowing east and south to the Gulf of Mexico. At the Divide, the observer can look out onto two monumental drainage systems—small rivers flowing into larger rivers—extending farther than the eye can see: two enormous patterns impressed upon the continent by the downcutting of rivers over millions of years. Who could not sense the wonder of that?

At Silver City we turned north on State Route 15, and in a few more miles officially crossed the Continental Divide at Pinos Altos, elevation 7,080 feet. We continued deep into the Gila National Forest, turning east on Highway 35 and arriving shortly at Lake Roberts where we pulled in to Mesa Campground on a hillside overlooking the lake, a very pretty spot nestled among juniper and pinyon pines.

I stepped out of the camper into a scene alive with birdsong. Bluebirds, woodpeckers, sparrows, and blackbirds provided the music. Clearly this was rich birding territory, but birding would have to wait for a while. I had been sitting behind the wheel all day and needed exercise. I changed into running shorts and shoes and ran several laps around the campground loop, a hard run at that elevation and in the heat.

Later, Susan and I hiked the nearby Purgatory Chasm trail. The trail started out along a ridgeline through the dusty green of junipers and pinyon pines but then dropped down via a ladder into a slot canyon where walls of fine-grained, light gray volcanic ash, sculpted by water and wind into sinuous curves, closed in on us. In places knobs of rock overhung the trail and we had to squeeze through narrow corridors. Occasionally, a turn in the canyon would unexpectedly widen to reveal a hidden grotto with small pools and green grass. Alone in the canyon today, it was easy to imagine that we were the first explorers in this enchanting place.

Tuesday, May 18, 1982

Early this morning I walked from camp down to the lake, encountering an amazing variety of birds. At lakeside I looked back up the hill and realized I had passed through four distinct habitats in the short distance from camp to lake: pinyon-juniper woodland at camp, riparian scrub along the stream, marsh at lakeside, and the lake itself. Each habitat yielded its own species, everything from bluebirds and woodpeckers around camp, to sandpipers and coots at the lake. Back in camp I reported my findings to Susan whose interest in the natural world was growing daily.

We left at mid-morning for Gila Cliff Dwellings. The last few miles into the monument were the curviest I had ever seen, and steepest, at 10% and 12% grades. I put a stranglehold on the steering wheel and kept my foot pressed on the brake. At times it seemed we would lose traction and roll like tumbleweeds to the bottom. I was glad I was driving nothing larger than my trusty VW camper and mightily glad when we came to the end of the road and parked.

But the hair-raising drive into the park brought its rewards. It was quiet and beautiful when we stepped out of the camper and there were very few visitors. To view the cliff dwellings visitors must hike a one-mile loop trail from the parking lot through the forest and up into the cliffs. Susan and I walked at a leisurely pace peering through the trees for our first glimpse of the mysterious dwellings tucked into alcoves in the volcanic rock. These were the homes of the Mogollon people who had lived here about seven hundred years ago, snug in their recessed shelters. They were hunters and farmers, cultivating corn, squash, and beans. And they were artisans, too, crafting pottery and jewelry, which they traded with other tribes. But they weren't here long. Sometime in the early 1300s they abandoned their home after only twenty to thirty year's residence.

Susan and I probed into all the caves and dwellings, trying to imagine the fifty or so inhabitants going about their daily lives. It was a beautiful home, obviously, so why did they leave? No one knows for sure, but likely they had exhausted the resources of the canyon environs. I thought about the present day strain on planetary resources imposed by modern civilizations and unchecked global population growth. How much longer could my own affluent civilization continue, and would I be able to adapt to catastrophe if our own society should collapse?

I thought about these things as I walked in the footsteps of the Mogollon. There was something very alluring about the place. It seemed far removed from the ills of the world, peaceful and comforting. This was one place we were in no hurry to leave.

But leave we did. We had a bit of business to conduct before returning to camp, a telephone call to Mile Hi Ranch in Ramsey Canyon in Arizona. Mile Hi Ranch was a Nature Conservancy preserve noted for the fourteen different species of hummingbird that could be seen there. The Conservancy maintained four small rental cabins at the preserve, and we wanted to reserve a cabin for four for two nights.

We stopped at Campbell's Trading Post on our way out of the national monument and made our call. Fortunately, Mile Hi had a cabin available and we booked one for May 28 and 29. I sent a money order to reserve the room, bought beer and ice, and drove back to camp.

Wednesday, May 19, 1982

After coffee and breakfast I hiked the Purgatory Chasm trail again. I had companions this time, five mule deer at the trailhead, which was fine, and a group of noisy children on the trail, which wasn't. Walking back to camp

I saw a flock of pinyon jays moving from tree to tree. I recognized them by their uniformly, sky-blue bodies and their distinctive *queh queh queh* calls.

Later on there was nothing much to do but sit around and watch things. Fine with me. At 3:00 I went for a run, foolishly choosing the hottest part of the day to do it. The heat and altitude sabotaged my breathing, but I kept going anyway. On each lap around the campground, Susan looked up from her book and gave me a limp wave.

She must have felt guilty watching me struggle through my run because, later, she pulled herself up from her chair and said, "Guess I'd better go for a run, too." She was capable of running several miles, but she was slower than me and not used to heat and high elevations. As she passed me on her first loop, she was already panting. I gave her a grin and a cheery wave, but the mere sight of her tripped a spring-loaded alter ego inside me, a zany, devilish side she had often seen before. She needed some lightheartedness to keep her going. As she approached on her second loop, red-faced and panting, I was hiding behind the camper waiting. Just as she started to pass I jumped out and flapped a two-handed salute. She laughed and kept going. Next time around I was lying prone beneath the camper with my arm sticking out waving. This time she doubled over laughing and gasping, but she kept going. The fourth time around I was hiding behind a bush. When she came around the turn all she could see was an arm waving wildly from within the bush. But that was the end of my shenanigans. I had had the last lap's last laugh. She'd had enough and I was out of ideas.

Thursday, May 20, 1982

We broke camp early this morning and drove to Silver City stopping for breakfast then pushing on to Lordsburg and into Arizona. Off to the southwest I could see the Chiricahua Mountains, a forested "sky island" rising abruptly from the desert floor. We would spend a few days there when Greg and Denny joined us. The mountains had a mysterious, ghostly look, as though haunted by peoples from the past. And, indeed they were. This had been the stronghold of Apache chief Geronimo as he and his warriors fought off the U.S. military in the late 19th century.

We finally reached a KOA just off the freeway on the outskirts of Tucson. It was noisy and urban, not a nice place to camp, but convenient to freeway travelers, and easy for Greg to find when he arrived late tomorrow night. I was close to bursting with excitement and impatience to see him.

Expenses:	$25.00	breakfast, gas, ice, camp

Friday, May 21 – Sunday, May 23, 1982

It was 11:30 p.m. when Greg pulled in after a fourteen-hour drive from Fresno. He stepped out of his car, grinning widely, and opened his arms to me. We set up his tent and crawled in to greet each other properly.

Greg and Susan met in the morning and seemed to get along fine. We three packed up and moved to Crazy Horse Campground, still on the outskirts of Tucson, but a pleasanter place with cactus and mesquite to lend more of a desert feel. Here we would stay until Denny's plane arrived from Eugene Sunday evening.

With most of Sunday at leisure, Susan, Greg, and I visited the Arizona-Sonora Desert Museum west of Tucson, an exceptional museum and zoo with first class exhibits of Sonoran desert biota and geology. We stayed most of the day, until time to pick up Denny at the Tucson Airport.

Denny and Greg, both amiable men, became friends instantly. Denny had expressed an interest in learning about birds, and Greg was more than happy to become his tutor. We returned to Crazy Horse for one more night.

For accommodations, I relinquished the greenhouse to Susan and Denny, while Greg and I shared his tent. This seemed to be the only practical arrangement, and I had readily agreed, but I had to acknowledge a twinge of dissatisfaction, a feeling of sorrow. Giving up my camper to Denny and Susan seemed to symbolize a shift in the nature of my journey. Now it was no longer a solo affair. Although I had experienced loneliness on my travels, I had also relished being alone, going where I wanted and doing exactly as I wanted. Now I was obliged to cede territory, like a queen exiled from her realm. Already I could feel crankiness festering within me. The next few days would be a test.

Monday, May 24 – Wednesday, May 26, 1982

Monday morning we left for the Chiricahuas, Susan and Denny in my camper and Greg and I in his car. We were backtracking toward New Mexico where we would approach the area from the east. Greg and I drove along in high spirits, for the time being, happy and in love, looking forward to our week together.

At Roadforks, just across the border into New Mexico, we turned south on Highway 80 then crossed back into Arizona at Rodeo. From Rodeo we continued on a few miles to the village of Portal, well known to birders as the entry to one of the nation's best birding hotspots. After a rest and a visit to the Portal store, we continued on to Idlewild Campground in Cave Creek Canyon, surely one of Arizona's most beautiful places. Towering, rose-colored cliffs and spires matted with doilies of pale green lichen framed the entrance to the canyon. Nearby Cave Creek gurgled cold and clear and over all a canopy of Arizona cypress, white-trunked sycamore, and live oak provided shade.

Birders were everywhere, setting up scopes, hanging feeders, peering through binoculars. Most of them were here to see the elegant trogon, a tropical bird more commonly found in Mexico.

Before we were finished setting up camp we heard it, the call we had studied well, low and harsh, *ko-ay, ko-ay.* It only took one sweep with our binoculars to find the trogon perched on a sycamore branch nearby. Susan and Denny saw it, too, and Denny proudly declared the elegant trogon to be the first bird on his life list.

Within a few minutes of seeing the trogon, Greg and I also spotted a bridled titmouse, Arizona woodpecker, blue-throated hummingbird, magnificent hummingbird, and hepatic tanager—my most incredible birding hour to date. I was passionate about seeing these beautiful birds and adding them to my life list, but I was soon to rediscover that Greg's passion far exceeded mine and verged on what I considered obsessive. It wasn't like me to be single-minded about any pursuit, and I certainly had my limits where birding was concerned. I could bird for a few hours, tramp through brush and along streambeds to find a particular species, but I was not a dawn-to-midnight birder. I wouldn't risk bodily injury or endure a sleepless night to pursue a rare bird. I feared Greg would chide me for this, and, at the time, I didn't want anything to jeopardize our future together. For the sake of the relationship, I reminded myself, I had pledged to be a more adaptable, flexible person. That resolve would soon be put to the test.

Tuesday, after a morning of lazing around camp, the four of us drove further up the canyon to Rustler Park where we birded and tramped around most of the afternoon. Back in camp we all pitched in to make supper. I was content to stay around camp enjoying the sights and sounds of evening, but Greg wanted me to join him in search of the common but rarely seen flammulated owl, a tiny owl only 6½ inches long that lives in pine forests and upper oak woodlands. The owl is strictly nocturnal and silent until well into the night when it's call, a single, low hoot given at regular intervals is easily missed.

The best place to find it, we were told, was on the Vista Point Trail out of Stewart Campground farther down the road. I could see that Greg was annoyed at my reluctance to go out into the forest after dark, so to avoid discord I grabbed my binoculars and a flashlight, and we drove to Stewart Campground. The night was pitch black and it took us a while just to find the trailhead. We hadn't walked far when Greg halted and said, "Listen." After a few seconds we heard the faint, low hoot, a flammulated owl off in the woods.

Without hesitation Greg strode off the trail into the brush, the owl's infrequent hoots guiding him on. I followed, but with each step into the forest I became more worried about finding our way back in the blackness. Still, Greg pressed on, following the hoots and swinging the flashlight beam up into the trees. We pushed on until we heard the owl's soft hoot almost above us. Greg shone the beam upward and there it was, a tiny owl, no bigger than a sparrow, perched on a branch staring straight ahead. Admittedly, I did feel a surge of wonder at the sight of this delicate creature, and I was glad, but mainly because now Greg would be ready to get out of the forest and back to camp.

We turned around and started out, but the trail was nowhere to be seen.

"This way," Greg said. But I was sure he was wrong.

"No, Greg. We came this way," I protested pointing in the opposite direction.

"No we didn't," he insisted, his voice rising in anger.

We argued back and forth, Greg irritated that I should doubt him, and me near panicked with fear we would be lost in the forest overnight. We went his way, of course, and still did not come upon the trail. I was sure we were only going deeper into the forest, and angrily told him so.

We bushwhacked on, quarreling, until finally the flashlight beam fell across the trail. Oh thank God, I thought, we're safe. We hiked back to the car in frigid silence and returned to camp just before midnight. Susan and Denny had begun to wonder if they should come after us. Greg and I crawled into his tent amid a cloud of tension. I was still seething with anger about his carelessness, but even more about his stupid, heroic, daredevil approach to birding.

The next day the tension between us slowly dissipated. It was our last day in the Chiricahuas and I mostly stayed around camp venturing out only occasionally with Greg to look for sulpher-bellied flycatchers. In the evening he went out again, without me, to look for flammulated owls. I had already seen one. That was enough.

Thursday, May 27 – Saturday, May 29, 1982

Today was our last day in the Chiricahuas. At breakfast we devised a plan for separating and rejoining again later in the day at Patagonia Lake State Park about ten miles north of Nogales. We had to decide which vehicles each couple would take. Much to my dissatisfaction, the decision was obvious. Greg and I couldn't take my camper because that would mean Susan and Denny would have to drive Greg's car, not acceptable to Greg. So I relinquished my camper to Susan and Denny, something I was loath to do. The greenhouse and I had been an inseparable pair, a unit, taking on the road together for most of a year. It had been my respite and haven during all the travails of my journey. Rendering it to strange hands made me feel I had broken an inviolate bond. More than just being a physical separation from my trusty steed, the parting seemed to have symbolic meaning, too. Sadly, my trip was coming to an end. The venture I had put so much emotional energy into was coming to a close. The taking over of my camper signified this, the end of a sweet, perfectly executed dream. Of course, I kept these thoughts to myself for fear of appearing selfish and uncooperative.

Greg and I drove off in his car, skirting the Chiricahua National Monument then slipping down into the grasslands on the west side of the mountains. We drove through the tiny town of Elfrida and on to Tombstone where we stopped to poke into the curio shops and gape at the OK Corral where Wyatt and Virgil Earp shot it out with the Clantons and McLaurys.

From Tombstone we continued to Sonoita Creek Sanctuary, a Nature Conservancy preserve, and the only known nesting site in the country for the rose-throated becard, a small flycatcher. We walked the creekside trail under cottonwoods and sycamores and saw a gray hawk and several other area specialties, but no rose-throated becards.

Finally, long after I had tired of birding, Greg consented to leave Sonoita Creek and move on to Patagonia Lake State Park where we would meet up with Susan and Denny and camp for the night.

We drove into the state park expecting a pleasant, shaded campground, but found instead what looked like a dirt quarry. The lake, man-made and ugly, as all man-made lakes are, sat in a bowl of sun-faded, reddish-brown dirt encircled by reddish-brown dirt banks. Powerboats screamed across the bathtub-like surface towing shrieking water skiers who evidently found the place delightful.

Greg and I were setting up his tent in our patch of dirt when Susan and Denny drove in. They parked in another dirt patch and came to greet us.

"This is a strange place for an Oregon boy," Denny said. "Where are the fir trees, the vine maples, and the water-rounded rocks? Great fun camping in the dirt, eh?"

With absolutely nothing else to do, we all retired early that night. As we were settling in, Greg and I had another tiff over some small matter I didn't fully understand. It left me feeling anxious and puzzled, since I didn't know what he was disgruntled about. I let him mope and hoped he would forget it by morning.

I lay on my back with my arms folded beneath my head, thinking. A good relationship requires give and take. I had heard it so many times it had the weight of federal law. I wished to hell someone would tell me how much, and when I was supposed to give, and how much I was supposed to take. I pondered this awhile until the truth struck home. I really didn't care because, frankly, whatever was to be gained from Give and Take wasn't worth even one single minute of my stomach tied in knots because of some infantile grievance of a sulking man.

Worth it or not, though, I continued to accept it as part of the deal, this splinter of angst embedded beneath my skin. It wouldn't be until many months later, after my journey had ended, that I would look back on my romance with Greg and shake my head in gentle self-derision at my blindness.

At 5:30 the next morning Greg stirred and groped for his clothes. He was going back to Sonoita Creek to search again for the rose-throated becard. Knock yourself out, I thought, snuggling deep in my sleeping bag feigning sleep and wondering if he was still in a snit. I wouldn't know until later when we met up again, meaning I would have the entire morning to deal with stomach knots.

After he was gone, Susan, Denny, and I drove to Patagonia for breakfast at a café and then to a laundromat to wash our clothes. As we hauled our clean laundry out to the camper, we spotted Greg pulling into a gas station down the street. We stashed our laundry and walked down to meet him. He was sweaty and dirty, with twigs and bits of brush sticking to his hair. What looked like a six-inch gash on his shin was leaking blood into his sock.

"What happened to you?" I asked, incredulous.

"Aw, I scratched myself climbing over a barbed wire fence," he said.

I shook my head, but said nothing more. What is it about this man, I thought, that would cause him to forego food and sleep and risk bodily injury just to go see a bird? Foolishness, I decided, and I confess it gave me some pleasure to sneer at him. Inwardly, of course.

"I found the rose-throated becard." He was triumphant and offered to show us where it was. To placate him and, admittedly, because I really did want to see the becard, we all went back to Sonoita Creek Sanctuary and followed Greg downstream.

Our James Lane bird book instructed us to look in the sycamores near the rest area. We crept along the trail to the sycamores and crouched down beneath them. There they were, a pair of becards hovering around their nest up in the branches, exactly where Lane said they would be, rare birds I would never have seen if not for Greg's bloodletting.

At last it was time to drive on to Mile Hi Ranch in Ramsey Canyon, south of the town of Sierra Vista. I so desperately wanted a hot shower and a soft bed with clean sheets. Greg seemed to regard me with disdain for desiring these luxuries—clean, dirty, it was all the same to him—but I couldn't help that. My enthusiasm for camping was taking a hit. Yet in a day or two, when Susan, Denny, and Greg would be gone, I would be back on the road camping solo again for a few more weeks. That is, if I intended to finish my journey exactly one year to the date after beginning it.

In high anticipation, we drove through Sierra Vista and south on Highway 92 watching for Ramsey Canyon Road. "There it is!" I called out, and we turned east up the winding road.

Ramsey Canyon is best known for its fourteen recorded species of hummingbirds as well as many other rare bird species. A perennial stream lined with lush oaks and pines runs through it. We pulled into the small parking area and stepped out into a frenzy of hummingbird activity. Hummingbird feeders hung everywhere, from trees, from wires suspended between trees, and from the eaves of the four rustic cabins. We sat on benches and chairs The Nature Conservancy had arranged near the feeders for easy viewing, and watched the show for a while. Hummers zipped to and from the feeders so fast we barely had time to check out their colors, except for one slightly larger bird that zoomed in and hovered, flashing its beacon of an iridescent, emerald green throat and purple crown while Greg and I watched in amazement. It was the aptly named magnificent hummingbird, one of the showcase birds of Ramsey Canyon.

After awhile, we unloaded our luggage and prepared to settle in. The cabins were tucked back among the trees and shrubs, secluded from the public bird-viewing area. We reached them across a little bridge spanning a small side channel of the stream, as enchanting an entrance as we could have wanted. Our cabin was cozy with a fireplace, deep sofas, and a tidy little kitchen. I noticed that Greg smiled broadly as he looked the place over. All traces of his earlier mood seemed to have vanished.

We chose bedrooms and unpacked things then went out to hike the nature trail, pointing out bird species to Denny and Susan. In the evening the four of us drove back into Sierra Vista to a cozy Italian restaurant,

LaTaverneta. It was a superb dinner of spaghetti, candlelight, and red wine. We raised our glasses and drank to new friends, then drank again to beautiful hummingbirds. We drank until the ruddy glow of conviviality suffused the room with amber light and reflected on our faces, while outside the first clear stars appeared in a darkening sky.

Back at the cabin Greg pulled from his pack a little something, in brownie form, to put us into even higher spirits. I hadn't had any marijuana since my graduate school days, and Susan and Denny, hardly ever, but we all partook that night. Music seemed in order, so we played something lively, but soft, and before long we were all grooving and Susan was tapping out a riff with two spoons against her leg.

That night Greg and I became passionate lovers again. All night long. Oh, how I loved him, all my apprehensions swept away by a night of passion. He would be the answer to the looming question, where will I go when my journey is over? What will I do?

I hadn't thought about this during my travels, and I hadn't intended to. The trip was to be a year of unencumbered pleasures, my last hoorah before returning to the world of work. The feasibility study I had scratched out back in 1980 while sitting at my city planner's desk included $3000 for start-up money when I returned, money to sustain me while I decided what to do: renew my search for a college teaching position, or seek a new career. That was the extent of my planning. Now I knew what I was going to do. I would hurry on to Fresno, California, move in with Greg and map out my future there.

In the morning when we roused ourselves and stepped outside on shaky legs, our neighbors smiled and asked if we had heard the music last night. They wondered where it had been coming from.

"Well, we did play some music, but we kept it low," I said, glancing at my cabin mates, who all seemed to be gazing off in different directions. Although I truly believed we had been reasonably quiet, apparently our libations at dinner, plus the odd dessert in the cabin, raised our sound level above Nature Conservancy standards.

Denny, Susan, and I seemed to be moving very slowly and solemnly through the morning as though we were pushing through water. But, not Greg. "How about a hike?" he suggested in his typically obtuse and cheery way. The very word "hike" made my stomach flip. But Denny said all right, so I went along. Susan opted to stay at the cabin.

Greg was in his element pointing out the birds to Denny. With each new species, he enlightened him with a lecture on the bird's habitat, behavior, and a multitude of other pertinent facts intended, as I firmly believed, to demonstrate his expertise. I was in no mood for a lesson on birds; I knew quite a bit myself, a fact that Greg blithely ignored. Could someone please tell me, I thought, is this a "give" moment? Am I supposed to recede into the background while Greg hogs the limelight?

Back at the cabin, I slipped into the bedroom for a long nap, awaking at dinnertime groggy and grumpy. Greg was still holding forth.

Sunday, May 30, 1982

I slept well last night and woke with my ardor toward Greg restored, yesterday's hard feelings forgotten. This was the day we would leave Ramsey Canyon, the day that Greg would return to Fresno. We lingered by his car door, sad to say goodbye but comforted knowing we would be together again in a few weeks. He drove off and I turned back to face Susan and Denny.

Suddenly, unexpectedly, I was walloped by a nauseating punch of despair. The prospect of one more night of camping was intolerable. All that had fired me up for the last eleven months, and the twelve months before that, died in an instant. The shock of it horrified me. How could this happen to me, the resolute, happy-go-lucky, intrepid traveler? I was profoundly disappointed in myself for the inability to sustain my enthusiasm. Blind-sided once again by romance, I was consumed by only one desire—to jump in my camper and drive west.

Greg was gone. Denny would be gone that evening, and Susan and I would be on our own again. I approached Susan and Denny, a wreck, barely able to conceal my anguish and resentment. The journey was no longer mine. It was out of my control. Over. Now, their travel plans overrode my own and I was utterly at their disposal, thwarted in my urgency to go home. But I had obligations to fulfill and more nights of camping to endure.

To pass the afternoon Susan and I took Denny on a tour of Saguaro National Monument, then to the airport where we saw him off on his evening flight. It would be the last time she would see Denny; I already knew that. Denny was a fine man, but far too mild-mannered for Susan's style. Besides, back at Big Bend she had accepted an invitation from Gordon to visit him in Santa Fe, and had already booked a flight for June 3.

Now she and I headed back to Crazy Horse Campground where we would wait out the next four days. I was beside myself with impatience, bedeviled by it. I couldn't stand being forced to bide my time at an RV park waiting for Susan's departure date. It was like being caught in a whirlpool, unable to break free. I loved my sister, but I could hardly contain my aggravation at having to wait. I wanted to leave for California immediately. I wanted to be with Greg. But now I had to mark time at Crazy Horse, then endure three more weeks of solo camping after that.

I tried to hide my annoyance from Susan, but she must have detected it. Far from being angry or offended, she understood. She sat down beside me and spoke in a soft voice.

"Lynnie," she said, "there's no law that says you have to keep camping until June 22. Why don't you just go to Fresno after you take me to the airport?" Her words freed me. She was right. I wouldn't lose face by returning to California a few weeks shy of a whole year. It wasn't like I was going AWOL, and who would I lose face with anyway?

Monday, May 31, 1982

Greg called me at the campground this morning to let me know he arrived home safely and that he couldn't wait to see me. How could I stand the remaining hours until I turned my little green camper home?

"Want to go to Madera Canyon?" I asked Susan half-heartedly. Madera Canyon was another birding hotspot south of Tucson. At this point I barely cared about birding, but I wanted to break the hideous monotony of languishing at Crazy Horse. We drove to Madera Canyon intending to camp there for the night. We were looking for a restful campsite similar to Idlewild in Cave Creek Canyon. What we found was a campground teeming with people, bustling and noisy. Garbage cans overflowed and dirty diapers had been tossed along the roadside. Susan and I didn't say anything to each other, neither of us wanting to admit to being repulsed. She headed off to the latrine, but when she returned, the look on her face settled things. "I couldn't even go, it was so filthy," she said.

"All right," I acquiesced. I really didn't want to stay, either. We turned around, drove back to Crazy Horse and spent the rest of the afternoon lying around the pool.

Tuesday, June 1, 1982

This waiting is straining my tolerance to the limit. I'm so sky high in love and eager to begin my life with Greg.

Wednesday, June 2, 1982

Soon my journey will be over. In the morning I will take Susan to the airport then, finally, head west.

We went to breakfast this morning at a nearby café, then spent the rest of the day around camp doing laundry and last minute packing. It is hard to believe that my trip is nearly over, my dream nearly fulfilled. In spite of the seemingly interminable waiting, the end has sprung upon me as if by stealth, like a beast pouncing unsuspected from an overhanging limb. This is a time for introspection, it would seem, but at the moment, introspection eludes me.

Thursday, June 3, 1982

I took Susan to the Tucson Airport to catch a 7:00 a.m. flight to Albuquerque. I watched her walk down the ramp to her boarding gate, wondering where she would go next and when I would see her again. My heart ached with loneliness, as it always did whenever I said goodbye to her. She had always been my anchor and support, as necessary to me as a vital organ.

Tears brimmed in my eyes as I turned and walked back to the terminal. The bright Arizona sun blazed through the huge windows. I raised my head and stepped out into the brilliant light, solo again and obligated to no one but myself. I climbed up into my camper, checked my maps, and turned the snub nose of my greenhouse west onto Interstate 10.

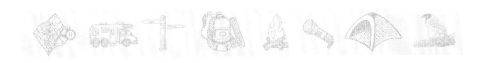

EPILOG

I began my journey seeking nothing more than birds and the beautiful places I had seen in my copy of *America's Wonderlands*. I was not on a life quest and I was not "in search of myself." It happened, however, although I was unaware of it, that I was on a parallel journey—a journey toward a discovery of self-truths.

After only a few weeks in Fresno with Greg, truths that had been squirming and wriggling inside me for months finally burst forth into the light. I was not in love with him, and in fact I had done what I had determined never to do again—package myself inside someone else's life for the sake of a relationship. I hated Fresno and couldn't abide Greg's condescending behaviors toward me. He crowded me with plans for our weekends and, with careful deliberation, chose a pet name for me as though I was a cat.

It was intolerable. I had traveled alone for most of a year, completely on my own, taking directions from no one, asking little from anyone. Without realizing it, I had become savagely independent, staunchly resentful of anyone trying to exert control over me.

I wasn't just ill-suited to Greg. Soon after my journey ended I came to realize I was ill-suited for a tandem lifestyle, or any relationship that prevented me from following my own path as a free agent, unencumbered by the wishes of another. The line of patter I had used on myself about compromise and give-and-take was all hooey, and the intense relief I felt when I left Greg confirmed that my instincts at last were correct.

I settled into a teaching career, but the journey I had recently undertaken was only a prelude to twenty-five more years of solo camping. I had been infected with an incurable longing to flee to the wild places, the mountains, the deserts, the coast, the plains. Whenever a vacation rolled around I packed up my rig, whether a new pop-top camper, a trailer, a pickup, or just a tent, and headed off to another wonderland. It was automatic; I couldn't help it. It's where my route from Cultus Lake was taking me.

ACKNOWLEDGMENTS

I extend my deepest gratitude to Susan Droz, my sister, who prompted me to write this book, and who listened patiently to countless telephone readings of my initial drafts. Her encouragement, praise, and editorial nurturing never faltered from start to finish.

Special thanks to Barbara Gleason and Dara Nichols for book and cover design, and Dave Imus, who created the map and line drawing of me in my camper, and offered friendship and encouragement throughout the process.

I am enormously grateful to Bob Welch for his fine writers' workshop, encouragement, and kind words.

Thanks also to my dear friend Linda Martin, who loved everything about my book and always listened.

I am indebted to Carol Brownson for her encouragement and editorial overview of the final draft.

Many thanks to fellow writers Roger Hite, Margaret Merisante, Carla Orcutt, Susan Wyatt, and Joyce Leader. Thanks to friends Tina Farley, Mary Brooner, John Hannah, Vic Martin, Carolyn Auker, David Guzzetta, Anne Newins, and the Thursday lunch group who listened, read, and shared.

236

Outside of Merrit SD: Rochford
H
P. 82 "general view of unworthiness"
axis.

24113292R00137

Made in the USA
Charleston, SC
12 November 2013